The Kingdom Within

THE KIN(

DOM WITHIN

Genevieve Caulfield

EDITED BY ED FITZGERALD

Harper & Brothers Publishers New York

. . . And on being asked by the Pharisees, "When is the kingdom of God coming?" he answered and said to them, "The kingdom of God comes unawares. Neither will they say, 'Behold, here it is,' or 'Behold, there it is.' For behold, the kingdom of God is within you."

—SAINT LUKE 17:20-21

To my Mother
to whose understanding and devotion
this book bears witness

The Kingdom Within

Chapter I

I was only seventeen years old when I made up my mind that what I wanted to do with my life was to go to Japan as a teacher and do whatever I could to make the people of Japan and the United States more friendly. I conceived this ambition as I sat on a porch swing listening to one of my teachers read aloud a magazine article entitled "Should Japanese Children in California Be Sent to Separate Schools?"

One minute I was relaxing in the swing, listening idly; the next, I was sitting up straight, angry and aware. I didn't know, or, at that point, particularly care, any more about the Orient than the next person, but I was an avid student of history and I had been intensely interested in the outcome of the Russo-Japanese War, which had ended a short time before. I had been under the impression that most Americans admired the courageous stand little Japan had made against the giant of the North, and I couldn't believe that one of our own United States was seriously considering a law that would bar from its schools children whose only sin was that their parents had come from this brave country. It didn't make sense to me.

I had read, or heard, about other injustices in the world without becoming nearly so excited, but this one hit me hard. "Do you think they'll actually pass that law?" I asked the teacher in outrage.

"I doubt it," she said reassuringly. "It's against everything this country stands for."

She was partly right. That specific piece of discrimination never was enacted into law. But the spirit that generated it didn't die. Other savagely discriminatory measures, like the anti-alien land laws, did pass, and scattered the seeds that later bore the bitter fruit of a destructive war.

I don't know why I felt so much sympathy and affection for the Japanese, but I did, and I never got over the shock I felt at the discovery that my country could consider telling them bluntly that, of all the peoples of the world, they weren't welcome here. I made up my mind right then and there that, with the help of God, Who certainly couldn't think much of such stupid prejudice, I would do something about it. I promised myself that I would learn all I could about Japan, and as soon as I possibly could I would go there and work and teach, and do anything within my power to create better feeling between our countries.

It was, I realize now, a mighty resolution for a schoolgirl in her teens who had no money, no resources except those of the spirit, and who was blind. It simply never occurred to me, though, that any of these things, including my blindness, might stop me. I had been brought up to believe that being blind merely means that you can't see; it doesn't mean that you can't live a full life—provided, of course, that you're willing to fight for it and to rely with utter faith on the help of the Almighty every step of the way.

My blindness was the result of an ordinary household accident, the mere upsetting of a bottle. It happened two months after my birth on May 8, 1888, in Suffolk, Virginia. I've never been told exactly what was in the bottle, except that it was some strong medicine, but I was a helpless baby, and when the doctor who was examining me knocked over the bottle with his elbow, the caustic fluid splashed all over my face and into my upturned eyes.

My mother and father never told me much about what

happened in those first dreadful minutes as my burned eyes grew shockingly disfigured. But I can imagine the frightened haste with which they must have rushed me to the hospital, and then, as the days went by and it became obvious that I was unable to see, took me from one specialist to another. Nothing did any good until, when I was seven months old, a young doctor in Nashville persuaded them to let him try a new operation called an iridectomy. The doctor operated only on my right eye; the left eye was totally dead. By making a delicate incision in the iris, he was able to allow a little light to penetrate the eye, giving me two two-hundredths vision in that eye. Legal blindness is twenty two-hundredths, and my vision is exactly one-tenth of that. What I have in that one eye, and I treasure it, is faint light perception. I can see a shadow when a person stands near me, and I can make out the glow of a lighted electric lamp in a room.

The operation in my seventh month is the only one that has ever been performed on my eye. The doctor urged my parents never to allow any further surgery. He predicted that other suggestions would be made in the years to come but he warned that, while another operation might possibly provide me with more sight, it might just as easily cost me the tiny ray of light I have. Since I have grown up and been in a position to make my own decisions, I never have disagreed with this sensible advice. I have no wish to risk losing the ability to detect daylight. It's a lot better than living in absolute darkness.

Because I was only an infant when I lost my sight, I have taken my condition for granted all my life. We seldom talked about it in the family; I rarely asked any questions, and Mama and Papa, who probably never got over their feeling of responsibility, tried hard to give me as normal a life as possible. Very few special provisions were made for me as a blind child. The one great concession was the extra amount of reading that was done for me.

No effort was made to disguise or escape the fact of my

blindness. It was simply there, to be accepted and lived with. I fell more than the other children did, for example; I was never allowed to go out on the streets alone; and I can remember crying bitterly because I couldn't have a bicycle, which I wanted badly. Otherwise, I lived a fairly normal life.

I was about four years old when the family moved to Pawtucket, Rhode Island, where my father had obtained a job as chief engineer in charge of the Central Falls plant of the American Electrolitic Copper Company. Papa never went to college but he held down some surprisingly good positions. The only trouble was that he kept getting tired of them. If his intellect and his ability had been balanced by a steady character, Papa might have become a truly successful engineer. But there was a frivolous, pleasure-loving bent to his nature, and his early success had encouraged him to give in to it. I think he knew what his trouble was, but instead of trying to correct it he grew increasingly resentful toward those who tried to advise him. He developed the fatal notion, common among bright young people to whom success comes too soon, that he couldn't work for anyone else. This quirk of his made our family life nervously uncertain, although it was my mother, not my little brother Henry and I, who did the worrying.

Like any child, I liked to play, but my greatest delight was listening to someone read aloud to me. Mama and Aunt Genevieve, whom I always called Aunt Ducky, were never too busy to read to me. In the evening, when the grownups sometimes went out, Nannie would take over. Sometimes she would read new stories but more often I would choose some well-loved tale for her to read for the seventh or eighth time.

Nannie, whose real name was Evelyna Holland, had come to us from Suffolk, after Henry was born, to be our nurse and general factotum. She was a bright, attractive mulatto girl of about sixteen, and she endeared herself to us all and stayed with us until I was almost ten years old, when she married the elegant coachman of one of Pawtucket's first families. Nannie combined the warm qualities of the traditional Southern Negro with a decidedly modern outlook on life and some firm ideas about the disciplining of children. She could read beautifully and was most particular about what she read to us. No matter how much we begged her, she wouldn't read us the funny papers—not even the Katzenjammer Kids, which seemed to us the height of cruelty. "Cinderella" we could have, and *Black Beauty,* and *Grimm's Fairy Tales,* but nothing that did not meet Nannie's standards.

I did manage to get in some reading that no one knew about. In the evening, when Henry and I were supposed to be asleep, Mama and Papa liked to read grown-up books aloud to each other. I was usually awake, and I made certain that I didn't miss a word. The books they read were good ones, but I doubt if Nannie would have approved of them for me. I listened raptly, for example, to *The Scarlet Letter,* and I can still remember how excited I was during the forest scene when Little Pearl refused to go to her mother until she replaced the scarlet letter on her dress.

It was really a blessing that I was deprived of sight, for I'm sure that if I had been able to see and to read I would have become a bookworm of the most objectionable kind. Even today, whenever I get hold of a Braille book or magazine, it takes all the will power I possess not to read it from cover to cover with no thought of other duties or responsibilities. I have never given much thought to feeling sorry for myself, but from time to time I have wished fervently that I could pick up an ordinary book and read it.

It was taken for granted by my family that I would have to be sent to a school for the blind, but in those days children didn't go to school as early as they do now, and particularly because I would have to go to a boarding school it was thought best that I absorb as much home life as possible before going away.

I got my first unofficial taste of school life when Henry
and the children who lived in the apartment upstairs began
to go. I went right along with them. I couldn't, of course,
read their books, nor could I learn to write as they did; but
I could and did soak up what the teacher said. Furthermore,
I had an advantage over the other children in that, when I
was bored with the kindergarten classes, I was free to wander
off to the higher grades and listen to what was going on
there. My advanced reading made it possible for me to understand and enjoy many of the more difficult subjects. I must
have been a nuisance to the busy teachers, but they never
let on that I was. They were so kind and patient that I felt
encouraged to go to school almost every day.

The spring before my first official year in school, I made a
trip to Camden, New Jersey, to visit Grandma Caulfield,
who had married for the second time and whose name now
was Mrs. Hillman. For as long as I could remember, Grandma
had come to see us every summer, bringing exciting presents
of trains for Henry and dolls for me. Everyone said my dolls
were beautiful. Their wardrobes must have taken Grandma
weeks to make. My first one, which I named Eintsy, was a
wax infant with real eyelashes. I was far too young to own
such a treasure, as I promptly proved by putting her in a
steaming hot bath with disastrous results. The luckless Eintsy
was followed by a procession of others, some of whom I took
to school with me. I still can't remember any dolls except
those that Grandma gave me. She was a kind of fairy god-
mother to me, and when Aunt Ducky told me she was going
to take me to see her I could hardly wait to get started.

On the appointed day, Aunt Ducky and I took a local train
from Pawtucket to Providence and then changed to the
Colonial Express, which ran between Providence and Philadelphia. Aunt Ducky was the best traveling companion any
little girl could have wished for. She was just about fifteen
years older than I, and she always seemed more like a big
sister than an aunt to me. She was small and lively, with an
inquiring mind and a quick sense of humor. I loved her.

Near the end of the trip, we took a ferryboat ride from Philadelphia to Camden. When we were getting off, a quiet, pleasant old gentleman joined us. Aunt Ducky called him Mr. Hillman and assumed that I knew who he was, as well she might, for I had met him on various family occasions. But I had forgotten all about him.

When we got to Grandma's house, one of a long row of marble-front dwellings of the kind so characteristic of Camden and Philadelphia, I seized the first opportunity to ask Aunt Ducky about the status of Mr. Hillman, who seemed to be making himself very much at home. "Who is he?" I wanted to know. Aunt Ducky explained to me that he was Grandma's husband, that she had married him a few years after Grandpa Caulfield had died.

"Why?" I asked relentlessly.

"Because Grandma didn't like to live alone," Aunt Ducky said, "and Mr. Hillman is a very nice man."

"But, Aunt Ducky," I protested, "he's so old."

"No, dear," she said, gently but firmly, "he's only a year or two older than Grandma."

Aunt Ducky took me everywhere she went, and I had a good time visiting friends and relations. The only thing I didn't like was shopping. There is something about a department store, or a shop of any kind for that matter, which quickly gets on my nerves. I love pretty things, but buying them is a trial to which I have never grown accustomed. One day, crossing on the ferry to Philadelphia, I began to cry, because I had heard we were going shopping. Aunt Ducky, surprised by my demonstration, was considering staying on the boat with me and going right back home, when suddenly Mr. Hillman appeared.

"What's the matter with the little girl?" he asked kindly.

"I don't want to go shopping," I told him, sniffling.

"I don't blame you," he said sympathetically. "How would you like to just ride on the ferryboat until your aunt has finished shopping? Then she can pick you up and take you home."

"Oh, I'd love it," I said hastily. "May I?" The tears were all gone.

Mr. Hillman took me by the hand and led me up a steep flight of stairs and into a little room where he seated me in a comfortable chair. He told me he had to leave me for a little while, and in a moment I heard the bell ring for the boat to start. I didn't see him again until we had reached Camden.

"Well," he asked, "how did you like it?"

"It's very nice," I told him. "Is this boat yours, Mr. Hillman? May I ride on it every day?"

"You may ride on it every day if you wish," he told me, laughing, "but it isn't my boat. I'm only the captain."

Only the captain! All the captains I had ever read about came crowding into my mind. I had often dreamed of meeting a real live captain in the flesh, and here I was actually talking to one. I couldn't have been more excited sailing through the South Seas. Mr. Hillman, who up to now had been the dullest and oldest and most uninteresting of men, suddenly had become a hero. The five-minute ferryboat ride between Camden and Philadelphia was an adventure. From that day on, I never called him Mr. Hillman again; I always called him "the Captain."

When we returned to Pawtucket, Aunt Ducky was married. For more than a year, Dr. Leonard Kiernan, a young doctor from Providence, had been coming to the house to take her out, and we often had driven in to the city to spend Sunday afternoon with him and his three sisters. I wasn't surprised when I was told that he was going to marry Aunt Ducky and that in the future Henry and I should call him Uncle Leonard.

After the wedding, they went to live in Providence, where Uncle Leonard had his practice. We had always been so close I missed her terribly. If I hadn't had the exciting prospect of going away to school in the autumn to occupy my mind, it would have been a long summer. As it was, I found myself hardly able to wait for the great day to come.

Chapter II

These days, when there is scarcely a city or town in the United States where there aren't people working at transcribing books into Braille for the blind, or in some other way helping them to overcome their handicap, it is hard to realize that in the so-called Gay Nineties there were relatively few schools for the blind in the entire country and most people knew little and cared less about the education of the "unfortunate" children who attended them. There were virtually no state or private agencies for the blind, and the schools that did exist were so far removed from ordinary life that my family had no idea how to go about trying to get in touch with one.

My parents, understandably, were reluctant to have me go away at all. It wasn't customary for American families to send small children off to boarding school, and it seemed unnatural to Mama and Papa to send me away simply because I was blind. While they were thinking about it, resisting what they knew in their hearts had to be done, one of Uncle Leonard's sisters told us of having heard about a woman in Providence who had gone to the Perkins Institution for the Blind. This was too good a lead to pass up, so the entire family, including Henry, went in to Providence to see the lady. I've forgotten her name now but I remember clearly how dark and musty her parlor was and how old she seemed. It turned out that she had graduated from Perkins only a year or two before, but to me she seemed a parchment person of greatly advanced age. Instantly I wondered if I would become like that if I went to her school. The poor woman probably gave such an impression only because she was totally inactive, completely isolated from the mainstream of life, which was the case with most blind people, especially women, at that time.

We learned that all Papa had to do to get me into Perkins was write a letter to Dr. Anagnos, the director of the school, and make an appointment to call on him. The rest, the kind lady said, would be easy.

Papa wrote the letter and it wasn't long before he received a cordial answer and we were on our way to South Boston, where the school was located.

The first thing I was shown when I walked through the front door of the Perkins School was a huge globe which, when gently rotated upon its axis, introduced me to an embossed map of the world. I was greatly excited by this first geography lesson. The shapes of the different continents were all new to me, and I couldn't have had an introduction better calculated to impress upon me the wonders of knowledge.

When I last visited the beautiful modern Perkins, at Watertown, not long ago, the old globe, with its promise of wonders to be unfolded, was still standing in the entranceway, and as I stood in front of it and ran my fingers over its raised surface, spanning oceans I have sailed and flown across, exotic cities I have visited and faraway countries I have lived in, I felt a lively sense of gratitude for the first push this school gave me on the way.

The founder and first director of the Perkins School was Dr. Samuel Gridley Howe, the famous abolitionist and husband of Julia Ward Howe, who wrote "The Battle Hymn of the Republic." Among Dr. Howe's many interests was a passionate sympathy for the people of Greece in their struggle for freedom from Turkey. He spent six years working in Greece as a soldier, surgeon and relief administrator, and when he finally returned to the United States he brought with him a young Greek protégé, Michael Anagnos, who later married his daughter, Julia Romana Howe, and upon the death of Dr. Howe became the second director of Perkins.

When I first met Dr. Anagnos, he was well past middle age. I was instantly attracted by his kindly, gentle manner. After I had answered all his questions, he told Papa that I could be admitted to the primary department of the school, which was situated in Jamaica Plains, a suburb of Boston, and that I could begin when school opened in September. I was overjoyed, and at first I didn't understand why Mama and Papa didn't fully share my pleasure. But I soon understood that it was only because they were reluctant to have me go away from them, alone, into a strange world of which they knew nothing. I was sorry I had to leave home, too, but I didn't shed any tears over it. The adventure ahead filled my mind, and I was eager to get started.

The kindergarten and primary department at Jamaica Plains was Dr. Anagnos's pride and joy. He had built it after he took over the school from Dr. Howe. The number of pupils had been increasing steadily and expansion was imperative. Instead of trying to enlarge the plant at South Boston, he decided to restrict South Boston to the older grammar and high school students and to build a new primary department at Jamaica Plains. The new plant had two main buildings, one for boys and one for girls, containing both residence and class rooms. Between the two was a common assembly hall and gymnasium. Our building, which housed thirty-two girls the year I began, was an ideal place for children obliged to be away from home; it was beautifully equipped and as much like home as a school could possibly be. There were single rooms for the teachers, comfortable double rooms for the pupils, a dining room, kitchen, several parlors and spacious classrooms. With four teachers and two matrons to supervise thirty-two girls, there was ample opportunity for individual attention.

My chief desire was to learn how to read, and I embarked on this great adventure almost before Mama and Papa had left the building after delivering me to the school. I'm sure they felt much worse about the separation than I did. Being so young, I was innocently unaware that they had another grave reason for their heavy hearts. All was far from well between them. Papa always was a restless man, unable or unwilling to stay long in any one position or in any one place. All through the years of my childhood I was well aware of his rolling-stone qualities, but it wasn't until I had grown up that I understood that it was a roving eye as well as a restless spirit that took him away from Mama and the family so much.

The excitement of learning how to read was exactly what I needed to keep me from feeling homesick. I settled quickly into the busy routine of the school.

At that time, beginners at Perkins were not taught Braille. We were taught to read raised letters, known as line, a system in which a firm impression was made on heavy paper by a wooden block, creating a letter that the reader could feel with his fingertips. Line was much harder to read than Braille, and required a more sensitive touch. If you could master line, it was easy to learn Braille, but, if you learned Braille first, it was very difficult to distinguish letters in line. Braille is easier to read because it is sharper than line, which is never used any more. But for a long time educators thought it was important for the blind to become familiar with the same kind of print that is used by the sighted. The truth is, of course, that the only thing that matters is that the blind person be able to read and write easily.

The greatest drawback to the line system was that it couldn't be written. Even though we might become skillful enough in line to read the most profound classics, we still couldn't write a word of our own. The teachers at Perkins tried to overcome this by having us practice the art of writing with a pencil. Relying entirely on the sense of touch and the directions of the teacher, unable to see a thing I had written and just guessing at the approximate length of each line, I found it one of the most laborious and frustrating tasks I have ever tried. We used a grooved board to help us guide our writing, but it was pretty bad. The one good thing I can say for this method, aside from the fact that I still use it to place my signature on checks, passports, and other documents, is that all my letters home were written this way, and Mama seemed to be able to read them. I think it's safe to say, however, that it would take a mother to make the effort.

These days there is a universal Braille system in use throughout the United States, and Braille has been adapted to most of the other languages of the world, including such difficult ones as Chinese and Japanese. But when I was going to school, three different versions of the basic Braille idea, a code of raised dots, were fighting for supremacy. English Braille, the original system invented by young Louis Braille, a French teacher of the blind who was infuriated with the line method because it left him unable to write, was considered the most difficult. It contained many contractions and only the best readers used it. In our country the great rivalry was between the systems known as American Braille and New York Point. The struggle was bitter. The advocates of both the rival methods had the interests of the blind at heart, but they become so absorbed in the battle to win government appropriations that all too often they seemed to forget the real purpose of their work. Not only was there scandalously wasteful duplication of badly needed books, but blind readers schooled in one system often had to learn one or both of the others in order to read books in which they were vitally interested. It was by no means easy to go from one system to another; they were greatly different. But I, brought up on American Braille, had to learn New York Point when I began to study Latin because that was the only system in which the required grammar book was printed. If any of us wanted to read a book published in Great Britain, English Braille was called for. A pupil in a New York school, using New York

Point, couldn't read a letter from a friend in Philadelphia, where American Braille prevailed.

Luckily for the blind population of the United States, and for that matter of the whole world, reason and common sense finally got the upper hand, and after a blazing controversy, which sometimes threatened to undermine the entire program of education for the blind, it was decided to make the English Braille system universal for all readers of the Roman alphabet throughout the world. The universal system wasn't adopted in the United States until I had nearly finished college, but I was glad to give up American Braille and set to work mastering the highly contracted English system, thankful that, at last, I would be able to read the many fine books that had been embossed only in that system. Everyone co-operated so enthusiastically that most pupils in schools for the blind today have never even heard of American Braille or New York Point.

In addition to reading and the painful pencil writing, my early lessons at Perkins included arithmetic, handicraft and music. We were given a lot of poetry to memorize, too, and the teachers spent hours reading all kinds of interesting stories to us. It was a well-rounded schedule, generously broken up by play periods.

We ate our meals in a spacious dining room equipped with four large tables. The sixteen older girls sat at two of the tables with one teacher at each, while the sixteen younger girls had both a matron and a teacher at each of their tables. That way our table manners could be carefully supervised.

I had been there about a week when the teacher at our table spoke to me about my eating habits. "All our girls are expected to eat whatever we have," she said firmly. "It's not only bad manners to pick and choose, but when you grow up it will be very hard for you to travel if you can't eat and enjoy every kind of food. However," she added understand-ingly, "if there's something you really can't bear to eat, tell me about it now and I won't serve it to you when we have it." That was fair enough. Vastly relieved, I gave the teacher my list of pet aversions—baked beans, sweet potatoes and boiled cabbage, with particular emphasis on the beans. Even during the acute food shortage in postwar Japan, when we were given baked beans as our canned food ration in place of the usual corned beef, I managed to get by without eating them. I'm sure that my ability to miss a meal without minding it too much dates from my Perkins days, when the entire school ate beans every Saturday night and Sunday morning while I managed successfully with brown bread. Our teacher never complained about my occasional fastings because, except for my three aversions, I stuck faithfully to our bargain and ate everything that was put in front of me.

The teachers at Perkins were strict, but they were so gentle and understanding that the rules didn't hurt; they instilled in us very definite ideas of right and wrong. Little misdemeanors might be overlooked but infringements of fundamental principles were not tolerated. This was made abundantly clear to me once when I trifled with the truth. We weren't allowed to leave our own rooms and visit others, and one day, when one of the teachers called me and I didn't respond right away, she asked me where I had been. I told her quickly that I had been in my room. But I hadn't been; I had been in a friend's room, and the teacher knew it. I had lied because I was frightened. It was only a small matter but I can remember to this day how humiliated I felt when the teacher showed me how low I had fallen in her regard. For a long time, she scarcely noticed me. She may have overdone the silent treatment a little, and perhaps modern advocates of pampering the young would tremble with fear of lasting inhibitions being planted in the shunned child, but as far as I've ever been able to see the only effect the punishment had on me was to teach me a wholesome respect for the truth, which has never hurt me.

When I went home for summer vacation at the end of my second year at Perkins, I found to my surprise that the family was getting ready to move to Hartford, Connecticut. It was another phase in Papa's long history of restlessness. Convinced that he owed it to himself to apply his talents to a business of his own, so that he could reap all the profits of his genius, he had quit his job. I can remember hearing the glum news being repeated over and over again to relatives and friends of the family. "Harry has resigned." The words were spoken with such a doleful air that they assumed in my mind the most sinister implication, like "Carthage must be destroyed."

It was indeed a serious matter. Papa's severing of relations with American Electrolitic marked the end of our family's prosperity for a long time to come.

Papa's first venture as an independent capitalist was an unmitigated disaster. He had a nice little savings account put by from the excellent salary he had been earning, and he decided to use the money to underwrite the publication of a history of Pawtucket. Papa had met the prospective author of this work, become interested in the idea, and, upon learning that all the man needed was a backer, had made up his mind that Fate had singled him out for this fortunate role. Fate had singled him out, all right, but there was nothing fortunate about it.

The book was handsomely printed and illustrated and was made available, according to your taste and pocketbook, in either cloth or leather binding. Unhappily, the cost of publication was considerably higher than Papa and his author-partner had anticipated, and in order to have any chance of making a profit on the deal, they were compelled to fix a steep price on the book. The good people of Pawtucket did not rush to buy up the edition. The bound volumes piled up unsold in our house, and the author, who had worked on a salary paid out of Papa's dwindling capital, sought other communities to conquer. Papa was left holding a very large and expensive bag.

Badly in need of another business opportunity, he had turned up something in Hartford. I don't remember much about Papa's business ventures during the next two years, the first of which we spent in Hartford and the second in Albany, New York. The only one that sticks in my mind was an installment-plan clothing business, which, I'm afraid, was so far ahead of its time that Papa's sharply depleted capital was reduced almost to the vanishing point. We saw very little of him in those two years; most of our contact with him was through the irregular letters he wrote Mama, with money orders enclosed. We lived comfortably enough, but there were no more luxuries like Lemuel Brown, the coachman, and the horse and carriage we had had in Pawtucket. Between our tightened financial circumstances and Papa's long absences from home with their undertone of another claim on his affections, Mama must have been worried to death; I was old enough to sense that she was often anxious and preoccupied. But she was never too wrapped up in her own troubles to take time out for us.

I had expected to return to school at Jamaica Plains, which would constitute no drain on our family finances because tuition and board were free for any resident of the New England states. But Mama discovered that there was a primary school for the blind right in Hartford which also prepared pupils for the upper grades of the Perkins School. This was a pleasant surprise, for though I had been very happy in my old school, the prospect of being near enough to be able to come home every weekend was an appealing one. The Connecticut School for the Blind actually was within walking distance of our house, and I could have come home every night if the rules of the school hadn't required pupils to board there all through the week.

We had, I think, about twenty-five pupils living in adjoining duplex houses that at one time had been ordinary homes. We had comfortable rooms, although nothing so grand as the relatively new quarters at Jamaica Plains. The food was good, and we were well taught.

One of the things I remember about that year was the

night I outwitted Death. My two roommates and I concocted some medicine for our dolls, using a mixture of tooth powder, soapsuds and water dye extracted from strenuously washed hair ribbons. We bottled the mixture carefully and tried it on the dolls. When they failed to respond in any way, one of the girls suggested that I try it on myself to see how it acted. Unhesitatingly, I swallowed a generous dose of the unappetizing mixture. My friends, aghast at my bravery, told me I would surely die. It happened just before bedtime, and, prudently rejecting the idea of taking my troubles to the school nurse, I went to bed. I was petrified with fear but I was grimly determined that I would not die.

I had no idea what people did when they died, but I was quite sure it had something to do with going to sleep. So my first step in my struggle against Death was to make certain that under no circumstances would I go to sleep. I was sure that everything would be all right if I could just keep my eyes open all night. It was, too. I never shut my eyes once. All night long I counted sheep, thought about places I had been and places I would like to go, and went over my favorite stories, scene by scene. And, sure enough, in the morning I was still alive. I got out of bed with the triumphant feeling of a conqueror.

Henry and I began to learn something about our religion during that year in Hartford. Papa was a Catholic, although far from a zealous one, and Mama didn't join the Church until we had grown up. But Mama had promised to raise us as Catholics, and she did her best for us. Most of the responsibility for instructing us fell upon Aunt Ducky's shoulders, but she didn't seem to mind. I also got a great deal of help from Miss Neil, our school nurse, who had the added duty of looking after the spiritual progress of the Catholic pupils. She not only gave us an excellent foundation in the Catechism but worked hard to make us understand that religion is something to be lived, not merely memorized. Miss Neil did much to awaken in me a desire to know more about my religion.

Whenever I hear people say, "We shouldn't teach children religion when they're young; we ought to wait until they grow up and can choose for themselves," I am filled with wonder at the reasoning processes of human beings. It makes just as much sense to say, "We shouldn't insist upon feeding children while they're young; we ought to wait until they grow up and can choose for themselves what they want to eat."

After a year in Hartford, we moved to Albany. I didn't know it at the time but Mama told me later that Papa's business affairs had gone from bad to worse. We saw him only every now and then, although he still sent money to us by mail. It's too bad Mama, who could be very firm with Henry and me, was such a clinging vine where Papa was concerned. She almost never took a stand in opposition to him. Whatever he said, she accepted. She was an old-fashioned wife who believed in deferring to her husband. Unfortunately, that was, I am convinced, the worst way to handle Papa, who badly needed a stronger hand. It was pleasant that they never quarreled but it might have been better if Mama had forcefully awakened him to his responsibilities.

There was no school for the blind in Albany for me to go to, but my days were far from empty. Henry was in the third grade of the public school and I went along with him nearly every day. His third-grade teacher, Miss Redmond, and the fifth-grade teacher, Miss Vaversaur, took as much interest in me as if I had been a regular pupil. They allowed me to attend their classes as often as I pleased, and even invited me to take part in the recitations, which gave me a glorious opportunity to show off my extensive reading. Whenever blackboard work came up, I silently drifted away to the other classroom, looking for something that was more in my line. When Miss Redmond or Miss Vaversaur had to go out, they would appoint me monitor, and I would be happily "in charge" until they returned.

Mama continued to read to me by the hour, from authors

like Scott, Thackeray and Dickens. The world of books held
me enthralled. My interest in foreign lands was aroused first
by a book called *Thaddeus of Warsaw,* an exciting story which
led me to search out the only Polish girl in the fifth grade
and share her seat for weeks in a vain attempt to learn from
her some more information about the land of her origin.
Even her name was disappointing; instead of a long and
beautifully unpronounceable one, hers was Annie Green. I
was crushed. I had thought it would be something like Lud-
mila Jedrezejowski.

Both of my teacher friends were Catholics, and with Mama's
permission they took Henry and me to a wonderful Domini-
can sister who gave me instruction for my First Communion.
Henry helped me faithfully. He would read the questions out
of the Catechism and I would recite the answers that I had
learned from the sister.

I received my First Communion on a beautiful summer
morning, after having spent three memorable days of preparation living in the convent with the sisters. They put me in a
private room of my own, served me my meals in solitary
splendor in the otherwise empty guest dining room, and allowed me to go to Holy Mass with them every morning.

Late that summer we packed up once again and went back
to Pawtucket. This time, though, Mama put all her own
household effects into storage and we moved in with Mama's
sister, Aunt Belle. In September, I was readmitted to the
Perkins School primary department at Jamaica Plains. I was
glad to be back. I learned Braille, began taking piano lessons,
and made my first attempts at writing. The trouble was, I was
interested in writing only love stories, and my teachers discouraged me rather sharply.

All the pupils at Jamaica Plains lived for the time when
they would go to the upper school at South Boston, and
eventually the great day arrived for me. I had attained my
first major goal in life.

The boys at South Boston lived in a big building called

"The Old School." The girls lived and studied in five cottages and two classroom buildings situated in the spacious court-yard. Each cottage housed fourteen or fifteen girls, along with a house mother and three or four teachers. We lived together just like a large family. Each cottage had a cook, but the rest of the work was performed by the students. It wasn't play work, either; it was the real thing. We all were assigned specific duties by the house mother—sweeping, scrubbing, washing dishes and waiting on table. If we didn't do our as-signed task properly, we were promptly summoned to do it over. It was just as much a part of our education as arithmetic or American history.

Every afternoon we went out for a walk, not in a procession but two by two, a girl with a little sight walking alongside a totally blind one. In those days the streets were compara-tively free of traffic and we had little to fear. Everyone in the neighborhood knew us and we were as much a part of the community as anyone else as we hurried or dawdled along, depending upon our mood, doing a little shopping or stopping to talk to acquaintances. The only restriction the school au-thorities placed upon our outings was that we girls had to take our walk at a different time from that allotted to the boys.

Among the things that made the year memorable was the big fire one evening in midwinter. We were taking our handi-craft lesson in the school's newest building, the only brick building on the campus, when the cry of fire went up. The teacher told us to get out as fast as we could and not to stop in the cloakroom downstairs to look for our coats. We had never had a fire drill but we didn't need one. From the teacher, who was blind herself, to the smallest child, we all scurried out of the building without a moment's hesitation. There was nobody to guide us. We simply relied on our memories and our senses of touch and sound. In no time at all we were all out in the courtyard, where we stood around shivering while noses were counted. Then we were taken up to the boys' building, a rare adventure which, in our minds, far outweighed the fire.

I couldn't have been happier than I was at school that year, and I was looking forward to many more years of all that Perkins had to give. But just after Easter one of the girls in our cottage was stricken with scarlet fever. As a matter of precaution, all the girls in the cottage were sent home. I thought it would be only for a week or two, but when I got home Mama told me I wasn't going back.

Uncle Leonard had become interested in the treatment of alcoholism, and he had opened a sanitarium in a large house in Haverstraw, New York, a pleasant brickmaking town on the west shore of the Hudson River just below West Point. Things had gone from bad to worse between Papa and Mama, so Uncle Leonard and Aunt Ducky had invited us to come and live with them in their big house.

Once we were settled there, Papa appeared less and less, and finally he didn't come home at all. I can't remember that he actually ever said good-by to us. He was, of course, always leaving on trips and therefore always saying good-by; this time, he simply didn't come back. Mama heard from him from time to time, and after I grew up he sent Mama and me a little money, but that was all.

Aside from the blunt fact that we needed a home, Mama felt good about our move to the sanitarium because it gave her an opportunity to help Aunt Ducky, whose health, never robust, was slipping. I was intensely interested in our new surroundings. The patients, confirmed alcoholics, came from all parts of the country and from all walks of life. Aunt Ducky, Mama and I weren't allowed to see them when they first came, but as soon as they were "straightened out," we were allowed to be with them just as though they were members of the family. Sometimes we talked to them about subjects of mutual interest, sometimes we played games with them, and sometimes we just listened to their troubles. Uncle Leonard felt it was just as important to make the patients feel welcome in our family circle as it was to provide them with the medical treatment they needed. In a way it was a miniature, and pioneer, Alcoholics Anonymous, and it worked. Most of the patients were able to go home, well and able to face the world, after staying in the sanitarium about a month. Uncle Leonard kept careful track of his "graduates," and many of them made it a point to visit us every now and then after they had resumed their own lives. Among them were mechanics, farmers, traveling salesmen, doctors, lawyers and newspapermen, and they provided powerful examples to other men and women who were still trying to conquer their weakness. One of them was the mother of one of America's greatest playwrights.

Naturally, I missed no opportunity to draft willing patients to read to me, and since many of the professional men were voracious readers themselves they offered little resistance. They read many a book and magazine to me during the long summer afternoons on the spacious porch of the big house. Then, when fall came, and Henry went to the Haverstraw school, where he was a schoolmate of James A. Farley, who grew up to be President Franklin D. Roosevelt's campaign manager and Postmaster General, I was enrolled in the Overbrook School for the Blind in Philadelphia. Mama selected Overbrook not only because it had an excellent reputation but also because it was near Grandma Hillman's home. I would be able to use Grandma's address as mine, and thereby qualify for free tuition, and I would have a place to go for occasional weekend visits.

Overbrook's main building was a dazzling white. It was built along Spanish lines with two inner courts or cloisters, one for boys and the other for girls, off which both classrooms and living quarters opened. It was an up-to-date plant, and I was lucky to be able to spend nine years there, four of them earning my diploma and five more studying music and preparing for college. It was at Overbrook that I seriously prepared for the business of living. The lessons I learned there—academic, social and moral—gave me the background

I needed for the years ahead. Some of the men and women I met there, and studied under, influenced not only my life but the entire course of American education of the blind.

Dr. Edward E. Allen, who was the principal of the school most of the time I was there, was a remarkable man. It isn't too much to say that I don't make an important decision even now without asking myself what Dr. Allen would think of it. We all stood in wholesome awe of him—in fact, sometimes we were scared to death of him—but his persuasive personality and his unshakable confidence in our ability to live full lives in spite of our handicap fired all of us with courage and enthusiasm. He was strict with us and exacting with his teachers, but he was never harsh, never unreasonable, and never petty. In every way he knew how, he instilled in us the desire to live like other people, to be independent and to contribute something to the world instead of just asking the world to take care of us. I firmly believe that his policy of never babying us was far better than the tendency in too many schools for the blind today to do everything for the child.

Every morning we had a short chapel service, after which, four mornings a week, Dr. Allen talked to us or read a carefully chosen story or article. Mostly he spoke to us about ordinary things, trying to make us familiar with what was going on in the world around us. He told us about his trips to other schools or conventions, of his occasional trips abroad, or perhaps about an unusually interesting lecture he had attended. He read to us about explorers, inventors, artists and writers, about all sorts of successful people, both blind and sighted. Often, he brought guests to speak to us, and sometimes he invited the guest to eat with us in the pupils' dining room.

I remember one day, while we were in class, he walked down the corridor with a guest, who remarked, in the unthinking tone that some people use in the presence of the blind, possibly with the idea that they are deaf, "Why do you have so many beautiful plants and pictures in the classrooms? They can't see them, can they?"

"No," Dr. Allen said, "they can't see them with their eyes, but their awareness of beauty is the same as anybody else's. It just makes sense that people who are surrounded by beauty will learn to love beautiful things."

We had many contacts with the outside world. Generous artists came to give us concerts and entertainments; our glee club performed at churches and clubs; and every week a group of teachers and pupils attended the Saturday-night concert of the Philadelphia Orchestra, using tickets supplied by members of the school board. We all attended our own churches and joined as actively as possible in their programs. Pupils who could see a little were encouraged to take totally blind pupils on trips around the city. Traffic wasn't much of a problem and it was comparatively easy for us to go all over Philadelphia, on foot or by streetcar, either alone or with friends. We were constantly being told that we simply had to learn to get around by ourselves, and after a while we thought nothing of it. As every blind person learns early in life, people are astonishingly eager to help; all it takes is a little confidence and good sense, and you can go almost anywhere. I suppose you might wonder why I wasn't killed during some of my adventures in the city, but even now, when traffic accidents are so frighteningly common, blind victims are rare. Our Guardian Angels are kept busy but they manage to take good care of us.

I had a difficult time convincing Mama and Aunt Ducky of this whenever it was time for me to make a vacation trip from Philadelphia to Haverstraw. There was no tunnel under the Hudson River at that time—and, for that matter, no sepulchral Pennsylvania Station to get lost in. The Philadelphia trains ended their runs at the Pennsylvania Railroad's terminal in Jersey City. In order to get home from there, I had to take a shuttle train to Weehawken and then change to a train for Haverstraw. Because of the complications, I always was met at Jersey City by either Mama or Aunt Ducky, and we made the rest of the trip together. But I wanted very much to be allowed to do it alone, and I kept pleading for permission. Finally, Mama said, all right, I could try it.

I was a proud young lady when I stepped off the train in Jersey City and started on the intricate journey home. I was even prouder when I finally settled down in a seat next to the window on the train to Haverstraw. I felt downright triumphant, because I had proved that my sense of direction was as good as I had said it was and that people were as kind as I had thought they were. I had hardly settled myself, though, when a lady sat down next to me and, to my astonishment, leaned up against me and kissed me hard. It was Aunt Ducky. She had met the train at Jersey City, and, without saying a word, keeping a discreet distance, had followed me through all my changes, thereby assuring herself and Mama that I was indeed capable of managing the trip by myself. After that, they raised no objections to my traveling alone.

Dr. Allen encouraged us in all these venturesome activities because his central purpose was to convince us that we could live full and normal lives if we would just make up our minds that we were going to.

Dr. David D. Wood, the director of the music department at Overbrook, himself a totally blind graduate of the school, shared Dr. Allen's fervent conviction that we should, for our own good, be urged to involve ourselves as much as possible in the world outside. The power of decision, he kept telling us, lay within ourselves. If we were determined to do it, we could do it. He stood shoulder to shoulder with Dr. Allen in objecting strenuously whenever someone praised one of us for doing something that our blindness made hard for us. I can still hear both of them saying, "Don't say it's wonderful! It's no more than they should do!"

Our school always prided itself on its concerts. But, typically, Dr. Wood said we could do even more difficult things.

He made up his mind that we should give full-scale oratorios, and for five years before Dr. Wood died we gave a great choral work each year. Accompanied by the Philadelphia Orchestra, with the members of St. Stephen's choir as soloists, we sang the choruses from memory. We copied every note of the intricate choruses in Braille, practiced each part until we memorized it, then put all the parts together when Dr. Wood paid his twice-a-week visits to the school.

The first work we attempted was Mendelssohn's "Hymn of Praise." We had only one rehearsal with the orchestra, and then on the great night we gave the first concert without a slip. We sang the unaccompanied chorale as though our lives depended upon every note, and maybe they did; I think we would have inflicted bodily injury upon anyone luckless enough to have come in on the wrong note. Then we waited tensely for the orchestra to take up the theme. Had we kept up the pitch? We had. It was a genuinely thrilling moment for us when the members of the famous orchestra greeted the end of the performance by pounding lustily on their music stands. The last words of the work, "All that has life and breath, sing to the Lord," still hung in the air. We were filled with exultation. We had made good. Dr. Wood and the school would not be ashamed of us.

When I graduated from Overbrook, I had no idea of going on to college. Only one girl and very few boys from the school had ever done so, and I gave little thought to the possibility. As a matter of fact, I had no idea what I wanted to do. Nor did I see any reason why I should hurry my decision; I had only just passed my seventeenth birthday, and I was in no great rush to assume a major responsibility. I took the easy course of returning to Overbrook as a practice teacher. They put me on the payroll at the rate of seven dollars a month. I greatly enjoyed the work and I might easily have gone on to become a regular teacher in the school if that sudden flash of inspiration about Japan hadn't put me on a different road.

After I was exposed to the *Outlook* Magazine article about the segregation of Japanese schoolchildren in California, I began to read everything about Japan that I could get my hands on. More than anything else, I wanted to go there, but I had sense enough to realize that the first thing I had to do was to learn something about the country. Then I might be in a position to influence the thinking of other Americans at least a little bit.

I inaugurated my career as an unofficial ambassador of Japan by trying to stir up some interest in the country among my friends at school. It wasn't hard because the girls always were ready to adopt a new cause, and Japan was as good as anything else. They even went along with a scheme I concocted to mount a debate on the question that originally had awakened my interest: "Should Japanese Children in California Be Sent to Separate Schools?" Aside from my interest in the merits of the issue, I was enthusiastic about the debate because I felt that it would give me a golden opportunity to accumulate material on Japan without making my teachers curious about why I wanted it. I didn't want to get involved in lengthy explanations. The only problem that remained unsolved was how I might get hold of the kind of material I had in mind. Today, when even some of the smallest foreign countries maintain information bureaus in the United States, this would be no problem at all. Then, however, it was a major project.

After I had racked my brain for days, I finally decided to seek out the Japanese Consul and ask him to assist me. I didn't want to ask any of the teachers to help me locate this mysterious dignitary because I didn't want to expose my big dream yet, for fear of having it stamped on; so, with the faith of the very young, I asked the man who owned our favorite drugstore if he had any idea how I might be able to get in touch with the Japanese Consul. He scratched his head and said, no, he didn't, but if it would help me any, he did happen to know where the office of the Belgian Consul was.

I didn't think there was likely to be much connection between the two, but at least it was a clue, so I called the number the drugstore man gave me, and, to my intense joy, I was given the name and address of the man I sought. The only disappointment involved was that the Consul wasn't a Japanese at all, but an American businessman hired to take care of the duties of the office. His name was Franklin McFadden, and he was a cotton merchant with an office on the Philadelphia waterfront.

Obtaining permission to go after material for the scheduled debate, I set out alone for Mr. McFadden's office at Second and Arch Streets. When I got there, with the combined help of a kindly streetcar conductor, a policeman and two or three passersby, I made my way up a flight of stairs lined with packing boxes and bales of cotton, and found Mr. McFadden. He was a most considerate man and he listened in a friendly manner as I explained to him that I needed some literature about Japan for use in a high school debate. He was very sympathetic, and he appeared to be genuinely interested in my problem, but he had no idea where I might be able to find what I was after. He didn't know any more about Japan than I did.

"I'd be glad to lend you some material," he said gravely, "but I don't have a thing in the office except the Japan Year Book. If you think that will help you, and if you promise to bring it back in two weeks, you're welcome to it."

I didn't have the remotest idea what the Japan Year Book was, but I accepted Mr. McFadden's offer with gratitude. Anything was better than nothing. So I walked proudly out of his office carrying a book as thick and as heavy as a dictionary. It was packed with facts about Japan, including data on courts of law, educational institutions, factories, prefectural governments and a variety of other organizations. It was such a big book that I had a hard time lining up enough teachers to take turns reading it to me. Typically, however, I persevered until I had drained the book of every line of information.

Japan was no longer an unreal fairyland to me, but more than ever I was determined to go there, to live there and to work there.

Chapter **III**

Making up my mind that I was going to cross the Pacific
Ocean and take up my life's work in Japan was one thing;
getting there was quite another. One thing was certain. It
wasn't going to be any tourist's joyride. I would have to earn
every inch of my way.

It seemed obvious to me that the natural thing for me
to do was to go to Japan as a teacher of the blind. I knew the
Japanese had schools for the blind because I had learned
about them from the year book, which also had informed me
that clinical massage and Japanese music were the principal
occupations of the blind. Surely, when I got there, I could
make myself useful as a teacher of blind children. But in
order to qualify I would have to be properly educated and
trained myself. That meant I had to go to college.

Mama, Aunt Ducky and Uncle Leonard were enthusiastic
about the idea. Talking it over, we settled on Trinity College
in Washington, a relatively new Catholic college for women
that was affiliated with Catholic University. But we agreed
that it would be best not to apply for admission until I had
made sufficient preparation to give me solid grounds for
asking the Sisters to accept a blind student.

As soon as I returned to Overbrook in September, I put
the matter before Miss Elizabeth Dunning, the Principal of

the Girls Department. It was Miss Dunning who had prepared Overbrook's other college girl for Vassar. She gladly agreed to give me all the help she possibly could; anything that would be helpful to one of her girls always found favor in Miss Dunning's eyes. She worked with me on my Latin for an hour every night, staying with it all the way through Caesar, Cicero and Virgil.

After writing to Trinity for a syllabus, we mapped out a course of study that included four years of Latin, three years of German, and extra work in English Literature, History and Mathematics. It was a heavy program but I buckled down to it with pleasure, and my teachers seemed to be as happy about it as I was. All they knew, though, was that I was determined to go to college; I hadn't told a soul about my burning desire to go to Japan.

My one regret was that I didn't know any Japanese people, but that was soon remedied. One of my classmates told me that she had heard there were two Japanese students at the Women's Medical College, and I went into action with the zeal of a private detective. I telephoned the college and found out their names and where they lived. Whenever I obtain such information over the telephone I have to memorize it until I can get to a Braille slate and write down what I have been told. It was quite a task memorizing the names of Miss Aizawa and Miss Nakagawa, and their address, but I managed it. They lived in a boardinghouse near Girard Avenue, and my next step was to call them, introduce myself, and ask permission to call on them. They were very friendly, and on the next Sunday I went to see them.

I told them immediately of my ambition to go to Japan. From the way I made my announcement, I'm sure they must have thought I was planning to sail the next day. But I soon set them straight and we spent many a pleasant hour together that year talking about their home country. They were charming girls, juniors in the medical college, gravely serious and hard working, determined to make the most of the opportunity that had been given them to study abroad.

I must have pestered those two girls to death. I was always dropping in on them or inviting them out to a flower show or concert, and every moment I was with them I was pumping them for information about their homeland. In a way, though, I think they rather enjoyed it. They were very reserved and didn't seem to have many friends. Sometimes, when their work was caught up, they must have been lonely. I often invited them to visit Overbrook on Sunday afternoons, and they always were warmly welcomed by everyone. It was unheard of for a pupil to invite guests to a meal, but Miss Lorimer, our understanding head matron, recognized the educational advantages of having such unusual guests, and she frequently asked the girls to stay for Sunday supper. After a while they were more the school's guests than mine.

Toward the end of my next to last year at Overbrook, I was stunned by the news that Dr. Allen, the principal, was going to leave. In common with most of the other older pupils, I couldn't imagine what the school would be like without him, but we were somewhat consoled when he told us that his successor was to be Olin H. Burritt, the principal of the New York State School for the Blind at Batavia, New York, whom we all knew because he was a close friend of Dr. Allen and had visited us many times. We knew that if we had to lose Dr. Allen, we could hardly do better than Mr. Burritt as his replacement. But, just the same, it was a blow to lose the principal we had known and loved so long. The only thing that made it any better was the knowledge that he was going to my old school, Perkins, to succeed Dr. Anagnos, who had died, and to build a new school on a beautiful site on the Charles River, at Watertown.

I was hoping to enter Trinity at the start of the 1910 school year, and I had little on my mind except the entrance examinations which the college authorities already had given me permission to take. Then, one morning at chapel, Mr. Burritt announced, "We're going to have a very special open

house guest on Overbrook Day. He comes from Japan."
Quite seriously, he looked around the room and said, "You
all know where Japan is, I'm sure." There was a very audible
titter, which may have puzzled poor Mr. Burritt but was
very clear to me. My one-track mind had made Japan almost
as familiar to the students of Overbrook as Philadelphia. "His
name," Mr. Burritt went on, "is Mr. Yoshimoto. Remember
that, Yoshimoto. If he should happen to speak to any of you,
I want you to be sure to remember his name and to pro-
nounce it correctly."

If the principal had said that the Angel Gabriel was
coming to our school, I couldn't have been more excited.
From that moment on, all the preparations for Overbrook
Day had only one meaning for me. Mr. Yoshimoto was
coming, from Japan, and maybe I would be able to talk to
him and get him to help me.

When the great day finally came, we were all busy showing
the work of the school to the hundreds of guests who flooded
the buildings and grounds. Mr. Yoshimoto walked around
with Mr. Burritt, inspecting our classroom work and handicrafts, watching exhibitions of gymnastics and folk dancing,
and listening to a short concert. I never found myself near
him. But that night, at the school dance which was the traditional climax of the day, I finally got my chance. Mr. Burritt
introduced me to Mr. Yoshimoto, and, as soon as the principal turned away to speak to someone else, I threw caution
to the winds and boldly invited the gentleman from Japan to
step outside on the cloister with me, where we wouldn't be
disturbed.

It was my first encounter with the imperturbable politeness of the Japanese gentleman. Mr. Yoshimoto didn't turn
a hair. He simply followed me outside, said something about
what an interesting day it had been, and waited for me to
speak. Without wasting any words, I told him that the one
thing in all the world I wanted to do was to go to Japan and
find my life work there.

For a long minute he was silent. Then he said, gently, "Why don't you stay in the United States? You can earn much more money here than you ever could in Japan."

It had never occurred to me that my cherished project might be looked upon as a money-making venture. I had realized, of course, that I would have to find a way to support myself, but I had thought of that only as a necessary evil. My object in going to Japan was to get to know the country and its people and to do anything I could to be useful there.

"Honestly," I told him, "I don't care about how much money I can earn. All I'm interested in is going to Japan."

Mr. Yoshimoto, a mature man with serious work to do, undoubtedly thought I was a silly, sentimental schoolgirl obsessed with the notion that Japan was a romantic land filled with Lieutenant Pinkertons and Madame Butterflies. He was patient. He told me a little about the difficult living conditions in Japan, and something about the blind of the country, in whom he was very much interested, partly because his own eyesight was steadily becoming worse. But he gave me no encouragement except to say that he would be staying at Overbrook for a week and would be happy to talk to me again if I still wanted to know more about his country.

He must have lost no time sounding out Mr. Burritt about my idea, because the next day, when I took my friends from the Medical College over to Mr. Burritt's house to meet their countryman, the principal demanded to know if I was serious about wanting to go to Japan.

The cat was out of the bag, and from then on I had to endure the questions and the discouraging arguments of my friends, who thought I was crazy even to think of such a thing. I was amazed to discover how little Americans knew about Japan and how much prejudice there was against the country. For instance, I kept hearing the old story that Japanese people were so innately dishonest that all Japanese banks had to employ Chinese cashiers. "They don't ever trust their own," I was told again and again. I wish I had known then that this ridiculous misconception was circulated by tourists who had visited American or European-owned banks in Yokohama and Kobe, where Chinese experts in detecting counterfeit money often were employed. Japanese-owned banks, on the other hand, never use Chinese in any capacity.

The cherry blossom and geisha enthusiasts were almost as hard to cope with as the anti-Japanese. They were guilty of just as much falsification in talking about the country as though it were a fairyland peopled with bowing men and dancing women and studded with exotic towns containing a few dozen fragile doll houses, each with a private view of Mount Fuji. Thanks to Mr. McFadden, the part-time Consul, and my educational exposure to the Japan Year Book, I knew better. From the beginning, I never fell for that "Mysterious East" nonsense. I looked upon the Japanese as real, matter-of-fact people, serious and hard-working, and that saved me a lot of heartache later on.

During the June week that Mr. Yoshimoto stayed with us at Overbrook, I virtually haunted him. On the day he left, he told me that if, after I had been in college for two years, I still felt that I wanted to live and work in Japan, I should write to him and he would help me. He gave me an address in Oxford, England, which I carefully memorized. I was satisfied that I was on my way, and I devoted myself with renewed energy to my preparations for college.

Naturally, I couldn't take the exams in the same manner the other applicants did, so arrangements were made for the questions to be forwarded to the Academy of Notre Dame in Philadelphia, a preparatory school for Trinity, operated by the same order of nuns. The plan was for one of the Sisters to read the questions to me and for me to copy them in Braille. Then, in the same amount of time given to the ordinary applicant, I would write the answers on the trusty portable I had been given when I learned to type. Problems in mathematics I worked out in Braille and then dictated to the Sister. The one concession made to me was that I was permitted to substitute an extra math course for science, because we had no science courses at Overbrook.

During the summer holidays, I got word that I had passed everything. The only hurdle I still had to clear was medieval history, which had been postponed until the autumn to give me an opportunity to study it through the summer. But, even before I got around to taking, and passing, that last examination, I was notified that I had been awarded a freshman-year scholarship that would pay for my tuition, room and board. I didn't see how I could ask for anything more.

One other matter I had wanted to take care of before entering college led me that summer to the Manhattan Eye and Ear Hospital in New York, where my useless left eye was removed. This was the operation suggested by the surgeon who had performed the iridectomy on my "good" eye when I was a baby. The dead and disfigured eye was replaced by an infinitely more attractive artificial one. My appearance, everyone told me, was greatly improved.

I was ready to go on to new things.

Chapter IV

I wanted two things from college, each with equal passion. I wanted to learn everything I could, and I wanted to prove— not only to the faculty and the students, but to myself, too— that I could compete on even terms with people who could see. The Sisters clearly intended to give me every opportunity to do exactly that. They had made it plain that they would be glad to accept me, if I passed the entrance examinations, but that, once I was enrolled, they couldn't give me any special consideration because of my blindness. That was fair enough; the last thing I wanted was to be treated any differently from the others.

When I registered at Trinity, two or three days before classes were to begin, the Dean, Sister Mary, asked me how I was planning to get the assignments read. I told her that I had assumed I would have to pay student workers to read to me.

"Well," Sister Mary said, "don't make any arrangements like that until you talk to me about it again. Unless I'm very much mistaken about the kind of girls we have here, you'll be able to get your reading done without having to pay for it."

She was right. For three years, every single morning, as soon as the lights came on at five-thirty, I would hear a gentle

39

tap on my door and I would open it to Mary Johnson, hud-
dled inside a flannel robe, holding the day's history assignment in her hand. In order to read it to me, she had gone
to the school library when it closed at nine-thirty the night
before, taken the book after everyone else had finished with
it, and arranged to return it by eight o'clock, when the library
would reopen. She read to me for a full hour from five-
thirty to six-thirty as the heat made its slow way through the
pipes and the winter dawn lighted the sky. The rules of the
library forbade anyone to read aloud to me there during
regular hours, so Mary did it the hard way.

Zoe Walsh read the English lessons to me, Mary Hayes read
the mathematics problems, and everyone else, upperclassmen
as well as members of my own class, did everything they
could to help Genevieve Caulfield get to Japan, for it wasn't
long before they all knew that was my goal.

Toward the end of my second year I wrote, as I had
promised I would, to Mr. Yoshimoto and told him that I still
wanted very much to go to his country to teach the blind.
Much to my joy, he answered, and said that he would do
everything in his power to help me. After that I wrote to him
from time to time, asking for advice as to the best way to
prepare for what I wanted to do, and he responded with many
a valuable suggestion.

I was still seizing every opportunity to add to the number
of my Japanese friends. Among them were Dr. and Mrs.
Toyokiko Takami, who lived in Brooklyn and who invited
me one memorable weekend to visit them at their home in
order that I might attend a dinner the Japan Society was
giving in New York in honor of the Japanese ambassador,
Count Chinda, and his wife. As often happens, that dinner
snowballed when Count Chinda invited me to visit the Embassy in Washington, where I found two more good friends,
Mr. and Mrs. Tamakichi Ohta. Mr. Ohta, who later became
his country's ambassador to Russia, was then the second
secretary of the Embassy. I got to know him and his charming

wife well, and for a long time I went to their Washington home every Saturday afternoon to give Mrs. Ohta an opportunity to practice her English with me, and afterward to have Japanese-style dinner with her and her husband. It was in their home that I had my first lessons in the art of eating with chopsticks.

In many ways, Trinity's location in Washington was a great boon to me. Aside from my special interest in the Japanese Embassy, I was able to make trips to such fascinating places as the houses of Congress, the Supreme Court and the Library of Congress. Also, Uncle Leonard's three sisters had moved to Washington and I was able to visit them whenever I felt a special need to be with someone who was close to my family. Nevertheless, despite all these advantages, I decided, at the end of my third year, that for my final year I ought to transfer to Columbia University in New York.

Even though what I wanted to do in Japan was to work for the blind, I knew I had better be thoroughly prepared to do a good job as an English teacher, in order to be sure of earning a living. The courses at Trinity would give me the basic qualifications, but I had to admit that a degree from Columbia would carry a lot more prestige in Japan. I left Trinity with a heavy heart but I was sure I was doing the right thing.

Blind students had attended other departments of the university but I was the first ever to enroll in Columbia Teachers College. My role as a trailblazer was made clear to me in my first interview with the secretary of the college. "One thing I'm very worried about," he told me, "is your using the elevators. I don't think that would be safe for you at all, and I wish you wouldn't try it, at least not until you've had plenty of time to get accustomed to everything around here."

I wanted to put his mind at rest, so I promised him I would be glad to walk up and down the stairs. I didn't bother to add that, on the whole, it was far more dangerous than a nice, comfortable ride on the elevator. He was plainly relieved, and I didn't mind the extra exercise.

I think my first day at Teachers College was the loneliest day of my life. Aunt Ducky had made the trip with me from Haverstraw, and it was raining pitchforks as our taxicab drew up in front of Whittier Hall, where I had been assigned a room on the second floor directly opposite the elevator I had pledged myself not to use. Aunt Ducky helped me arrange my possessions in the room, and sat quietly talking to me until, early in the afternoon, it was time for her to leave. After I said good-by to her I sat alone, struck by the astonishing quiet of the big dormitory. The only sound I heard was the regular opening and closing of the elevator door. I kept hoping that someone, stepping out of the elevator and passing my room, would stop and knock on the door, but nobody did. I felt very much alone.

As evening approached, I was so hungry that I couldn't bear it any longer. When I heard footsteps outside my door, I jumped up to intercept them. I poked my head outside and asked, hesitantly, "Can you tell me where the dining room is?"

"I was just going to ask if you could tell me," a cheerful voice replied. We both laughed at that, and we agreed to join forces in an all-out search. It wasn't long before we discovered that the dining room was high up in the building, on the eighth floor, a piece of information which caused me right then and there to abrogate my treaty with the secretary and take the forbidden elevator.

I found myself assigned to an interesting table group which included two Chinese girls, one from India, a journalist from New Zealand, a teacher from England and an American who was studying interior decoration. It was a genuinely international group, and I loved it, even when the two Chinese girls were at each other's throats. They came from different provinces of China and literally didn't speak the same language. When they talked to each other, which wasn't often, they had to speak English. When one of them was at the table and the other was not, the one who was present missed no opportunity to run down her countrywoman. About the only thing they had in common was that they both wore Chinese dress.

The girl from India contributed her share to the exotic character of the table by wearing a sari and sprinkling curry powder over everything she ate, including ice cream. I endured so much of the smell of curry powder that year that it was a long time before I was able to eat it myself. I was beginning to see what everyone meant when they said that a college education broadened one.

I ran into one snag which caused me all sorts of anxiety. When I settled myself in my room, I placed my Remington portable on a small table next to my desk. A typewriter, to a blind student, is what a fountain pen is to one who can see. I always typed my notes, my assignments, my examination papers, and of course my letters. I was hardly prepared for what happened when the social director of Whittier Hall came into my room on the second day of my stay and reacted with horror to the sight of the poor old Remington. "Miss Caulfield," she said in her chilliest tone, "hasn't anyone told you that students aren't permitted to have typewriters in their rooms?"

If she had asked me if I didn't know that we weren't allowed to sleep in our rooms, but were supposed to sleep on the floor in the Hall, I couldn't have been more surprised. I tried to explain how necessary my typewriter was to me, but she brushed aside all of my pleas. It was out of the question, she said, for me to have anything as noisy as a typewriter disturbing the academic hush of the dormitory. Even when I was bold enough to compare the gentle tapping of the typewriter with the harsh racket of the elevator, I was overruled. She was adamant.

Her first suggestion was that I keep my infernal machine in the dining room, where I could make all the noise I wanted to between meals. But the dining room was all the way up on top of the building, a long way from my second-floor cubbyhole, and even worse it was very much in use for a good two hours at each mealtime. There would be precious little "between" time.

The social director agreed at first to let me keep the typewriter in her office. But that didn't last long. The next haven was the general reception room where the girls were allowed to entertain their boy friends in the evening, and that was no haven at all. If I had been working on the kind of love stories I once had tried so hard to write at Perkins, I could have taken advantage of the situation to pick up a lot of useful material. But the tender scenes being enacted all around me didn't help my studying any, and I'm sure my incessant pounding on the typewriter didn't help them.

I felt frustrated enough to take up the matter with the Dean of Teachers College, who listened sympathetically to my tale of woe and promised firmly that I would obtain relief. With whom he settled the issue, whether with President Nicholas Murray Butler of Columbia, with the university's Board of Trustees, or with the Senate of the United States, I don't know, but in any case word soon was handed down that I was to be allowed to keep my typewriter in my room on condition that I never use it after ten o'clock at night. The Remington crisis was over.

There were a number of Japanese students scattered throughout the university, and I got to know many of them. I often went with some of them to the Cosmopolitan Club for Sunday-night supper, and I managed to participate in a wide variety of activities set up especially for Columbia's foreign students.

Besides the students, I acquired other Japanese friends, some of them residents of New York City and others visitors from the homeland, ranging from members of the Diet, the Japanese Parliament, educators and businessmen to just plain tourists. I met many of these interesting people at the home of Mr. and Mrs. Reitaro Ichinomiya, to whom I had been introduced by Dr. Takami and his wife. Partly because of Mr. Ichinomiya's position as manager of the Yokohama Specie Bank in New York, and partly because of their compelling personalities, the Ichinomiyas were leaders of the Japanese community in the city, a group numbering some three hundred persons.

Mrs. Ichinomiya, knowing that I not only had to earn some money but also wanted to get to know as many Japanese as I could, got me my first two Japanese students of English. She put me in touch with two of her friends who didn't want to enroll in formal courses but who were eager to improve their English by talking and reading with a congenial teacher. One of my pupils worked in the New York office of the Bank of Japan; the other was a newspaperman. The banker, Mr. Yamada, was a gentleman whose stiff, uncompromising manner gave no indication at all of his true character. The journalist, Mr. Horikawa, was an outgoing, communicative man who talked freely and easily. He was intensely interested in Japanese politics and he belonged to a small party of young liberals who had no taste at all for the militaristic policies of the men in power at home.

I was careful not to allow my full schedule of extracurricular activities to interfere with my studies. I worked hard, especially with my English courses, which I knew were going to be the staff of life to me when I got to Japan. My psychology course kept me busy, too. The assistant professor who was our instructor was devoted to experimenting, and he regarded me, his first blind student, as a gift straight from Heaven. I never knew when he was going to come upon me without warning, to test whether or not I recognized his footstep, or his voice, or could detect the direction in which he was walking. He delighted in testing me, in class, in competition with sighted students, on such simple experiments as fitting different-shaped pieces of wood into holes. Of course, this sort of thing was baby stuff to me; I was an old hand at making up for my sightlessness with my sense of touch. I always defeated my blindfolded competitors, much to the delight of Professor Ruger. It really was easy. The others would pick up a block of wood, fondle it carefully in an effort to memorize its shape, then reach along the row of holes searching for one that felt like it. Eventually, after a few false stabs, they would strike gold. But I employed a two-handed technique, holding the piece of wood in one hand and running my other hand over the holes until I sensed that I had the right one. I always finished up before they had more than one or two done.

On the day of our last psychology class, Professor Ruger told us that we had done so well all year it wouldn't be necessary for us to take the final examination. The rules permitted such exemption for students whose grades were 90 or better. When he had finished explaining this to the pleased class, the professor turned to me and said, "Miss Caulfield, will you be good enough to come to the laboratory at two-thirty this afternoon for your examination?"

I was crushed. I couldn't understand what had happened. My work in the class might not have been brilliant but I had thought it was as good as anyone else's. It didn't seem possible that I could have been the only one not to earn a 90. But it wasn't the kind of thing you can argue about, so that afternoon, as sweltering and humid a June day as New York ever produces, I reported to the lab as directed. Professor Ruger was there, bubbling with amiability and enthusiasm. From two-thirty until five o'clock I followed his directions, performing experiment after experiment, identifying sounds, solving problems by touch, lifting weights and guessing their approximate cubic contents, and generally testing my capabilities in all the special problems that the professor had posed for me during the year. Finally, he told me cheerfully and with satisfaction that we had finished.

"Finished what?" I said, considerably taken aback. "What about my examination?"

"This is all I wanted you to do," Professor Ruger said,.

laughing. "I only mentioned the examination because I wanted to be sure you would come."

One doesn't go around crowning assistant professors, but I came dangerously close to it. I have always hoped that he included the results of that hot afternoon's work in some learned volume. I would hate to think it was wasted.

At last, my Bachelor of Science degree was in my hand, and so was my Teachers College diploma for the teaching of English. At the age of twenty-seven, I was ready to begin my career. Life looked very pleasant on that June day in 1914 as I left for Haverstraw and a week's holiday at home. According to the plan that Mr. Yoshimoto had outlined in his letters, I was to spend a year doing practical work for the blind, and then leave for Japan.

As Mama, Aunt Ducky and I entered the house on Commencement Day, we were met by all of Uncle Leonard's patients, pressing upon me a huge armful of American Beauty roses. These good men, wanting to be part of our family, had ordered the flowers all the way from New York for the occasion.

After my short holiday I went back to New York, took a room at a Catholic hostel for girls, and went to work for the New York State Commission for the Blind. The commission hadn't been in existence very long and was engaged, as a necessary first step, in making a survey of the adult blind population of the state. My assignment for the summer was to travel through Westchester County, just north of the New York City line, and report on the names and addresses, living conditions, occupations and possibilities for further training of the blind. I was equipped with a list of those who had registered with the commission, but the list was fragmentary and it was my task to make it as complete as possible. I spent a week in each of the principal cities and towns of the county, making a habit of going first to the Catholic church and asking the pastor to recommend a place for me to board and a high school student I might employ as a guide.

I had some eye-opening experiences. In one Yonkers home

I found a family of Hungarian immigrants, father, mother and three daughters, living in a neatly kept flat that the newly blinded mother no longer was able to maintain. She sat all day in a chair by the window, her only positive contribution toward the running of her household being the delivery of a running fire of instructions to her youngest daughter, who stayed home from work half the day in order to do the necessary housework. The mother obviously was miserable in her unnatural inactivity. I decided to do something about it, and I sent the daughter out on a trumped-up errand.

"Don't you think you could do some of this work yourself?" I asked the mother.

"Sure," she said, "if they let me. But they all afraid I get hurt. They let me do nothing."

Such an attitude on the part of the husband and children was understandable enough, but after a couple of years of it the mother would be reduced to total helplessness, robbed even of her pride. I tried to find out how we might go about making a start toward putting her back to work.

"I like cooking," she said. "If I could only light fire, I could cook."

"How about making a fire right now and fixing us some lunch?" I suggested quickly. "What a nice surprise that would be for your daughter when she gets back."

"Do you think I could?" she asked eagerly.

"Of course," I said, with an air of confidence I was far from feeling. This was going to be as grim a test for me as for the woman I was trying to help. I was then, and still am to this day, mortally afraid of handling fire. It takes all the courage I can screw up to strike a match, and once I have struck it I don't know what to do with it. I'm always afraid I will set both myself and the house on fire. But I was in for it. I couldn't back down. We went into the kitchen and approached the stove.

"We burn wood," she said, going unerringly to the wood box and picking up a few pieces and some old newspapers.

Blind or not, she knew what she was about; she had done this all her life. She laid the fire carefully, arranging the paper on the bottom and the wood on top. She was gaining confidence quickly, which relieved me a great deal because it was all sheer bluff as far as I was concerned. When she had finished the first stage, she started back toward the wood box and said, "The kerosene is over here."

I tried to keep the panic from my voice. "No," I said, in what I hoped was an even tone, "I think we can light it without the kerosene."

She picked up a box of matches from their holder by the side of the stove and, without a moment's hesitation, struck a match and held it down by the rolled-up newspaper until she felt the flame start up. Then she dropped the match on the fire, held her hand over the grate to be sure it had caught, and replaced the stove lid. "Now," she said happily, "we cook something. What you like, lady?"

"What's your favorite?" I asked.

"The girls like fried eggs. All right?"

All that woman needed was someone to convince her she could still be a useful member of the family. She hadn't forgotten how to cook just because she had lost her sight. When I called on her the next afternoon, she told me proudly that her daughter had gone back to working full time and that she was busy preparing the family dinner. A year or so later, the daughter wrote to me to say that she thought I would like to know that her mother was doing almost as much work around the house as she had done when she could see.

I had another interesting experience that summer, with quite a different lesson. I had been staying with some friends in Mount Vernon, while I was working on commission business. At the end of the week, my friends took me to the railroad station and saw me aboard the train for New York. I explained to them that I was quite accustomed to traveling alone, but they must have asked the conductor to look out for me, for, just as we were pulling into Grand Central

Terminal, he approached and laid a kindly but insistent hand on my shoulder.

"You stay right here until I come back for you," he said firmly. "Don't move, you understand?"

"Yes," I said meekly, "I understand."

The train stopped at the platform and I waited impatiently in my seat until everyone had left. I could hear voices outside the vestibule, and then the conductor came hurrying down the aisle toward me. "All set now," he said cheerfully. "Come along, miss." I got up and he led me slowly to the door, where he had carefully placed a little plank for me to walk over. When I was standing safely on the platform, he said, "Now you can get in."

"Get in?" I asked, puzzled.

"Yes," he said in his gruffly kind manner, "we've got a nice, comfortable wheel chair here for you."

"But I can walk," I told him, dismayed.

"Now, miss," he said, "don't you worry. Just get right in and the porter will push you and I'll walk along beside."

I didn't want to ride in that wheel chair any more than the man in the moon, but I didn't see how I could refuse the courtesy of this man who had gone to so much trouble for me. If I did, not only would I be hurting his feelings, but when another person came along who really did need help he might remember my ungraciousness and not bother. It wouldn't do me any harm to climb into that silly wheel chair and let myself be pushed across the waiting room. So, praying that none of my old teachers was around to see me violating every rule of self-reliance I had been taught, I gave myself up to the luxury of being pushed to the taxi stand. There, with great care, the friendly conductor handed me into a taxicab, and I rode away in style. As soon as we had left the terminal a few blocks behind, I got out of the cab and took a more economical bus.

It is, of course, hard for people not accustomed to dealing with the physically handicapped to know what they can do for themselves and what they require to have done for them. Sometimes people give too much help and sometimes not enough. But the handicapped person must always remember the other's viewpoint. The dinner companion who asks if he can cut our roast turkey for us is not made happy by an abrupt, "No, thanks, I can do it myself." It makes him feel that he has committed a horrible breach of etiquette. As a result of this uneasiness, people sometimes hesitate about offering help that is badly needed. I remember asking a gentleman for some assistance in a crowded railroad car. "With pleasure," he said quickly. "I was just afraid you might not want me to help you."

I am getting to be an old lady and I can remember only twice when I was let down. Once a taxi driver insisted that I had given him a two-dollar bill when I knew it was a five. He must have needed the money. Another time a busy trainman told me to use my eyes and not bother him when I asked his help in locating my section of "The Lark" on my way to Los Angeles. I'm sure he must have been working overtime.

It seems to me that the worst problem sightless people face these days is not the generosity of other people, which can always be depended upon, but such modern devices as the self-service elevator. These infernal objects doubtless are convenient and efficient but there are too many makes of them and they all use different control setups. Nothing is more frustrating to a blind person than a spick and span New York office building with no elevator operators, only imposing directories which you cannot read and elevators that are obediently responsive to a series of buttons which, unfortunately, may rocket you as easily to the basement or penthouse as to the floor you are seeking. Even worse, your probing finger may press the button that sounds a shrieking alarm and brings dozens of people rushing to see what is the matter. However, you usually can find someone to help you if you are patient, and it is then that you must remember how important it is never to allow someone who offers you assistance to feel that he has made a mistake in doing so.

In September, I went to Perkins for some practice teaching. My old friend and principal from Overbrook, Dr. Allen, now held forth there in a magnificent set of new buildings at Watertown. Dr. Allen was interested in my ambition to work in Japan, but he wasn't at all confident that it would work out, so he tested me by assigning me to teach a class of the most backward boys in the school. He also gave me an opportunity to show my teaching skills by giving Latin and mathematics to two deaf-and-blind boys. I worked hard, so hard that, especially in these tranquil surroundings, I barely was aware of the turmoil that was gripping the continent of Europe. Aside from a growing feeling of shock that people could commit such unbelievable atrocities as those we were told about, the World War was as remote to us as though it were taking place on another planet. My personal life was filled with a deep sense of peace, and, in spite of my eagerness to press on to the next stage, I found myself almost wishing that these pleasant days would never end.

The Christmas vacation, however, marked the end of my stay at Perkins. I moved on to Overbrook to do some practice teaching there, and encountered a happy surprise when I was asked to stay not merely for a month, as originally planned, but for a whole half-year term as a substitute for one of the regular teachers. I was glad not only for the experience but also for the opportunity to repay a small part of the scholarship grant I had received from Overbrook to pay for my year at Columbia.

It was like coming back home. I had been away only a little more than four years, and I knew most of the teachers and pupils. At first it was a little awkward to be treated as an equal by the teachers, who had been so strict with us during our school days, and to be addressed by them as "Miss Caulfield," but I soon became accustomed to it, and liked it.

I was coming of age.

Chapter V

All this time I was keeping Mr. Yoshimoto in Japan informed of what I was doing, and from time to time he wrote and offered suggestions about the kind of preparation he thought might be useful. His letters always were friendly and always expressed interest in what I could do for the blind of Japan, but they never were very definite about the specific work I might expect to do there, or how I might be able to support myself while I went about it. He did tell me in one letter that he knew of a family in Tokyo who would be glad to have me live with them if I was satisfied to live simply—which, of course, I certainly was. In any case I thought it best to leave all such details in his hands. But my family and my many Japanese friends kept insisting that I ought to know more definitely what he had in mind for me, so, responding to their urgent prodding, I finally wrote to him and asked him if he would let me know what he was planning. I assured him that any arrangements he might make for me, as to income and living conditions, would be satisfactory; I just wanted to know what he had in mind. I tried to make the letter as humble and undemanding as possible, and it seemed to me to be a reasonable request for essential information. I was sure that Mr. Yoshimoto would understand.

It was some time before I got my answer. It came on a

bright spring day, while I was still at Overbrook, and if I live to be a hundred and ten, I will never forget the stunned, nerveless sense of shock that spread through me as my friend Harriet Totman read it to me:

"I have read your letter several times," Mr. Yoshimoto wrote, "and I cannot help reaching the conclusion that you are not as much interested in helping the blind of Japan as I thought. Your inquiries about the arrangements I was making for you to live in Japan seem to put more stress upon the material side of the matter than upon what you can give to the blind. For this reason, I think you had better give up your idea of working for the blind of Japan."

I didn't, either then or later, have the slightest thought that Mr. Yoshimoto had been deceiving me. I have met him, over the years, several times, and we never have referred at all to our momentous exchange of letters, but I know that there never was a more selfless worker for the blind of his country than Tadasu Yoshimoto, and I have always been sure that something serious went wrong with his carefully laid plans. My best guess is that when he proposed his idea to the authorities they weren't interested. They undoubtedly thought they knew more about the needs of the blind of Japan than a young American girl just out of college.

This logical explanation crowded into my mind even then, but it didn't ease the pain I felt as a result of Mr. Yoshimoto's accusation that I was too concerned with material rewards. That was unjust, and it hurt. I knew I had to provide for my living, so that I wouldn't be a burden to anyone else, but the thought of gain as such, of making money for its own sake, never had entered my mind. I had tried to make that clear to him in my letter, but he either misunderstood or deliberately used it as an excuse to call the whole thing off.

I promptly wrote him another letter, telling him how disappointed I was and asking him to please tell me the real reason why he had changed his mind about me, but, of course, he never answered. I shouldn't have written such a letter, but

I was young, disappointed and inexperienced.

As soon as I got over my first shock, I made up my mind that, Mr. Yoshimoto or no Mr. Yoshimoto, I was going to Japan anyway. If it couldn't be arranged for me to go as a worker for the blind, I would go on my own and pay my way by working as an English teacher. First, of course, I would have to find work here at home and save up enough money to book my passage and enable me to establish myself in Japan. I reconciled myself to the fact that it would take years for me to put away the amount I would need, but there was nothing else to do. I certainly couldn't be satisfied with enough money to buy a ticket to Japan. I couldn't place the responsibility for my upkeep there, and for my return ticket if one proved to be necessary, upon the shoulders of my Japanese friends. It would be enough to ask their help in obtaining work for me as an English teacher once I got there on my own.

The first step in carrying out my resolution was to find work. Late that summer I went to the employment office at Teachers College and registered as a private teacher of English. I also took a room in the apartment of one of my Columbia friends and arranged to eat my meals in a nearby restaurant. The room was to cost six dollars a week and the meals seven. In these days of inflation that may seem unbelievably cheap, but it was a lot of money then. Furthermore, the room was in one of the best apartment houses in the Columbia neighborhood, and the meals were excellent. The only problem I had was that the friend from whom I was renting the room understandably wanted it to be taken for the whole school year, so that, even though I had no idea how much work I would be able to obtain, I had to guarantee the rental through June. I decided to do it even though my total capital at the time amounted to thirty-five dollars which Henry, who had gone to work for the New York Central Railroad, had given me. It was a risk, but I was sure I could find enough work to pay my way.

I picked up a few students the first week I was in New York, thereby assuring my ability to pay the rent for a while, and as the weeks went by my "class" increased steadily. Among them were Cubans, French and Belgians, but, running true to form, I acquired a heavy majority of Japanese. The war in Europe had closed the Continent to them, so more and more Japanese were coming to the United States on business or educational missions, and my many friends from their country saw to it that my services as an English teacher were widely advertised and strongly recommended.

One of my first pupils was Mr. Yamada, the banker who had practiced his uncertain English with me four nights a week at Columbia. After he had begun his regular lessons, he brought several other bankers and officials of the Ministry of Finance into the fold. Although his manner was decidedly forbidding, Mr. Yamada proved to be a good friend. If you didn't know him well he appeared to be downright antagonistic, but once you penetrated his prickly surface you found generous measures of loyalty, warmth and understanding. The trouble with him was that he had been living in all sorts of rooming houses ever since he had come to the United States, and none of the boardinghouse mistresses ever had bothered to penetrate beneath his icy mien. As a result, he had moved thirteen times in the two years he had lived in New York.

At the end of my first year as a free-lance English teacher, Henry and I made up our minds that it was time we got together and made a new family home with Mama. We rented a seven-room apartment in the Morningside Heights section near Columbia. Shortly before we moved in, Mr. Yamada came to me as usual for his English lesson. He was characteristically blunt. "I saw the building where your apartment is," he said, "but a seven-room apartment is much too big for three people, isn't it?"

"Yes, it is," I agreed, "but we've been thinking that we'd like to have two other people live with us."

"Why?"

"I've found that most Japanese men in New York are lonely and badly in need of a little home life."

Mr. Yamada picked me up instantly. "Are you planning to ask two Japanese to live in your home?"

With a sinking feeling I thought of the thirteen times he had moved. "Yes," I said hesitantly, "that's what we've had in mind."

"Then," he said firmly, "I will be the first one to move in with you."

I was shaken. This was the last thing I wanted. This difficult, unyielding man, who had been unable to get along with a baker's dozen boardinghouse keepers, was hardly the kind of person Mama, Henry and I wanted to live with. "Oh, no," I said quickly, "you would never be happy with us. You've moved so many times already. It wouldn't be any good for us to have somebody as uncertain as that."

Mr. Yamada, the great stone face, laughed heartily. "This is quite different," he said. "The places I've been moving in and out of haven't been homes, they've only been rooms. I thought it was interesting to try out all the different kinds. But you and your mother and your brother are different. It will really be like home. At any rate, I'm coming, and I'll find another man who will be suitable. Leave it to me."

There was nothing I could do but submit to the inevitable, and the inevitable proved to be most satisfactory. We settled into our big, attractive apartment on Morningside Drive and 116th Street, just opposite President Butler's house, with all the prideful joy of a family long deprived of a home of its own. Mr. Yamada came soon after we moved in, and right behind him came a young man who worked for the Bank of Taiwan.

Mama took to my Japanese friends immediately and unfailingly treated them like her own children. Henry always got along well with them, too. And, of course, for me, it was the next best thing to living in Japan. But, after just a few months, Mr. Yamada came home one evening, looking sad. "I'm sorry to have to tell you," he said, "but I've been transferred to London." Seeing how disappointed we were, he added hastily, "I would appreciate it, though, if you would allow my successor, Mr. Sonobe, to take my place here. He'll be in town soon, and when he comes I'll go to a hotel and let him move right in here."

So, for the fifteenth time, Mr. Yamada moved to a new American residence, and Mr. Sonobe came to our apartment, where he stayed for three pleasant years. At the same time, however, the man from the Bank of Taiwan left, and I had to find someone to take his place. I thought of one of my students who was connected with the Navy Supply Office in New York, Commander Masato Sugi, and I resolved to ask him if he would like to move in with us. He agreed, I'm glad to say, and he, too, stayed with us nearly three years. But the part he played in my life reached long years into the future.

Mr. Sonobe and Commander Sugi were in every respect members of our family. If we were entertaining guests, they were included in the party as a matter of course, and they were as free to invite their friends to the apartment as we were to invite ours. Mama worried just as much about them wearing their overshoes and remembering their umbrellas as she did about us, and before many months had passed she even had learned how to cook some of the standard Japanese dishes, such as, for example, pickled vegetables, an essential part of every true Japanese dinner. Mr. Sonobe even taught Mama how to make *ozoni*, the traditional Japanese New Year's soup. At home, an old-fashioned Japanese gentleman of Mr. Sonobe's upbringing would rather be caught dead than in a kitchen doing a woman's work, but in America he could yield safely to Mama's hunger to learn the Japanese way of doing things. It interested me greatly to see that, although at home he would never deign to help make *ozoni*, or any other dish, for that matter, he knew exactly how to do it.

New Year's Day is the same for the Japanese as it is for us,

January first. But in our house it was celebrated Japanese-style. Mama always made the soup, without which New Year's isn't New Year's in Japan. Into it we put toasted pieces of pounded glutinous rice, which, together with other delicacies of the season, we were able to buy from Katagiri's, the only Japanese store in New York. On New Year's Day our table looked strictly Japanese, with the special holiday treats—all prepared, as is the custom, the day before—arranged on serving plates and in three-story lacquer boxes, ready for guests to be served at any time they might drop in. A good many Japanese did drop in, for the sight of their New Year's traditions being observed in an American home was a tonic for their homesickness.

Not just on holidays, but almost any time we gathered a group of friends together in our living room, it was likely to resemble a large section of the Japan Year Book come to life. These were all unusually able men, especially selected because of their special abilities to work, to study or to represent Japan in the United States. I was lucky to be able to get to know them, to talk to them about the million and one subjects that interest eager young people longing to remake the world in which they live, and, in a very real sense, to learn from them.

My daily hours of English lessons went on without interruption in order to keep the wolf away from the door. They became even more important after Henry and his fiancée, Beatrice Young, whom he had often brought to the apartment, decided to marry and set up housekeeping on their own. They found a little place farther uptown and began to make preparations for their new life.

Mr. Sonobe and Commander Sugi were intensely interested in this close-up view of a U.S.-style courtship, engagement and marriage, with the young people making their choices out of purely romantic considerations instead of submitting, as was the universal practice in Japan, to marriages arranged by their elders.

The Japanese concept of marriage was, and to a large

extent still is, based upon the idea of the union of families rather than of individuals—or, more accurately, the adoption into one family of a carefully approved member of another. It doesn't mean the disregard of women's rights, as is so commonly believed by Western critics, but rather the voluntary subordination of the interests of the young people to the larger good of the two families.

From ancient times, in Japan, when a young man reached marriageable age, his friends and relatives began searching for a suitable wife for him to bring into his family. When a promising young lady was discovered, the friend or relative informed the prospective groom's father, who, if he approved in principle, asked the go-between to investigate the girl's family. The investigation was a serious one and consisted of a thorough inquiry into the general reputation of the family and a careful scrutiny of the family's record for evidences of any diseases or mental disorders that might be regarded as hereditary. If all was satisfactory, the go-between approached the father of the girl, who then requested a similar bill of health from the family of the groom.

If any impediments were uncovered, the matter was quietly dropped without anyone except the two fathers and the go-between knowing anything about it. If, however, all was well, negotiations were begun to bring about a meeting of the two families.

The strict ancient custom did not allow the young people to meet until the day of the wedding, but since the time of World War I it has been generally considered proper to introduce them and encourage them to express their own approval or disapproval of the match. Etiquette, however, requires that the young people do not speak to each other at these formal introductions; the girl, with her eyes carefully averted, serves tea, and the young man sits quietly looking on.

If there was no objection on either side, betrothal presents were ceremoniously exchanged and preparations for the wedding got under way. In the old days the wedding usually took place at the home of the bridegroom, but now it is the custom for the ceremony to be held at a Shinto shrine, or, if the bride and groom are Christians, in church.

After the wedding, the young couple, especially in cases where the groom was the eldest son, lived in his parents' house, and the bride was trained by her mother-in-law in the ways of the family. In time, she would hand down all she had learned to her own daughter-in-law, and thus the family traditions and customs were preserved.

It sometimes happened that, either for real or manufactured reasons, a bride was not satisfactory to her husband's family, especially to her mother-in-law. In such a case, after a solemn meeting of the family council, she was sent back to her own home. But such tragedies were rare. Unless the girl was especially undesirable, or the mother-in-law impossibly hard to please, the marriage usually was much more satisfactory than Western people can imagine.

To Mr. Sonobe and Commander Sugi, who explained these things to me, Henry's approaching marriage must have seemed casual indeed. I'm sure they had grave misgivings as to its outcome. To their way of thinking, Henry should have brought his bride into our home to be trained by Mama. Instead, the young people were planning to set up a home of their own in another part of the city, even though they had no experience in such matters, and clearly Beatrice was going to have to train herself as best she could. This struck the Japanese members of our family group as both foolish and risky.

After the wedding, and Henry's departure, our life continued much as before. Mr. Sonobe was a treasure house of information on Japanese customs and ideas, and as, in the course of his English lessons, we read English literature together, we spent many pleasant hours comparing traditions and discussing the resemblances as well as the differences in our cultures.

As for Masato Sugi, if he hadn't borne the rank of a naval

officer, he surely would have been taken for an economist or a sociologist; a more unmilitaristic military man would have been hard to find. Yet this unassuming scholar, who was in charge of the Japanese Navy Supply Office in New York, had, during the Russo-Japanese War, been one of the brave volunteers to face almost certain death in the blockading of Port Arthur. I never learned anything about his wartime exploits from Commander Sugi, but his friends weren't slow to inform me that we had a hero in our home. I tried many times to coax him to tell me about the war with the Russians, but I never succeeded.

One day, while he was airing his dress uniform, Mama expressed interest in his medals, and we both pressed him to explain them to us. He carefully explained what each one meant, but they all seemed disappointingly routine, merely service decorations. Then Mama noticed that there was one, carefully packed in a small box, that he hadn't mentioned.

"What's that one?" she asked.

"Oh, that's just another one I got during the war," he said off-handedly, and that was all he would say about it.

Later we asked one of his officer friends about the hidden medal and learned that it was the Order of the Golden Kite, at that time the highest military decoration the Government of Japan bestowed. It had been given to him for his part in the Port Arthur blockade, which had played so decisive a role in the defeat of the Russians.

Another time, still probing for exciting stories of his adventures in the war, I asked the commander to tell me about the most dangerous situation he had ever found himself in.

"One day," he said, smiling, "I was thrown out of a jinriksha onto a muddy road."

It was no use. He simply refused to show off for me.

One day he came home and announced to us that he had been promoted to captain. "I must say in a way I'm sorry about it," he confessed glumly.

"Why, for Heaven's sake?" I asked, puzzled.

"Because now everybody will call me Captain," he said, "and to tell you the truth, I like the sound of Commander better. In America, it seems as though every old man you pass on the street is called Captain."

It pleased me to see that our exceedingly modest friend possessed enough human frailty to prefer the title that sounded more grandiose. I teased him about it a little. But I was proud that he had been promoted and glad that the high opinion Mama and I held of him was shared by his superiors. It was a sad day for us when Captain Sugi's tour of duty in New York was over and he sailed for home.

He was followed by Commander Sakaya, a quiet, shy naval architect who played the *shakuhachi*, the Japanese flute, very well, and could even perform parts of the *Noh* drama, the classical dance of old Japan. He was a student of the old times and the old customs, and I learned much from him.

Mr. Sonobe, of course, also had to leave after a while, but his successor, Mr. Yoshikawa, also was from the Bank of Japan, so we continued to have both the Imperial Japanese Navy and the Bank of Japan represented in our family circle.

About this time one of our friends asked if we could add another member to our family, a nineteen-year-old Japanese boy who had come to New York to study the violin. Mama and I weren't sure we ought to do it. The boy was so young that we wondered if he would be happy in our quiet, orderly household, and the fact that he would have to practice his violin playing gave us further pause. But the very fact that he was so young made it imperative that he have a secure home in which to live, and after we once heard him play we no longer worried that his practicing would annoy anyone. We decided to take him in, and our home gradually took on a musical and sometimes even a temperamental atmosphere which added considerable color and variety to our days.

The young musician's name was Iwao Fukui. He was the son of a director of the powerful Mitsui Company, and he had put up a long struggle to secure permission from his father to study in the United States. He had even threatened that, if his father refused, he would simply stay home all day and do nothing. After a protracted battle of wills, Iwao finally won his parent's consent and came to New York. He proved to be as diligent as he was talented. He practiced long hours every day and in the process familiarized Mama and me with some of the world's best music for the violin.

The more I learned about the Japanese, the more I was surprised by some of their attitudes and customs. For example, I was amazed by the number of men in New York's Japanese community who were separated from their wives and families for the entire period of their stay abroad. It was the almost universal conviction of the managers of the great Japanese companies that if wives were allowed to travel with their husbands they would interfere with their work. It didn't occur to them that a man living alone for three or four years might be more fundamentally disturbed by the unnatural life he was forced to live, among strangers, without the comfort of any of the home life to which he was accustomed.

The Bank of Japan was one of the strictest institutions in this respect. The agent in charge of the New York office was the only member of the staff permitted to bring his wife with him, and even in his case it was merely allowed, not encouraged. One of the young men in the office, Mr. Nishina, recently had married a girl who was an ambitious pianist, and he wanted to have his wife, Michiko, study music in the United States while he worked here. He requested permission from the head office, making it clear that his wife would come at the expense of the family. The company's answer was that there would be no objection to Mrs. Nishina traveling to the United States at the expense of her family, provided that when she got here she lived in another city. Under no circumstances would she be permitted to live in New York with her husband. Michiko made the long trip and enrolled at Oberlin College in Ohio as a music student. I got to know her when she visited her husband on vacations, the only time they were able to be together.

This rigidity is a good illustration of the Japanese inclination to sacrifice the good of the individual for the good of the whole, a characteristic which goes almost completely counter to the American attitude.

As the years went by, and I waited for my bank balance to reach the necessary level, I found myself strongly tempted to take the final step of preparation and learn the Japanese language. I had tried it once, while I was at Columbia. I had undertaken a reciprocal teaching arrangement with one of the Japanese students who wanted to learn English. But his method was simply to have me memorize words out of the dictionary. When I asked him to help me put the words I was learning into sentences, he said it would take away too much time from our work on the dictionary. I had been so discouraged by that experience that I had done nothing more about it. And now, thinking about it again, I decided that I would be better off to devote all my time to my English pupils, in order to give my savings every possible chance to increase. I would wait until I got to Japan to study the language. With three Japanese living in the house, and with so much social contact with others, I couldn't, of course, help but pick up a great many Japanese words and expressions. But the spoken language I left for another time.

I hoped that it wouldn't be too long before I would be able to get started on the great journey. My friends assured me that all I needed was enough money for the round-trip fare, with a little extra left over. There was, they said, a real need for English teachers in Japan, and I would easily be able to find enough work to support myself once I got there. Their encouraging words inflamed my eagerness to be about my chosen work. So it was with excitement that, late in 1922, I listened to Mama read a letter from Captain Sugi saying that he expected to be stationed in Tokyo for the next two years and that he and his wife would be glad to have me stay with them in their home for that time. "But," he added, "you had better come as soon as possible. There is no knowing when the Navy may change its mind and transfer me."

Suddenly, excitingly, my hour seemed to have come. The only thing I needed was money. I didn't dare go until I had at least five hundred dollars more. But on the other hand, if I waited until I had saved it, Captain Sugi might be transferred and this wonderful opportunity to live in his home while I was establishing myself would vanish. It was a perplexing dilemma.

Then, magically, a few months later, Providence took a hand in my affairs. I woke up one morning knowing exactly what I should do. Henry had been working for quite some time for the Durant Motor Company, and at his suggestion I had bought ten shares of stock in the company at twenty dollars a share. Now, in early 1923, the stock was rising phenomenally. I had Mama check the newspaper and we found that at the close of business the previous day it had been selling at eighty dollars a share. That meant my stock was worth an enormous eight hundred dollars.

It was raining, but I told Mama I was going right over to our neighborhood bank and ask the manager to sell the stock for me.

"If you're making so much money on it," Mama wanted to know, "why do you want to sell it?"

"It's worth four times what I paid for it," I said. "That's enough profit for me. Besides, I need the money now. I'm going to sell it."

"You'll get wet," Mama persisted. "Can't you at least wait until tomorrow?"

But I couldn't. I was determined to get it over with right away. I went straight to the bank, where the manager took his turn at trying to convince me I should hold on to the stock. "It's still going up," he said. "I think you're making a mistake." But, when he saw that I was insistent, he put through the sale for me.

The very next day, Durant Motor Company stock broke; it went all the way down to forty dollars a share, and it never did go back up again. The bank manager probably was convinced that somebody had given me an inside tip, but the only tip I'd had was from the kindly hand of Providence, giving me a small reward for my long years of work toward my goal. With that eight hundred dollars added to what I already had saved, I felt I could well risk setting out for Japan.

I decided I would leave about the middle of June, 1923, a date which would fit conveniently into the plans of our present boarders, Mr. and Mrs. Hajimu Horikoshi. Mama and I knew Hajimu's mother and father, and, when he went back home to marry the girl they had found for him, they wrote and asked us to take him and his bride into our home when he returned to his job in the New York office of his father's company. We were glad to do it, and Mama greatly enjoyed initiating the seventeen-year-old bride, Kikue San, into the intricacies of American housekeeping methods. Now the young couple were expecting their first baby about the first of May, and, upon being informed of my plans, they quickly suggested that they take over our apartment and keep Mama with them so that the young wife and mother might benefit from her help and advice. It promised to be an excellent arrangement, and I was grateful to them. I ex pected to allow myself two years to make good in Japan; at the end of that time, if I had failed, I would return home. Meanwhile, I would have the comfort of knowing that Mama was well provided for. If, however, all went well for me in Tokyo, I could send for her to join me.

I still had innumerable details to settle. It would be necessary to relocate my pupils with other English teachers; a simple but reasonably complete wardrobe had to be assembled; and I had to arrange for my transportation.

Among our Japanese friends in New York was the manager of the Nippon Yusen Kaisha Steamship Company office. I asked him if he would arrange passage from Seattle for me on one of the N.Y.K. ships. Several of our friends volunteered to look up someone who would be going to Japan at about the same time, with whom I might travel, but I said no, thanks. I wanted to make the trip entirely on my own. I felt that if I wasn't going to be able to manage by myself I had better find it out and adjust my ambitions accordingly. Anyway, I was sure that I could depend upon the kindness of the train and steamship personnel.

The steamship company informed me that my passage had been booked as I wished, from Seattle. A few weeks later, the manager called at our apartment to read me a letter he had just received from his home office. I'll never forget it:

"We are gratified to hear about the interest which Miss Genevieve Caulfield has shown in Japan for many years, and the kindness she has shown to Japanese people in New York City. As an expression of our appreciation to her, we are happy to give her a fifty per cent reduction on her steamship fare to Japan, and return, if she should desire to revisit her country."

It was hard for me to believe that a great shipping company, carrying all kinds of people and cargoes to all the ports of the world, for profit, would take the trouble to extend such a personal courtesy to an obscure well-wisher of the country whose flag its ships flew. I was still learning about the Japanese. Gratitude is one of their predominant virtues, and to them friendship and a consciousness of obligation is a kind of religion. I had done some services for them, and they were showing me that they were grateful.

The long-awaited day of departure finally arrived, after a last restless night of anticipation. It seemed as though just about everybody I knew was at the railroad station to see me off on the first leg of my journey. All of my Japanese friends appeared to have taken time off from their work to say good-by to me and wish me good luck in their country. Aunt Ducky and Uncle Leonard were there, and so were Henry and Beatrice and their two little girls, Mary and Joan. It was hardest of all to say good-by to Mama, but we knew it would be at the most for only two years. Mama insisted upon seeing me settled safely in my seat, kissed me good-by, and, in a few moments, the powerful transcontinental train began to slide smoothly out of the station. After fifteen years of preparation and waiting, I was on my way to Japan at last.

Chapter VI

As soon as I set foot on the lower deck of the Iyo Maru, I dedicated myself to the twin tasks of learning my way around the ship and proving to the crew and the other passengers that I wasn't going to be a liability. The stewardess promptly seized me firmly by the arm and escorted me, with great care and kindness, to my cabin. In a solicitous but very positive tone she told me to stay there until she came back to unpack for me and escort me to the dining salon for lunch. Just as positively, I made up my mind that this would never do. I was sure that the company had hired that stewardess to do something more than look after me, and I had a strong suspicion that she was already racking her brains to figure out how she was going to look after a helpless blind passenger and at the same time perform all her other duties. As for me, I had no interest whatsoever in a two-week voyage at the end of a rope. I was determined to settle the issue as quickly as possible.

My first step was to examine the cabin with the minute care that, I suspect, only a blind person can bring to the task. Using my hands, my knees, and my feet too, for that matter, I checked the exact location of every piece of furniture and equipment in the room. I covered the whole cabin twice, and I missed nothing. When I had mastered the room

71

plan, I unpacked all the clothes and accessories that I expected to use on the voyage and stowed them away in the closets and drawers and shelves. When the stewardess came bustling back an hour or so later, all she had to do was show me the way to the community bath and tell me what hour had been assigned to me for my bath, then show me how to find the dining room and the other public rooms I would be likely to visit each day. Finally, she showed me the location of the deck chair assigned me for the voyage. After that I dismissed her, telling her I would ring for her if I needed her again. She thanked me, bowed and disappeared, and except for passing her on deck or in the passageways that was the last I saw of her until we docked. Fortunately, unlike most of the passengers, I didn't get seasick.

From that day to this, traveling on a ship has been one of my greatest pleasures. It's like entering another world, a tiny world to be sure, but a benevolently totalitarian state relieving its citizens of all responsibilities except to follow the leader. I have always found it a pleasant change from the burdens of life on shore.

On the second day out, I was standing on the deck after a brisk walk when the captain approached me and asked my name. When I told him, I had the feeling that he was surprised, but he said nothing except that he hoped I would enjoy the voyage. He was a pleasant man who spoke only rudimentary English, and even that with a good deal of hesitation. Most of the ship's stewards spoke almost no English, a lack which caused considerable difficulty for the American passengers. The N.Y.K. luxury liners were staffed by English-speaking officers and stewards, but cargo ships like the *Iyo Maru* usually carried mostly Japanese passengers, and English wasn't a requirement for the stewards. On this voyage, however, the ship carried an unusually large number of Americans, and communication between the passengers and stewards was a real problem. I knew enough basic Japanese phrases and words by this time to be able to make myself understood without any trouble, but the other passengers and the bewildered stewards struggled constantly to get through to each other on such problems as misplaced pieces of luggage, eggs that were boiled instead of fried, and drinks that were made with lemon instead of lime. The passengers weren't unreasonable, but a certain amount of impatience was inevitable. It occurred to me that there was no time like the present for me to do something constructive about improving Japanese-American relations. I asked to see the captain and I told him I would be glad to gather the stewards together every evening after they had finished serving dinner and do my best to equip them with a basic fund of practical English. The captain accepted my offer immediately, and the stewards were pathetically grateful. Their lives had been made miserable by the problem. So every evening, after dinner, the boys pushed together a couple of tables in the dining room and we held an informal class. As the other passengers became aware of what we were doing, they got into the habit of bringing their unsolved problems to me, and soon everything was shipshape.

I spent most of each morning helping the purser translate the radio news from Japanese into English. The purser did the actual translation and I put it into the kind of English the passengers might be more likely to appreciate. We worked in the captain's cabin, which was high up near the bridge and was, I'm sure, the shakiest spot on the ship. It gave me an excellent opportunity to test my seaworthiness on the stormy reaches of the north Pacific.

Whenever the captain had some free time I sat with him and worked on his English, with particular emphasis on pronunciation. Sometimes, when the weather was pleasant, we walked around the deck, talking about the lore of the sea, the International Date Line, the anti-Japanese propaganda being carried on in the United States by the Chinese, the captain's family and home in Tokyo, and any other subject which interested both of us and which gave the captain a chance to practice his spoken English.

On one of our walks, he made a friendly confession to me. "You know," he said, "when I first heard from our Seattle office that you were going to make this voyage on my ship, I wondered what I would do. The Office had made it clear that we were expected to take good care of you and not let anything happen to you. Frankly, I was very worried about it. I couldn't understand what a helpless blind woman was doing traveling all the way from New York to Japan, and alone, at that. I gave strict orders to the stewardess that she was to give you her undivided attention, no matter what the other passengers said about it."

I laughed and told him I was sorry that I had caused him so much anxiety.

"Well," the captain said apologetically, "I expected to see you come aboard in a wheel chair. I didn't think you would be able to take a step without somebody holding on to your arm. I certainly didn't expect to find you walking around the deck and going into the dining room by yourself. And the last thing I expected was that, instead of us helping you, you would end up helping us run the ship."

A few minutes before the time for the traditional Captain's Dinner on the night before we were due to land, the chief steward came up to me on deck and asked me if I would be kind enough to accompany him to my cabin for a moment. Expecting that the formalities of landing were beginning already, I followed him obediently. When I stepped through the door, I found all the members of my evening English class lined up to shake hands with me and wish me success in their country. "Also," the chief steward announced, "we have a small cake baked especially for you, with a message from us on top. It says, 'To Miss Genevieve Caulfield, in appreciation for her kind teaching.' The carpenter has made a strong wooden box for it and he is here to nail on the cover, so you can carry it ashore tomorrow and enjoy it with your friends in Tokyo."

Although Monday, July 16, 1923, was an ordinary working day, a large group of Japanese friends I had known in New York was waiting at the pier in Yokohama to welcome me when the *Iyo Maru* docked. Also on hand was an energetic, pleasant young woman who introduced herself as Mrs. Sugi and told me that, on behalf of her husband and herself, she was happy to welcome me to Japan and to their home, which they hoped I would make my home as long as I wished. I wasn't surprised that Captain Sugi himself hadn't come. I knew him well enough to know that nothing short of a major disaster could induce him to leave his station during duty hours.

It was just about the end of the rainy season, which lasts roughly from the tenth of June to the tenth of July, and a fine, misty rain was falling as Mrs. Sugi and I rode in jinrikshas through the narrow streets of the city. The day of speeding taxicabs was only just beginning to dawn, and the little carriage for one, pulled by a powerfully muscled man, was the common conveyance. There were, of course, streetcars and buses, too, but they would have been inconvenient for me with all my baggage, including the carefully boxed cake, so we made our way from the dock to the railroad station in jinrikshas which were curtained to keep out the rain.

As we rode through the muddy and bumpy streets of Yokohama, with its old-century atmosphere, I enjoyed the realization that, although it might not seem like it, I was in one of the great seaports of the world. I enjoyed every sound, every smell, every taste of my first Japanese city. It was, after so many years of dreaming about it, a heady experience to know I was actually on the soil of Japan.

A fast electric train took us to Shimbasi, then the principal terminal for Tokyo, the city which was to be my home for the next fourteen years. This time we got into a taxicab for the trip to the Sugis' house; we took only my smaller bags with us, leaving the trunks to be delivered by the Nippon Express,

Japan's version of the American Railway Express. Captain Sugi and his wife lived in Go Chome, which, up to then, I had thought meant Fifth Street. But it turned out that *Chome* doesn't mean street at all but a small section which, in the city's early days, might have been a separate little village or town, or even the estate of a feudal lord. The method of numbering houses in little blocks or sections made it most difficult for any stranger, blind or sighted, to find his way around Tokyo, and even now finding the house you are looking for is like solving a complicated puzzle. Number 37 Go Chome, for instance, might designate four or five, or even, in some cases, a hundred houses.

A sliding wooden gate led into the tiny concrete-paved space in front of the Sugis' house. A sliding door, gently pushed open by a maid, admitted us to the concrete entrance-way of the house, where we took off our shoes before stepping up onto the soft mats of the *genkan* or entrance proper of the house. There I was warmly greeted by Captain Sugi, who was informally dressed in the kind of summer kimono usually put on in the hot weather by Japanese men upon their return home from work. Seeing and talking once again to my old friend made me feel very much at home. I spoke the truth when I told him that I was most happy to be with him and his gracious wife.

The formalities of landing, the pleasure of renewing old acquaintanceships, and the trip from Yokohama had used up the whole day, and soon after I had settled myself in my cozy room dinner was announced. I hoped I would do justice to it. For months before I left New York I had practiced sitting on my heels in proper Japanese style, and I had acquired considerable flexibility in the difficult art, so I was able to take my place on the big square cushion in front of the low table with less awkwardness than otherwise would have been the case. I have never been particularly adept at handling *chasi,* the Japanese chopsticks, but I always manage to use them, when Japanese food is served, without suffering from undernourishment. Somehow they seem to go with the dainty lacquerware and the tiny dishes.

The Sugis lived in a traditional Japanese house opening onto a small but picturesque garden in the rear. It contained a drawing room, study, dining room, bedroom, kitchen and a small room for the maid. The study had been designated as my room.

Japanese rooms are measured by the number of mats, or *tatami,* they contain. The *tatami* are roughly three feet by six feet and are quite different from the American idea of mats. They are actually shallow wooden boxes about two inches deep, filled with straw and covered with a finely woven matting. Each mat is bound with black, brown or sometimes white binding, which marks the outline of each mat when they are laid side by side on the floor. The Sugis' drawing room was a ten-mat room, which meant that it was roughly fifteen feet by twelve feet. Their bedroom was an eight-mat, or twelve-by-twelve, room, and the study, which had been turned over to me, was a six-mat or nine-by-twelve, room.

In a typical Japanese drawing room there is no furniture except a pile of cushions in one corner, and perhaps a low table no more than fifteen inches high in the middle of the floor. At meal time, the family and guests sit around the table on the cushions. At one end of the room is an alcove containing a low platform upon which is placed a flower arrangement or some other ornament, perhaps an incense burner. Behind the platform hangs a roll picture or scroll, which is frequently changed to suit the season or a special family celebration. The guest of honor is always given the seat directly in front of the platform, or *tokonoma,* and that was where I sat for dinner that night.

I had hoped I would sleep on the soft Japanese bed cushions, called *futons,* which are stored in roomy cupboards during the day and spread upon the mats at night. But the Sugis had thought that might be too great a change for me and they had gone to the trouble of providing me with an

American daybed—just, they assured me, what they had always wanted to own. I also had an armchair, a table on which to write, and a desk chair. I had a cupboard of my own in which to keep my things.

Incredibly, I am still asked, on my lecture tours in the United States, if the Japanese really live in paper houses. Of course they don't, but the reason for this stubborn misconception is that the sliding doors and partitions separating the rooms are covered with paper that resembles our wallpaper, and the latticed windows which open from the rooms onto the narrow, glass-enclosed verandas are covered with translucent white paper. All of the rooms in the Sugis' house opened on to this veranda, which ran the entire length of the house and faced the south so that the rooms would be warmed as much as possible by the sun.

An encouraging number of English-teaching opportunities already had been booked for me by my friends. The most promising was an arrangement for me to go to Yokohama every Friday afternoon to the home of a Mr. Nakamura, the wealthy president of a Japanese silk company. I would give English lessons to his family, stay at his home overnight, take care of the English-language correspondence at his office on Saturday morning, and then start back to Tokyo at noon. The work would pay well and would be the core of my income. It was decided, however, that I shouldn't begin work until September, partly because the children were on vacation from their schools and partly because late July and August are so hot in Tokyo that hardly anyone does any more than the law requires. I settled down cheerfully to enjoy the Sugis' home, to meet old and new friends, and to devote myself to getting to know the country.

I saw, in that restful period before going to work, most of the Japanese men and women I had known in New York, and I visited many of their homes. Mr. Sonobe, of the Bank of Japan, lived, I was glad to discover, very near the Sugis, and I saw him and his charming, self-effacing wife frequently.

Mrs. Sonobe seemed to work so hard at anticipating and satisfying her husband's every wish and whim that I thought it would amuse her to hear the story of how he had instructed Mama in the art of making *ozoni*, the New Year's soup. She obviously doubted that he knew enough about it to dare tell someone else how to make it. "Was it really fit to eat?" she asked, astounded. I assured her that it had been enjoyed and praised by the most discriminating of our Japanese friends, but she just shook her head doubtfully. She was much too polite to question the accuracy of my storytelling but it was plain that she thought me guilty of an outrageous exaggeration.

I noticed that the more conservative the home the more certain the hostess was that I could not possibly enjoy Japanese food. Some of my hostesses went to a great deal of trouble to have restaurants deliver various foreign dishes which they thought I would be more likely to appreciate, and I'm sorry to say that most of them were pretty bad. I, of course, had been eating Japanese food for a long time, and I liked it—at least most of it. I tried, for that matter, to conform to Japanese customs in every way I could because I knew that only in that way could I live among these people comfortably and inconspicuously, and do my work efficiently.

I even decided to try Japanese dress. Not on the street, of course, but in the privacy of the house. I bought a summer kimono with everything that goes with it, including the *obi*, the tight sash, and all the little strings and fastenings that hold the kimono secure. I also acquired a pair of the white, mittenlike stockings, *tabi*, which are worn both with outside footgear and in the house after the wooden clogs or straw sandals have been removed. With Mrs. Sugi's help I put on the whole outfit and gave it a thorough trial. But I found that, in the first place, it was too tight, and in the second place, at least in August, it was much too hot. The experiment was a complete failure. As long as I sat quietly on a cushion, I didn't feel so ungraceful, but as soon as I began to walk around or do any work, I felt awkward and uncomfortable. I decided I would look better, feel better and work better in the kind of clothes to which I had been accustomed.

The Japanese language, of course, was something else again. I had to learn it and I worked at it steadily. I had resolved to spend the first year getting into the spirit of the language before studying it formally, and I found the plan to be a good one. My vocabulary increased rapidly and I had no inhibitions about using it, sometimes with embarrassing results. Once, for example, in asking the wife of a high Government official if she would "bring" her daughter to see me, I used the Japanese word that is applied only to inanimate objects. The lady politely said that she would, but Mr. Sugi pointed out my mistake and I never confused the words again.

While I was thus occupied with customs, costumes and language, Mrs. Sugi and I were getting to know each other better and making the most of our summer leisure. I couldn't have picked a more easygoing household in which to live. Captain Sugi was still the most unmilitary military man imaginable. He never wore a uniform on his daily trips from home to office, and back. He simply kept his uniforms in the office and dressed for duty every morning when he got there. He loved the Navy but he abhorred any kind of show and he didn't feel it was necessary to wear a uniform except when the performance of his duty actually required it.

He was the most thoughtful and loyal of friends, a point that was hammered home to me when he returned from work one evening with the news that he had been promoted once again, this time to Rear Admiral, and had been transferred to the naval base at Yokosuka, where he was to assume charge of the engineering section. He told us that it wouldn't be necessary for him to give up the house in Tokyo, that he would stay at the base during the week and return to Tokyo every weekend. It didn't occur to me at the time, and neither he nor his wife ever hinted at the matter, but I found out later that if I hadn't been with them, and if they hadn't undertaken to help me establish myself in Tokyo, Mrs. Sugi simply would have moved to Yokosuka with him and occupied the official residence provided for him, as a flag officer, there. When I discussed it with Mrs. Sugi later, she said that the subject never was mentioned between them; it simply was taken for granted that they would go ahead with the plan they had drawn up for me. Their own interests were firmly put aside.

They are good friends, these Japanese.

Chapter VII

I was supposed to begin my work for the Nakamura family in Yokohama on the thirty-first of August, but Mr. Nakamura called me a few days before to say that inasmuch as the thirty-first was a holiday, the anniversary of the death of Emperor Taisho, the lessons would have to be postponed for a week. I had been looking forward to my first weekend with the Nakamuras, but I decided to make the best of the postponement by spending the time with a friend of mine from New York, Mrs. Sekikawa, who had just returned from America and had news of mutual friends and, especially, of Mama.

Mr. Sekikawa had remained in New York, and his wife and their children were living in Otsuka, a suburb of Tokyo, about an hour's ride from the Sugis' house. We had a great deal to talk about and we sat up late on Friday night, long after the two children had gone to bed. It was hot that night, and when we went to bed the scent of a storm was strong in the air.

When we got up Saturday morning, it was raining hard and the wind was blowing with the force of an equinoctial storm. I wondered how I was going to be able to get back to Admiral Sugi's house by noon, as I had promised Mrs. Sugi I would. After breakfast, we settled down to talk some more while I waited for the weather to clear up a little. But the rain didn't stop beating down until half past eleven. The sun came out then, but it was so late that we decided it would be better for me to stay for lunch and then go home. We sent Mrs. Sekikawa's little boy to the corner store to telephone Mrs. Sugi, and we relaxed in the two U.S.-style wicker chairs in the living room. Then, without any warning at all, the house began to move.

"It's an earthquake," Mrs. Sekikawa said with a gasp.

The giant hand of Nature had seized the little house and was shaking it, and everything in it, like a toy in the mouth of a puppy. Dishes, books, pots and pans tumbled and clattered to the floor. We sat in our chairs, rocking and trembling, not daring to move, while the house shook as if the next upheaval would surely smash it to pieces. It seemed like an unbearably long time before the terrible convulsions slackened off to an occasional shuddering and trembling, and then, finally, stopped altogether. We stood up, dazed, our hearts still pounding with shock, and tried to think what had happened.

People were running past the house, babbling excitedly. Mrs. Sekikawa said that the ground was littered with heavy tiles blown off the roofs. In the distance we could hear the ominous sound of booming explosions. I couldn't understand why the Sekikawas' frail little house hadn't disintegrated, but I found out later that the Japanese, accustomed to these assaults, build their houses to withstand them. They may rattle and clatter and shake, but they usually remain upright.

The big question now, of course, was whether the house would be able to hold up against a second quake. An old woman who had lived through the last great earthquake to convulse Tokyo, some sixty years before, gave us the cheering news that the second shock had been worse than the first. That was a big help to our peace of mind. We sat, tense and almost unmoving, as the stricken earth caught its breath every five minutes or so with another convulsive jerk. The ground trembled constantly, with occasional violent shocks, for twenty-four hours, and the dread of a second violent visitation was with us every minute.

During the afternoon, as the people of the town began to come out of their houses to pick up the debris, returning neighbors reported that fires were raging out of control in every section of Tokyo. Mrs. Sekikawa and her young son went out at about four o'clock to see if they could learn anything, but they encountered nothing except more rumors, even wilder than the earlier ones. Telephone connections were disrupted and all transportation was at a standstill. The women in the houses outside the city had no way of knowing what had happened to their husbands, and the men could do nothing but walk slowly from their crumbling or burning office buildings to homes which might, for all they knew, already be consumed by fire. Nobody knew anything except what he could see with his own eyes.

When night came, we decided to go out into the garden; another earthquake might easily bring down the house about our heads. We took the wooden shutters from their little closet at the end of the veranda, laid them on the ground and spread bed cushions and sheets over them. Then we surrounded the improvised beds with our big mosquito nets, to protect us not only from the mosquitos but also from stray dogs and cats.

As darkness settled over the stricken city, a deathly stillness enveloped everything. My courage was at a low ebb. The world that only a few hours before had been so tranquil literally was crumbling around us. Even the dependable earth seemed to have deserted us; it never stopped trembling. I didn't know what to do, where to go or whom to trust. There was nothing except the acrid smell of fires burning and the shaking ground. Then, suddenly, as if in answer to everyone's doubts, another light appeared, soft, serene, steady, cool and comforting. "There's a full moon," Mrs.

Sekikawa said softly. The Universe was still there, calm and unshakable, proclaiming the glory of God. Cities might be crushed by death and destruction, but He was in His heaven and the world would go on, no matter how much it might seem to have come to an end. I wondered how many people in stricken Tokyo were being comforted by the sight of the Moon of Promise.

With the dawn, we heard, as the sun came up, the hum of a lonely airplane coming nearer and nearer. Someone was flying over the city to see and to report the extent of the disaster. The earth still trembled, as it had all night, and frequently shocks continued to fill us with dread of what might yet happen, but there was hope, too, brought to us by that single little plane.

Early that morning, Mrs. Sekikawa's brother brought us news from the city. In addition to the buildings wrecked by the earthquake itself, tremendous explosions had destroyed factories, bridges, and gas and water mains. Fires were burning everywhere, thousands of people were homeless, countless families were separated, and over everything hung the fear of another earthquake.

After a makeshift breakfast we decided that we had to do something, no matter how little, to help. Mrs. Sekikawa cooked some rice and made it up into little balls with a dried plum in the middle of each. She packed them into a market basket and we went out into the road to give them to anyone who was hungry. The tired refugees from the city marched by endlessly. Some of them carried a few precious possessions but most of them had left with nothing but the thin summer kimonos they were wearing. Our pitifully few rice balls were nothing among so many, but Mrs. Sekikawa tried to single out the weakest marchers. She asked a mother who was leading a little boy by the hand when they had eaten last. "Yesterday morning," the woman said shyly. "We had to leave the house before lunch." We gave each of them a rice ball but the woman gave one back to us. The other she broke in two, giving the larger piece to her son. "Thank you," she said as they moved on. "There are others."

We got back to the house at about eleven o'clock, just in time to meet an officious policeman who was going from door to door announcing that there would be a second earthquake at one o'clock in the afternoon. The Japanese were trained to place implicit trust in their policemen, and hearing such a portentous announcement from one of them filled everyone with a nameless dread. But, as one o'clock approached, struck, and passed without anything happening, their fear was replaced by a righteous anger. It was obvious that the pompous policeman didn't know anything more about another quake than they did.

That was only the beginning. The rumors came one after the other, the newest one wilder and more frightening than the last. The worst one, calculated to completely unnerve the already troubled people, was that the many Koreans in Tokyo were banding together to take advantage of the opportunity to sabotage the city by poisoning the old wells which, with the mains out, would be the only source of drinking water. This vicious report made the rounds like wildfire. There is nothing like a guilty conscience to arouse suspicion, and the Japanese knew that there was much resentment in Korea over some of the things that had been done since Japan took over control of the country in 1910. It wasn't hard for them to believe that the Koreans would welcome the chance to strike back. Bands of young vigilantes, armed with clubs and other primitive weapons, scoured the countryside and the streets of Tokyo searching for anyone who even resembled a Korean.

Each hour brought a new report of tragedy. Crowds of people fleeing from the fires in the city had sought refuge on the wooden bridges over the Sumida River, only to feel the flimsy structures tremble and collapse underneath them, plunging them and their meager belongings into the water. Thirty thousand others thought they had found safety in a huge open space in front of a downtown army supply depot, but sparks carried by the relentless wind set fire to the bundles they clutched in their hands and burned to death the entire multitude. Houses were gone, shops and factories in ruins, public utilities either shattered or in flames. The country was thrown back into the days before the seaports of Japan were opened up to the outside world by Commodore Perry.

Still unaware of the true scope of the disaster, I went to the telegraph office with Mrs. Sekikawa to see if I could send a cablegram to Mama, to let her know that I was all right. *"Dame,"* the man said, *Dame* meaning out of commission, no good.

I wanted to go back to Mrs. Sugi's, but there was still no way of getting through. I had been told that the district in which the Sugis lived had escaped the fire, but all I could do was wait. Finally, on Wednesday, four days after the earthquake had struck, a jinriksha man told us that he could take us. He had only one jinriksha at his disposal, but we thought it was best to hire him while we had the chance and try to pick up another on the way. I rode, as we set out, and Mrs. Sekikawa walked alongside the jinriksha, looking around constantly for another carriage. I sat there, in my solitary splendor, most reluctantly. But I knew it was a two-hour trip, and I felt that, if I rode at first, Mrs. Sekikawa's pride would be appeased and she would be willing to take my place in the jinriksha seat for the rest of the journey. I was reckoning, however, without the character of the Japanese woman. No other jinriksha ever came into sight, but nothing would induce Mrs. Sekikawa to change places with me. I would have been far happier doing my share of the walking, but my friend wouldn't even consider it.

Mrs. Sugi greeted us warmly but I could sense that her feelings were mixed. I knew she was relieved and happy to see that I was all right, but it was equally clear that she was worried about what was to become of me. My own feeling was that I never had been happier to arrive anywhere. Mrs. Sekikawa had been wonderfully good to me but Mrs. Sugi's was home and I wanted to be there. When I went into my room, I found everything I owned packed carefully in my two trunks, and the trunks themselves covered with heavy, oiled paper. My precious typewriter was entirely wrapped in the same paper and placed for protection in one of the trunks. Mrs. Sugi had used the oiled paper to guard everything from the rain that had been expected every day since the earthquake, and that would be bound to pour through the roof, from which just about every tile had been shaken loose.

Everybody talked endlessly about what they had been doing at the time of the earthquake, and we heard as many stories as we had friends, but I think Mrs. Sugi's was the best. "I was just beginning lunch," she said, "and I knew it was going to be terrible, that I would have a lot to do, and that there was no knowing when I would have a chance to eat again. So I made up my mind that I would sit down and finish my lunch before I did a thing." And that was just what she did, sitting at her lunch and eating methodically while destruction rained around her. When she had finished, she went out and got enough oiled paper to make all the valuables in the house reasonably waterproof, taking pains to pack and cover my things first.

People came from all over the city to find out how we were. Some of them were able to hire jinrikshas, but most of them walked. I was amazed that, in spite of all their own troubles, these old friends would take time out to check up on my safety. Even the policeman who had taken care of registering me as a foreign visitor the day I arrived at the Sugis' came to ask if I was all right. He greeted me warmly and expressed the hope that I wouldn't find Tokyo too uncomfortable.

After I had been back a few days, Mr. and Mrs. Horikoshi, the parents of the young couple who had taken over our apartment in New York and were making a home for Mama, came to call. Their house had been burned to the ground and they had saved nothing except the clothes on their backs. Mr. Horikoshi, who was nearly seventy, was in a highly nervous state. He thought I ought to go back to America as soon as I could get on a boat. "I'm afraid it will take Tokyo, and the whole country for that matter, a long time to recover," he said mournfully. "There is sure to be a business panic. Conditions are going to be very bad."

I didn't dismiss his suggestion lightly. I realized that it probably would be sensible to go back home. I knew Mrs. Sugi also was very worried about how I was going to manage. But my heart rebelled at the thought of giving up and going back so soon, after it had taken me so long to get here. In the end, I made up my mind that I would do nothing until Admiral Sugi came home and I had a chance to talk over my situation with him. I knew I would get calm, reasoned advice from him, and I promised myself that I would do whatever he thought best.

We heard nothing from him for a whole week. What made it worse, especially for Mrs. Sugi, was that we had heard that Yokosuka had been much nearer the center of the earthquake than Tokyo and had suffered almost complete destruction. Tokyo had been ravaged chiefly by fire, but in the coastal cities like Yokohama and Yokosuka the shock of the earthquake itself had done immense damage. We kept telling ourselves that, if anything had happened to the admiral, Mrs. Sugi would have been notified, but just the same it was a long, anxious wait.

There wasn't much to eat or drink, but we managed to get along with pears, which seemed to be plentiful, *takudani,* preserved fish, and unpolished rice. Our biggest triumph that week was getting the roof repaired. We had been using every available basin, pot, pan and tub to catch the water that cascaded through the sievelike roof, and it was a signal accomplishment when Mrs. Sugi persuaded a roofer to replace the tiles that had been shaken off by the quake. No men in all of Tokyo were more in demand that week than the roofers.

I shouldn't have been surprised by Mrs. Sugi's resourcefulness. I already had had ample opportunity to observe that Japanese women are prodigious workers and to verify at close range that they do not shun responsibility. It was another good lesson for me—further proof, if I needed it, of the fallaciousness of the Western notion that the Japanese woman is a passive slave to her lord and master. The truth is that a woman who proves her worth in the home wields great influence over her husband and exercises absolute authority in the bringing up of the children. In most families of men working for salaries, the wife even takes charge of the weekly pay envelope, much as women do in the United States. She pays the household bills, sets aside something to be saved, and gives the man of the house what she considers a fair allowance for his personal needs.

Japanese women may be old-fashioned in their relationship to their husbands, but they are not doormats. They have the gift of letting the men reign while they rule.

We continued to glean bits of news, a little more each day. The most important message was delivered by a courier from Yokosuka. Admiral Sugi was safe and sound, although desperately busy, and in another week or so he would be home for a visit. That was all, but it was enough. There also was word that the American Embassy in Tokyo had burned and that the Ambassador barely had escaped with his life. The Embassy offices, we were told, had been shifted to the Imperial Hotel, the world-famous creation of the American architect Frank Lloyd Wright. The Imperial was one of the big Tokyo buildings which had withstood the earthquake, although it wasn't, as has often been written, the only one to survive. Lots of brick buildings had crumpled to bits, but a good many concrete structures, such as the Mitsubishi

Bank Building, designed and constructed by Japanese, withstood the shocks without a crack.

On September fifteenth, two weeks after the quake, Admiral Sugi came home. He was tired but in good health. I tried to stay in the background while he quietly expressed his pride and appreciation to his wife for all she had done so bravely in his absence, and it wasn't until after we all had eaten dinner that I mentioned my problem. I told him of Mr. Horikoshi's feeling that I ought to go home right away, and I said that Mama, too, had cabled me suggesting that I be prudent and return.

"Do you want to go back?" the admiral asked bluntly.

"No, I don't," I told him honestly. "But neither do I want to cause my friends any extra trouble."

He leaned back in his chair. "So far," he said thoughtfully, "you have caused trouble to no one. Certainly not to us. If, after you've been here a few months longer, you decide that you can't fit into the new situation, you can consider going home. But right now I think you ought to remember that everybody is having trouble adjusting. If you don't mind the inconvenience and the discomfort, which certainly won't last, you ought to stay. We'll be glad to have you."

I felt comfortable for the first time in two weeks. I knew that Admiral Sugi wasn't just being polite. He wouldn't encourage me to stay if he felt it would be bad for him or his wife. At the same time, I realized that it was up to me to plan what I would do. One thing was sure—I couldn't go to Yokohama to work for Mr. Nakamura and his family. The earthquake had taken care of that, and it was a miracle that it hadn't taken care of me, too. For, if I had gone to Yokohama as I was supposed to, I almost certainly would have been walking with Mr. Nakamura just before twelve o'clock on that fateful Saturday when he was struck down by the earthquake and killed.

I wondered what I could do to make myself useful. When I heard that people had scarcely anything to wear, I began to knit, an occupation for which I have never had much enthusiasm. I knit from morning to night, making scarves, baby jackets and anything else that people could wear. Fortunately we were able to get enough wool, and I knit until my fingers were sore.

Two people came to my thoughts. One was Caroline Mac-Donald, an old friend from New York. In America she had been doing rehabilitation work among prisoners, and I remembered that she had told us that her next project was going to be a settlement for working people in Tokyo. I had been much attracted to her, but in the excitement of actually going to Japan I had forgotten all about her. I decided to write to her, tell her of my arrival in Tokyo, and ask if she knew of anything I might be able to do.

I also thought of Mr. Choshichi Ito, the principal of the Tokyo Prefectural Fifth Middle School for Boys. Mr. Ito had visited New York just before I left for Japan, and one of my friends had brought him to see me. We had spent an absorbing evening discussing education in Japan, and I had been interested in his advanced ideas. When he said good-by, he told me, "When you come to Japan, I want you to teach in my school." I wondered, now, if he had meant it. I decided to find out. I had never been especially eager to teach in a school; private teaching always has seemed more rewarding to me. But I had to make a start somehow, and I already had observed that in Japan the prestige of teaching in a good Government school is considerable. It would be an excellent stepping stone to what I really wanted to do.

As soon as the telephone service was restored, toward the end of September, I called Mr. Ito. Our conversation was short and to the point.

"Mr. Ito," I said, "do you remember Miss Genevieve Caulfield, whom you met in New York?"

"I certainly do," he said. "Where is she?"

"This is she," I said, eagerly, and without further preliminaries I plunged right in. "Do you really want me to teach in your school?"

His answer came without hesitation. "I certainly do," he said firmly. "Where are you now, Miss Caulfield?"

"I'm in the Aoyama section, number thirty-seven Go Chome, at the home of Admiral Sugi. I've been staying here with him and Mrs. Sugi."

"I'll be there in half an hour," he said decisively. "Will you wait for me?"

I certainly would wait for him. And within half an hour, as he had promised, he was there, shaking hands with me, welcoming me to Japan, and offering me a position as an English teacher in his school. I didn't want to teach in a school every day, so we arranged a two-day-a-week schedule. It was exactly what I had hoped for. The salary was small, but it was a good beginning; the prestige of the appointment would make it much easier for me to secure private pupils, and I still would have most of the week free in which to do other things. It was an ideal arrangement.

Astoundingly, Mr. Ito had not been in the house five minutes when Miss MacDonald arrived. She told me that she had just taken over a building not far from the center of Tokyo, which she was planning to use for a settlement house. One of her projects was a night school for working people, and she would like very much, she said, to have me teach there one or two evenings a week. The center also would be a place where men released from prison might find temporary shelter until they could obtain suitable work. I was intensely interested, and I was glad to accept an assignment to work in the settlement one night each week. What I was doing, in fact, was signing up for a liberal education in contemporary Japanese life, although I didn't realize it at the time. Once I was firmly anchored at the Fifth Middle School and the settlement house, private pupils began to appear from all directions. To help me find my way to all the places I had to go, I took on a young girl companion. I had made up my mind never to risk going out alone in Tokyo. I suppose I could have managed it if I had tried, but it seemed to me that making my way along busy streets wasted energy which I might better put to use doing less dangerous things.

The earthquake, which had contributed so heavily to my problems, accidentally eliminated one of the main ones. The manager of the Yokohama office of the Mitsubishi Company, whom I had met in New York, had been killed in the earthquake. I went to his funeral and met his sister-in-law, whom I also had known back home. This lady, Mrs. Tsugita, asked me what my plans were.

"I've been invited to stay as long as I want with Admiral and Mrs. Sugi," I said. "But I'm worried about it because he has to spend all week in Yokosuka and then come all the way back here every weekend. I'm sure they would both be happier if Mrs. Sugi were in Yokosuka with him."

"I think I have a solution," Mrs. Tsugita said. "I'd like you to live in the house of my mother and father, Mr. and Mrs. Eguchi. We have four girls and five boys in our family, and two of the girls and four of the boys are still living at home. If you'd like to try it, we've got two good-sized rooms you can live in all by yourself, and in your free time you can do whatever you want, including your work at the Fifth Middle School. All we would ask of you is that you help my brothers and sisters with their English. What do you say?"

I thanked her and told her I would think it over, but I knew right from the beginning that I would say yes. By the time Admiral Sugi came home for his next weekend visit, I had made up my mind that it was the right thing to do, and I told him about it with so much enthusiasm that he agreed instantly. He was pleased that I was going to have an opportunity to see, at close hand, the life of a Japanese family of the wealthy upper class. He went with me to see Mr. and Mrs. Eguchi, and we decided that the first of December would be a good time for me to make the change.

In the meantime, I had to make good as a teacher at the Fifth Middle School. I was noticeably nervous on my first day there. I had been teaching English to foreigners for more than seven years, but only in private lessons. My classroom experience was limited to the required practice teaching at Teachers College and to the year divided between Perkins and Overbrook. It wasn't very much preparation for teaching a class of fifty high school boys.

Mr. Ito showed complete confidence in me as we sat in his office and talked over the work. But he did have one doubt, which he wasted no time bringing up. "Would you like to have a Japanese teacher in the classroom with you," he wanted to know, "so you won't be troubled with maintaining discipline?"

"No, thanks," I said hastily. "Please, no. I'm sure I can manage the class alone. If I can't, I'd rather give it up. I couldn't very well have a third person between me and the class. I wouldn't be a teacher then, I'd only be a phonograph." Mr. Ito willingly agreed to let me try it my way, and that was the only reference he ever made to the fact that I couldn't see.

Things worked out very well. Undoubtedly this was partly due to the grimly serious approach the boys took toward their schooling. Only two hundred boys were accepted in the Fifth Middle School each year, and there always were between fifteen hundred and two thousand boys competing for the prized places. Once they got in, they had to work just as hard to advance their chances of being selected for the higher schools. There was absolute democracy in these schools; position or family wealth meant nothing. The students who did best in the long series of harrowing examinations, from kindergarten through the university, could aspire to the highest positions in the land. One boy, I remember, when I asked him what he wanted to be when he grew up, said, seriously, "I want to be a baron."

With so much at stake, the boys worked hard, studied eagerly, and were easy to manage. Not one of them ever gave me the slightest bit of trouble, and I obtained from them an insight into the Japanese character that I don't think I could have gained in any other way. I taught in the Fifth Middle School twice a week for fourteen years, half frozen in winter but always happy.

The temperature in the building was a real problem to one who, like me, was a product of American central heating. As my first autumn wore on, I became colder and colder. A Japanese winter is an experience. The temperature doesn't go down to zero or anywhere near it—usually about twenty or twenty-two is the lowest it will get—but the damp air penetrates to the marrow of your bones in the unheated or at best badly heated buildings. It isn't so bad when you're walking around outside, but comfortable living indoors becomes impossible.

I always kept my coat on all day at school during the winter months, but the poor students were obliged by the strictest etiquette to take theirs off. No wonder the Japanese soldier proved during the war to be a hardy specimen.

From the first of December until the first of March, we kept a wood fire burning in the classroom stove. It would be kindled red hot in the morning, but during school hours it would gradually cool off. At recess time the boys always ran to it and, instead of going outside to play games, they would pile on fuel and cluster around the cherry-red glow, rubbing their blue fingers and thoroughly enjoying themselves. I was supposed to send them down to the playground but I didn't have the heart to do it, for I, too, wanted to get as close to the stove as possible.

I don't think I could have endured that first winter of teaching if Emma Kauffman, a kind-hearted woman who had been in Tokyo for ten years as the head of the Y.W.C.A., hadn't lent me a fur coat which she steadfastly insisted was a spare one. I always felt guilty standing in front of my coatless boys, knowing full well that they were shivering while I was burrowing deep within Emma's furs. But, guilty or not, I wore the coat gratefully.

I enjoyed my work at Caroline MacDonald's settlement house, the Shinrinkan, too. Caroline spent most of her daytime hours visiting men in prison, meeting their families and trying to find work for men who had been released or were about to be released. It was no easy task, especially because a man's crime and the sentence he had served were entered prominently on his family registration record, which every prospective employer required him to show.

One of the officials with whom Caroline was associated in her rehabilitation work was Governor Arima, the warden of Kosuge Prison, where serious offenders sentenced to serve long terms were held. Despite the fact that the men in his care included some of the most dangerous criminals in Japan, Warden Arima believed firmly in the honor system. When the earthquake struck, he was confronted with a dramatic opportunity to prove the practical value of his theories. The prison was virtually destroyed by the terrible shock, and the fifteen hundred convicts were hurried out of the cell blocks to a huge open space in front of the tottering main building. In many of the other Japanese prisons, the men were kept securely locked up despite the danger of recurring quakes and, even worse, fire. But Warden Arima had his fifteen hundred men led outside to safety, and then he spoke to them:

"You can see," he said, "that the walls of our buildings are tumbling down. Tonight we shall all have to sleep out of doors. You know as well as I do that I cannot possibly provide an adequate guard for you. If you want to escape, I fear there is nothing I can do to prevent you except to endanger your lives by putting you back in the cells. This I do not propose to do. I expect you to behave accordingly. You know that you have been sent here by the law of your country. Some of you may think you are here unjustly, but most of you know you are not. Even those about whom a mistake may have been made have had a fair trial and are serving a sentence which your country regards as just. Think carefully before you do anything you may regret."

With the earth still trembling, the men made preparations to bed down for the night on the ground. They didn't sleep any better than anyone else in the area did, but when the roll was called in the morning not one man was reported missing.

When martial law was declared throughout Tokyo and its environs, a company of soldiers came to guard the prison. Warden Arima met them at the gate and told them it wasn't necessary for them to come in, but the commanding officer insisted that he had to obey the orders that had been given him. The warden, acutely aware of the damage that would be done to the morale of the men, begged the officer to hold off at least until he could go into Tokyo and consult with his superiors. To this, the officer agreed.

It took Warden Arima a long time to cover the distance to the city, traveling over hopelessly blocked roads past fiercely burning buildings, but he finally reached military headquarters and put his case directly before the commander-in-chief. At first, the general was firm. Martial law was martial law. He could not leave the prisons unguarded. It was his first duty to protect the citizens of Toyko and their property.

"And it is my duty," the warden said firmly, "to administer my prison. I have been working for ten years to instill in these men confidence in me and in society. If the soldiers go in now, everything I have accomplished will be destroyed. I'm sure I can control my men but I'm not sure your soldiers can. The minute one soldier enters my prison, I go out. These are men who simply can't be played with. I know them, and they trust me, but I won't have my discipline disrupted by strangers."

The general knew when he was beaten. Not one soldier marched into the Kosuge Prison compound during that whole troubled time.

As the first of December drew near, I made ready to say a grateful good-by to the Sugis. I wasn't going to lose touch with the Admiral and his wife by any means, for Mrs. Sugi had promised to visit me at least once every week, but it was time to move on to my new home.

The Eguchi house, at Yotsuya Mitsuka, was on one of the main streetcar lines in Tokyo and was within walking distance of the Jesuit University. It was a mansion constructed in Western style and containing rooms furnished in both Western and Japanese style. It was a big house, easy to get lost in, and at first I had a good deal of trouble finding my way around in it. There were nine children in the family, and each of them had a separate room. In addition there were a generous number of guest rooms, parlors and reception rooms for the endless stream of visitors who sought out Mr. Eguchi on business matters at all hours of the day and night. The house was solidly and well constructed; it combined the advantages of both schools of architecture, the principal contribution of the Western influence being thick walls which kept it amazingly warm for a Tokyo house.

I was assigned two rooms on the second floor. Both had mats on the floor, but one also was covered with a rug and furnished with chairs, a table and a desk. In the other room, the bedroom, bed cushions were spread on the *tatami* in traditional Japanese style. It was a most comfortable arrangement. I would be able to use the sitting room to meet with the Eguchi children and my private pupils. It was a bright, sunny room and it contained a Perfection oil stove, a prized possession in chilly Japan. The Eguchis lived well.

Families like the Eguchis scrupulously limited their spending to family purposes and occasions. Their homes were luxurious, their parties were lavish, their wedding ceremonies for sons and trousseaux for daughters were expensive. But individual members of the family were restricted to the simplest sort of living. It wasn't uncommon for families traveling with children of school age to let the children, especially the boys, go into the third-class carriages while the parents took first- or second-class tickets. The family car was strictly for the use of the head of the house or the family as a whole. It was never used for the convenience of the children. I remember going with the Eguchi children in the rain to a concert. We walked down to the fast-line express station while the family car stood idly at the door of the house. This wasn't because the parents were inconsiderate but simply because it would never occur to the children, even the grown-up ones, to ask for the car for their own use. If their mother took them shopping, or to visit the doctor, they would use the car, because that was family business. But on ordinary occasions they traveled exactly like other people. Their clothes were simple and their food was simple. The children of the rich, like those of the poor, took small lunch boxes to school containing rice, a little fish, and pickled vegetables, and they ate it cold, winter or summer. It was a matter of pride not to be different from the others.

I taught girls and boys from families of the nobility as well as families possessing great industrial wealth, but I cannot remember one of my pupils ever coming for an English lesson in an automobile.

Both Mr. and Mrs. Eguchi spoke excellent English. He had been abroad on business trips several times, and his wife had graduated from a mission school where English had been well taught. Whenever Mr. Eguchi had a little spare time, he liked to practice his English by bringing a copy of Robert Louis Stevenson or Mark Twain to my sitting room, where we would spend a pleasant half hour reading together. He was an understanding and cultured man. I'm sure he must have been a dominating personality in his business operations, for he had amassed a considerable fortune, but there was nothing of the lord and master about him at home. There is an old Japanese saying which goes, "Earthquake, Fire, Thunder and Father," but it never could be applied to Mr. Eguchi.

Indeed, in his household it was just the opposite. No one who knew Mrs. Eguchi could talk about the "servitude" of Japanese women. She was a strong woman, forceful and temperamental, and she ruled her domicile with a firm, often stern and sometimes downright unreasonable authority. Her word, which was carried out by the members of her family to the letter, was law.

There were times when I didn't see her for a week or ten days. She might be in the country or she might simply be staying in her own room, withdrawing from the family for a time to indulge her own interests. She often took her meals by herself, perhaps because, like most Japanese businessmen, Mr. Eguchi seldom was home in the evenings. He was occupied night after night with elaborate banquets at which, between exquisitely served delicacies and picturesque entertainment by geisha, important business was said to be transacted. As a result, I usually took my dinner with the children. When Mrs. Eguchi did appear for dinner, she was excellent company; she was well read and she had a quick sense of humor. She wasn't an easy person to deal with, however, and I had a few memorable set-tos with her regarding the children. I discovered from her that the famous politeness of the Japanese does not prevent them from telling people exactly what they think of them.

I had kept a fair number of private pupils to fill in the time left to me after my work at the school and my commitment to teach the Eguchi children. Some of them came to me for lessons, but if there were two or more pupils in a single family, I went to them. One of the families I visited every week as long as I was in Japan was the Fukuis, who sent their car for me every Saturday. My traveling arrangements weren't always, of course, so elaborate. I made my way to the Fifth Middle School two days a week with the regular assistance of a young girl to whom I paid a modest sum for the service. Whenever I had to go anywhere else, I took a jinriksha.

At first, I greatly disliked the idea of being pulled through the streets by another human being, but I gradually came to understand that these men were earning an honest living in the way they had chosen. They owned their own carriages and they liked the freedom of the work more than running errands or working in the fields or factories. They knew their business, too, and they were thoroughly trustworthy. They took me all over the great, sprawling city and found the most cunningly hidden addresses for me without fail. Modern taxi drivers in Tokyo don't even pretend to know how to find their way to where you want to go, and unless you are able to direct them you simply don't get there. But it was never that way with the extinct jinriksha men. They never missed.

A bonus for me was the incalculable amount of information I picked up from them. I learned about the kind of living conditions they knew, how much money they earned, that they never drank anything cold in the summer but quenched their thirst only with steaming hot tea, and even how long the average jinrikshaman expected to work at his trade before turning to something easier or retiring altogether to live on his son's earnings. These hard-working men became my friends and I trusted them absolutely. Gradually, inevitably, they gave way to more modern forms of transportation, but as long as they ran swiftly through the streets of Tokyo, I lived an independent life despite my blindness.

Chapter VIII

On January 15, 1924, I got up early to go to the Fifth Middle
School. Shortly before six o'clock the maid came to my room
to light the oil stove, and I went into the bathroom to wash
up. Just as I started out of the room, with towel and soap in
hand, I felt an ominous trembling, and in a moment the
earth was shaking violently. Remembering the terrible fires
that had laid waste to so much of the city after the other
earthquake, I thought first of the lighted oil stove. I dropped
the towel and soap on the floor and hurried back. I knew
every inch of the room and it was no problem for me to find
the stove. But it wasn't so easy for me to turn it off. I knew it
was operated by a little round screw, but whether the screw
was at the back or the front of the stove I didn't know. The
only thing I could do was put my arms around the stove and
feel gently with my hands until I found it. I forced myself
to ignore both the hot metal and my rising fear, and finally
I found the screw and twisted it until it was off. Then I
knelt on the floor and breathed a prayer of relief.

This earthquake turned out to be only half the intensity
of the earlier one, but it didn't do our morale any good. In
a way, we were probably even more frightened than we had
been the first time.

Actually, there wasn't much destruction in the city, partly

because there was so little left to be destroyed, but the Eguchi family gathered apprehensively in the drawing room, in varying stages of undress. The temperature was well below freezing, and we were cold. It made us realize how lucky we had been that the great September earthquake at least was accompanied by mild weather. We sat around and talked in subdued tones about what had happened to us the other time, exchanging stories of experiences that made us thankful for our present situation. At about half past seven, when we were just beginning to think about eating some breakfast, the doorbell rang sharply. Someone, the maid said, wanted to see Mr. Eguchi. Still wearing his indoor kimono, Mr. Eguchi went to see who it was. He came back in about ten minutes, plainly annoyed.

"Can you imagine?" he said. "That was a man asking me to join the Imperial Way Association."

The Imperial Way Association was an ultra-nationalistic organization of super patriots whose avowed goal was to drive Japan to a position of world power, at whatever cost.

"I wonder what will happen to us," Mr. Eguchi said thoughtfully, "if we ever fall into the hands of men like them."

Another caller, later that day, was Mrs. Sugi. Feeling certain that I would have stayed home from school, she had come all the way from Yokosuka to see if I was all right. She insisted upon taking me downtown to Mr. Horikoshi's office to send a reassuring cable to Mama. It was typical of Mrs. Sugi to think of Mama back home worrying as she read the news.

The Horikoshis were living with relatives while their new home was being built. The house they had lost in September had been in the heart of the city, but they had decided it would be more prudent to move out to the suburbs this time, and they had settled upon Azabu, a residential section which had withstood both the quake and the subsequent fire. Every time I saw Mr. Horikoshi or his wife they reminded me that

I was to move in with them as soon as the new house was ready. We felt very close to each other. Mama, of course, was still living with the young Horikoshis in our old apartment in New York, helping Kikue San master the mysteries of homemaking. So it was natural for Mr. and Mrs. Horikoshi to regard us as part of their family.

Zenjiro Horikoshi was a remarkable man. He was the son of a farmer but he had made up his mind at an early age that he was going to be a businessman when he grew up, and, instead of conforming to his duty as the eldest son by following in his father's footsteps, he defied all the stern family traditions of his country by running away from home as soon as he was old enough. He wanted more than anything else to go to America, but he knew he would have to wait until he had accumulated the knowledge and resources to start a business of his own. He found work in Tokyo, and as his meager earnings increased he put himself through business school. After years of surviving the hardships of an incredibly Spartan existence, he was graduated with an excellent record. Soon afterward he obtained a position with an export company, and finally he was sent to the land he had dreamed about for so long.

The salary he was paid in New York was so small that he couldn't afford to eat lunch. He would have a quick bite for breakfast and then fast until dinnertime. He got into the habit of spending his lunch hour at the public library, studying. Working hard, living frugally and tenaciously saving his money, he ultimately established his own company, Z. Horikoshi and Company, silk importers. His son and grandson are still operating the business.

I decided that the time had come for me to deal seriously with the Japanese language. My first teacher was a retired army officer who had absolutely no experience as a language teacher but who was grateful to me for taking his son on a vacation trip to the seashore and wanted to do something in return for me. As things worked out, he proved to be an ex-

cellent teacher; what he lacked as a pedagogue, he more than
made up with his instinctive feeling for drill. By the time
I had finished learning Japanese verb forms, I knew just
how the soldiers who had served under him must have felt
at the end of a field problem. He had no use for anything less
than perfection.

Later on, I had other teachers, and I often thought back
wistfully to my experience with this strict military man. For,
almost without exception, the kind people who taught me
were too polite to correct my mistakes. They would let me
make one error after another and cheerily congratulate me
on my handling of the language. Too often, I wasn't handling
it at all; I was manhandling it. But they couldn't bring themselves to tell the poor blind American lady that she had done
something wrong.

The autumn and winter slipped by, and I moved into the
handsome new foreign-style home the Horikoshis had built
in Azabu. Living with them and their daughter, Yukiko San,
was almost like being back with my own family.

With a full list of private pupils, my income had increased
to the point where I felt secure in writing to Mama and suggesting that she make plans to join me in the fall. The only
problem was to find a house. I began to look seriously for
one, and finally, with the help of Masako San, my assistant
and guide, I found one in Mita, one of the residential sections
of Tokyo. It was a two-story, Japanese-style house, far from
new but clean and comfortable. On the first floor there were
four good-sized rooms, a bathroom, and an empty space with
a cement floor and a cold-water tap which the imaginative
landlord described as the kitchen. There were three bedrooms upstairs, enough to take care of our requirements
nicely. Every room in the house had *tatami* on the floor, so
my limited budget had to be strained only by the purchase
of a dining-room set, some wicker furniture for the drawing
room and grass rugs for the dining room and drawing room.
I also arranged for a carpenter to reinforce the wooden floor

at one end of the drawing room so that we could safely place our piano there. To me, a home without a piano isn't really a home, and Mama was going to send ours over ahead of her.

We moved into the house in June. Masako San lived in one of the downstairs rooms and we installed a maid in the fourth room. We needed a maid to do the housework while Masako San and I were busy traveling around the city keeping teaching appointments; in addition to the work she would be able to do for us, I knew the maid would also be valuable merely to look after the house while we were gone, which was most of the time.

There was so much to do, the summer fairly flew by. Now that the time for Mama to come was so near, I found myself more impatient than ever to be with her again, to introduce her to this country I had found so fascinating and these people I had learned to like and to respect so much. There were so many wonderful experiences in store for her. Just an ordinary visit to the Tokumis, for example, where I went every Saturday to teach their two elder daughters. They lived in a pure Japanese house in which the *tatami*, the soft, richly covered *futons* and the exquisitely appointed *tokonoma* spoke as eloquently of their good taste as of their wealth. I visited their home every Saturday afternoon, after leaving the Fukuis, and when the serious work of the English lesson for their two daughters was over, Mrs. Tokumi insisted that I stay with them for an hour or so. One of the girls served tea and Mrs. Tokumi always produced some new delicacy to tempt my alien palate. One week it might be fancy rice balls wrapped in crisp seaweed, another week a bowl of steaming noodles with fried shrimp, another week the rice ball again, this time wrapped in a thin, sweet omelet or topped with raw fish. Mama, I was sure, would love Mrs. Tokumi.

I so seldom felt any qualms at all about how Mama would like Japan that, on the pleasant October day when Mrs. Horikoshi drove me to Yokohama to meet her, I was suddenly seized by a fit of apprehension. It would be terrible if

she didn't like it. But as soon as she came down the gangway
and embraced me all my fears vanished. Perhaps it was a
good thing that it was dark when her ship docked, and she
wasn't confronted with the battered face of earthquake-
ravaged Yokohama as her first sight of Japan.

Mama loved our house. Understandably, the only aspect
of it she took a dim view of was the kitchen, that little
cement-floored hole in the wall with its cold-water faucet,
its almost complete lack of storage space, and its two gas
burners and tiny oven which I had bought. Of course, in time
these failings were remedied; we put in a wooden floor, a gas
range and a hot-water heater. But such improvements required substantial sums of money and they appeared slowly.

Mama, however, cheerfully accepted everything as she
found it and fitted into the household so smoothly that by
the end of the first month it seemed as though she had always been there. The one fly in our ointment was Masako
San, my companion. Her duties, which were anything but
onerous, were to go with me on my teaching rounds, to help
me practice my Japanese, and to supervise the maid when I
was busy with other matters. Her free time, which there was
a lot of, was hers to use for study or anything she wished. She
was an intelligent girl, with a good mind, and when she
wanted to be she was very capable. But she was also lazy,
domineering and underhanded. Mama didn't like her at all,
and, because Mama's arrival had made her considerably less
necessary to me, Masako San plainly reciprocated the feeling.

Something had to be done. I didn't want to send her away
without helping her to find some other work, for she had
some younger brothers to help support, so I compromised by
sending her to the Y.W.C.A. to learn typing. If she could
complete the course, she would easily be able to find work as
a typist. Masako San was highly pleased with my plan, and
for several months she played to the hilt her role of young
lady of the house. She went out every morning to her classes
and returned so late for her lunch that she had to have special

attention from the maid—and woe to that poor child if Masako San's lunch was cold. Finally she completed her typing course and left us, leaving Mama in undisputed charge of the household.

Mama managed nicely even though she never learned to speak Japanese. Neither did she resort to the pidgin English so many people seem to think necessary in speaking to Orientals. I have heard otherwise intelligent Westerners address Japanese and Chinese university graduates as though they were totally illiterate. Mama had no such complex. To the maid, the butcher boy or the iceman, she spoke correct, complete sentences, and by some occult power they grasped her meaning. In fact, if the maid stayed long enough or the butcher boy came to our door often enough, they usually picked up Mama's expressions and began to use them themselves.

We found ourselves living among an interesting cross-section of Japanese society. Directly opposite our house, which was about halfway up the hill from the tram-car stop, was a little shrine. At the top of the hill was the estate of a marquis. Near us were a tiny Buddhist temple and a little ink factory. The homes around us were occupied by a doctor, a Government official, a charcoal dealer, an army officer, a carpenter and a dignified loafer who was always in search of a "position" and whose house finally was taken over by his unpaid landlord.

By Japanese law, landlords aren't allowed to eject delinquent tenants, so they resort to the tactic of forcing them out. First they take the doors off the house, then the shutters, then they turn off the lights and the water, and, in the end, they invariably succeed in emptying the house.

We lived among these people for nearly twelve years. Mama loved to sit in the sun on our upstairs veranda, watching the neighbors walking along the street or visiting the shrine opposite our house. She was righteously indignant the first time she saw a young family going out on a day's outing, the husband strolling ahead, smoking and enjoying the sights, very much the lord of all he surveyed, while his wife followed a few steps behind, the baby on her back and a heavy wicker basket in her hand. I had a hard time convincing Mama that the man wasn't a cruel, inhuman tryant and that he was merely fulfilling his role as the head of the family, probably more out of respect for long-established custom than from any sadistic desire to lord it over his wife. Undoubtedly he loved her just as much as any American husband loved his more assertive helpmate.

Slowly but surely we came to understand the customs and habits of the Japanese and to realize that, while at first glance they may seem startlingly different from us, actually the differences exist only on the surface. East is East and West is West, but they are very much the same where it counts.

Chapter IX

As time went on, I decided that I would like very much to adopt a Japanese girl. I began to look around for a young girl who might want to come and live with us. After a while, through a friend, I found Haruko.

Haruko was the middle child in a family of eleven children, and she wasn't, I gathered, very happy at home, where she felt crushed between the upper and lower layers of brothers and sisters. She was fourteen years old and was still going to school, which she didn't like much. She would have preferred to be allowed to study art, to which she felt strongly attracted. Her interest in it was no flight of fancy, either; everything she put her hand to reflected her imagination and her sense of beauty. When she came to live with us, I had her take lessons in flower arrangement, the exotic Japanese art of arranging flowers so skillfully as to suggest whole landscapes. At the same time she took lessons in Japanese painting, not because I expected that she would become a great artist but simply to strengthen her artistic background for what we both had in mind for her future, dress designing.

Haruko's family was living in Toyko when I first heard of her, but originally they came from the country, Kanagawa Prefecture. Her grandfather had been the mayor of the town and president of the bank and was, from all accounts, a highly respected citizen. His son, however, inherited little of his ability and none of his ambition. His principal talent seemed to be a capacity for dissipating his father's fortune and any other money he was able to get his hands on. It wasn't long after the old gentleman's death that the bank failed and the family moved to Tokyo. Haruko had finished elementary school two years before and was in her second year of middle school. Her mother had died and her father had married again, and her stepmother did little to improve the girl's unhappy condition. Neither did her eldest sister, a rawboned, masculine type of woman, who treated her with a mixture of contempt and studied cruelty. When she had been with us for a while, Haruko told me that she had been unable to go to her elementary school graduation ceremony because she had no suitable dress to wear for the occasion. Her sister, who had an excellent position, was financially independent and had a closet filled with handsome dresses and a chest packed with costly dress goods. But she refused either to lend Haruko a dress or to give her an inch of material with which to make one for herself. Such cold-blooded selfishness is almost unheard of in a Japanese family, where every kind of sacrifice usually is made to put children through school properly.

Mama taught Haruko housekeeping and English, and in turn Haruko helped me with my Japanese. All she needed was a little encouragement and she responded with a flood of loyalty and love. She was just what we needed to bring youth and beauty into our home. Her love of life, her spontaneous enjoyment of beautiful things, her capable hands, her almost uncanny judgment of people, her loyalty and her honesty carried her straight into our hearts. Haruko wasn't all sweetness and light, however. If she happened not to like someone, her untamed frankness could be embarrassing. She reacted to snobbery or pretense with a blunt directness that could not be mistaken. As she grew older she developed more tact but she never lost her intense dislike for any sort of sham.

We made a habit of giving regular Sunday-afternoon teas, and we had all sorts of interesting callers. There was, for example, Father Joseph Eylenbosch of the new Sophia University, who came frequently to see us and often brought one or more of his colleagues with him. One memorable figure to whom Father Eylenbosch introduced us was Father Farmer, a sixty-year-old priest who had been a Presbyterian missionary in China for many years. After his wife died and his children grew up and went off on their own, he became a Catholic and was ordained as a member of the French Province of the Jesuits. He asked to go to Shanghai, where he had formerly worked as a Presbyterian minister. He discovered that there were a considerable number of Japanese Catholics there but that not one of the priests assigned to the area was able to speak the language. So he had come to Tokyo to learn it. It was an inspiration to see this determined, sixty-year-old priest applying himself to the mastery of the complex idiom of the Japanese tongue, and to hear the sermon he preached in Japanese, without notes, just six months after he had begun to study it.

It saddened me to see the power and prestige of the ultra-nationalists becoming greater daily. They were obviously out to widen the distance between the people and their beloved Emperor and thus make sure that the people's grievances would be kept away from the one man who could overrule the ambitious, power-hungry militarists who were gradually penetrating the Government and leading the country toward war.

Mama and I found ourselves, one day, on a street which had been closed to traffic. The only thing we could do was to slip into a nearby garage, where we had to wait for an hour until the Emperor passed by in his car. It was as if a sudden wind or plague had swept the streets clean of people. I wondered how the Emperor felt as he rode swiftly through streets empty except for long lines of police standing with their backs toward him.

The whole temper of the country was changing. The army was going full speed ahead, bent on conquest or ruin. The Black Dragons and other secret organizations were increasing their activities. Every now and then another liberal spokesman was assassinated. Finally, in 1932, came the so-called "Manchuria Incident" with the Japanese army occupying Manchuria and setting up a puppet government there presided over by the impotent figure of the dethroned Manchu Emperor. Things being what they were in China, Japan might have been able to extend her influence there peacefully, but the arrogant militarists couldn't wait. When they forced the establishment of the kingdom of Manchukuo, they made their first great mistake.

I was troubled by the relentless crowding of events, but I had much to fill my mind. One problem to which I gave a good deal of thought was Haruko's ambition to become a successful dress designer. She had taken a year's course at a Tokyo dressmaking school, but neither of us thought she had gained much from it. The answer came quite unexpectedly. One of my English pupils, a student at Tsuda College, was planning to go to the United States to study, and I had recommended her to Trinity. Shortly before she was due to leave, her mother asked me if I would accompany them on a shopping tour and help them select what she would need to be properly outfitted for life at an American college. Since the girl was from a well-to-do family, we went to the Mitsukoshi Department Store, where, we had heard, there was a new modiste who had just come from Paris. Miss Odette proved to be most accomplished and when our young college girl was outfitted, I asked the modiste if she ever did any teaching. She told me, through an interpreter because she spoke only French, that her contract with the store stipulated that she could not teach. Then, babbling on in friendly fashion, she apologized for her inability to communicate directly with me. "I do so want to learn English," she said. "It's very inconvenient for me here not being able to speak either Japanese or English. I find that hardly any of my customers know French." When I told her that I was an English teacher myself, she seized upon it right away. "Would you," she asked eagerly, "teach me English?"

I had an inspiration. "Do you think," I suggested, "the store might agree to a fair exchange? You could teach dress designing to Haruko in exchange for English lessons for yourself."

Miss Odette laughed approvingly as this was translated for her. "It's an excellent idea," she said. "Let's go ask the manager."

The manager saw no reason at all why it shouldn't be done, and the bargain was sealed.

Haruko was overjoyed. It was exactly the kind of opportunity she had dreamed of. She had worked hard at the dressmaking school but the results had been so discouraging that she had begun to despair of ever getting anywhere. Now she would have a real chance to find out, once and for all, whether she had enough talent to be anything more than merely a proficient seamstress. Miss Odette soon settled this by informing me that she was both pleased and surprised by the natural instinct Haruko displayed for the work.

Haruko was an endless source of satisfaction and joy to me, and to Mama, too. When she first came to live with us, I took her to Mass on Sunday. I didn't want to press our religion upon her, so I made the suggestion just that one time. After about a month, she asked me why I hadn't invited her to go with me again. "Did I do something wrong?" she asked with that implacable honesty of hers. "Goodness, no, child," I said. "I just didn't want to seem to be insisting upon it. I don't want you to go only to please me. That wouldn't make sense at all." Haruko took a deep breath of relief. "I loved it," she said seriously. "I've been waiting all this time for you to ask me again."

From then on, she went with us every Sunday, usually to the Jesuit University. When I thought she was ready for instruction in the faith, I sent her to Mother Kiyoko Iwashita at the Sacred Heart School. I asked permission of her parents to have her baptized, and they offered no objection. Soon after that, Haruko asked me if I would adopt her.

"I want to be sure I will be able to stay with you always," she said gravely. "I would like to know that I am really part of your family."

From ancient times, adoption in Japan has been based upon the necessity from a religious standpoint of perpetuating the family name and making sure there would always be someone to make offerings at the family shrine of the ancestors. It was common for childless couples to adopt a child, preferably a boy, from a relative or friend who had a number of children. Since the social status of the adopting family usually was about the same as that of the family from which the child came, the adopted boy or girl could count on obtaining more advantages as the only child in the family than he would have as one of many.

Most families didn't especially mind giving up one of their children; they generally knew the other family very well, and the adoption brought the two groups closer together. Sometimes the system was abused, as in cases where the proprietors of geisha houses legally adopted the girls who worked for them and thus were able to exercise the rights of parents over them. But, as a rule, it worked very well.

When you adopted a girl, you had to plan to adopt a son, too, when it came time for her to marry, since, under the old family law, only a legal heir could actually inherit property and make offerings at the shrine. What happened in such cases, of course, was that, while the name was preserved, the true blood of the family ceased to run through the veins of its members.

Haruko, of course, wasn't thinking about perpetuating the Caulfield family name, and neither was I. All we had in mind was our love for each other and our desire to be together and to help each other. I was very much aware of the responsibility I was assuming, and I fully understood that she might not be with me very long, for girls do fall in love and marry, and I had no intention of adopting a son. But I felt that there was much I could do for Haruko before that time came, and I began to inquire about the procedure of adopting her.

First, I had to obtain the consent of her parents, which turned out to be an easy matter. They seemed glad to be rid of her. Then there was the problem posed by my American citizenship. I knew that, even though I adopted her, Haruko, being Japanese, could not become an American citizen. What I didn't know, but soon found out, was that under Japanese law a child adopted by a foreigner automatically lost his Japanese citizenship. Since Haruko couldn't become an American citizen, she would, if I adopted her, become a woman without a country—an impossible situation.

After long and careful consideration, and many consultations with legal minds, Haruko's parents and I signed a document assigning to me full responsibility for her. They relinquished all parental rights, and those rights were assumed by me. Since I couldn't legally adopt her, it was provided that her name would remain in her family register, thus assuring her of the rights of Japanese citizenship. I realized that the retention of her name in the family register might cause difficulties in the years ahead, especially if her parents decided to become troublesome about her marriage, but I decided the risk was worth taking. The paper was duly signed and witnessed, and Haruko became, to all intents and purposes, my daughter. I was proud and happy to have such a daughter, and I loved her as if she had truly been my own flesh and blood.

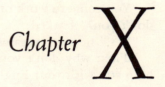

Chapter X

Along with my Japanese daughter, I also found myself "adopting" half a dozen policemen. One of the duties of the police was to maintain a careful check on the households in their district. Every month, like clockwork, a patrolman would appear at the house to ask the routine questions: "Are there any changes in your family? Have you any guests?" If there were changes, or if you had guests, it was necessary to explain the details carefully. If you had foreign visitors, you weren't even allowed to wait for the regular monthly visit; they had to be reported to the police station within twenty-four hours.

The policeman who usually took our family report was a pleasant young man and we had long conversations whenever he came to the house. I asked him once how he spent his free time, and he said, "I don't have much of it. Whenever I get a chance, I go to night school to study law. I have to pass an examination in law before I can be promoted."

"Do you have to study English?" I asked him.

"Yes, we do," he said. "It's very hard, too. The classes are so big it's not easy to keep up with the lessons. I'm afraid I don't understand it very well."

In other talks, he had explained to me that the police worked out of small subdivision stations called *kobans,* each of which consisted of a covered platform on which a patrol-man stood day and night, and a small room in which the men off duty rested. Nine policemen were assigned to each *koban,* and each man had a three-day cycle of duty, eight hours of work the first day, then a full twenty-four hours on duty, and then a day off. I had a pretty clear idea of what the schedule involved.

"You come to work on your eight-hour day at nine o'clock, don't you?" I asked.

"Yes," he said, pleased that I remembered.

"Then why don't you come here at seven? I'll be glad to help you with your English before you go to work."

"That's very kind of you, Sensai," he said, calling me by the Japanese word for teacher. "I wish I could. But I can't afford private lessons."

"Of course you can't," I said. "That's why I'm suggesting that you come so early in the morning. Seven to eight in the morning isn't one of my private lesson hours. I have nothing at all to do at that time, and if you want to come, I'll be glad to help you."

For a moment, he said nothing. Then, glad to accept my offer, he said, formally, "If it will not trouble you, Sensai, I will come once a week."

That was the beginning of my happy association with the men of the Mita Police Station. It wasn't long before my young friend introduced me to two of his fellow patrolmen who also were taking the law course with a view toward promotion, and who were eager for an opportunity to improve their English. Then their superior officers came to call, and before long our house was being referred to jokingly as the branch of the Mita Police Station. I put our extra up-stairs room at the disposal of these men, and it became a busy study for aspiring policemen. They would come into the house at odd hours of the day, whenever they happened to be off duty, carefully hanging their uniform hats and swords in the entrance, and thus, incidentally, advertising their presence to itinerant vendors and confidence men and making our manless home one of the most efficiently protected houses in the district.

One of my private English pupils, Dr. Muto, a general in the medical corps of the army, asked me to visit the military hospital and see if I could be of any help to a group of ten patients there who had been blinded during the fighting in Manchuria. I jumped at the chance. It was the first opportunity I'd had to work for the blind in Japan. That was what my original goal had been, and I still wanted to do it very much, but there simply was no need for me. The agencies and institutions concerned with the work were well organized and effective, and it had been necessary for me to turn to other ways of making myself useful. But General Muto's request captured my interest immediately.

They were a dispirited, discouraged group, these ten young men suddenly deprived of a gift they had always taken for granted. I told them, on my first visit to their ward, that I was going to teach them Braille, and that they would soon be able to read again, but they were unimpressed. I decided that a demonstration would be the surest way of convincing them, so I took out a copy of the Osaka *Mainichi*'s special Braille edition and began to read to them. At first they couldn't believe that I was reading only with my fingers, but after several of them had come up and touched my hands and the Braille newspaper, they were tremendously encouraged. If I could do it, so could they. They went to work with a will, and by the time they were discharged they were ready to study at schools for the blind.

I conducted these classes for two hours two afternoons a week, for two years. The hospital always sent a car for me, and because it was an army vehicle we sped through the city with little or no regard for ordinary traffic rules. I must confess I enjoyed it; human nature succumbs quickly to the joys of even a little power.

Shortly after I finished my work at the hospital, I was sitting in my living room one afternoon talking with an inspector from the Mita Police Station. He was wearing civilian clothes. An unexpected guest was announced, and when he came into the room he proved to be a rather pompous young man who obviously enjoyed informing us that he was an officer of the Kem Petai, the dreaded military police. Knowing that there was no love lost between this organization and the civilian police, I introduced the inspector only by name, making no mention of his official status. After we had exchanged greetings, the cocky military policeman said, abruptly, "Why did you go to that military hospital every week for two years? I want you to tell me why you went." His tone was distinctly unfriendly.

"If you want to know," I said, annoyed, "you had better go to the director of the hospital and ask him."

"I want you to tell me," he insisted.

"And I want you to hear it from the director himself," I said challengingly. "Is that all you want to know? If it is, perhaps you had better go right now and ask him."

I wondered if he would say anything more, but he simply got up and walked out of the room without a word. The inspector, who had enjoyed every minute of the little scene, congratulated me on standing up to him and said he only wished the police could do the same.

After the inspector left, I telephoned the director of the hospital. "I'm sorry to bother you," I said, "but I've just had a visit from a Kem Petai man who wanted to know what I was doing on my trips to the hospital."

"You didn't tell him, did you?" he asked right away.

"Of course I didn't," I said. "I told him that, if he wanted to know, he could ask you."

The general forgot his manners long enough to unleash an angry epithet. Then, quickly, he said, "Good for you. I'm sure he'll never even show up here, but if he does, I'll take care of him. Some of these whippersnappers just try to see what they can put over, and everybody is so afraid of them that they usually get away with it. I'm sorry you were bothered this way after all you did for our men."

"It's all right," I said. "I didn't mind. I just wanted you to know about it." I didn't add that I wanted him to make sure it didn't happen again, but that was hardly necessary.

The visit of the man from Kem Petai did, however, suggest to me the difficulty of my position as an American living and working in Japan. The military men were tightening their grip on the country, and restrictions were increasing. Every book and magazine that came into Japan was examined for Communist or Socialist propaganda, or, for that matter, any liberal ideas which might encourage "dangerous thought," the common description of any idea that did not conform to "The Imperial Way." Free discussion was discouraged and it took a brave editor to exercise fully the traditional Japanese freedom of the press.

As the policy of the military party stiffened, anti-Japanese sentiment increased in the United States. It probably would have been bad enough if it had been left to the Americans alone, but it had for years been encouraged and strengthened by skillful and persistent Chinese propagandists. In speeches and writings, in their business and social contacts, even at receptions and cocktail parties, Chinese officials and students missed no opportunity to buttonhole an American and run down the Japanese. The steady barrage gained in effectiveness, of course, as the Japanese militarists gave Americans more and more cause for disapproval. With Germany and Great Britain also interested, for different reasons, in setting Japan and the United States at each other's throats, the whole force of international propaganda and prejudice was turned on, playing right into the hands of the Japanese militarists, who needed no encouragement to hasten their own preparations for the make-or-break adventure they had in mind.

What could any one individual, let alone a blind woman with no weapons except her mind and her heart, do in such an atmosphere? I was allowed to continue my teaching unmolested, but it was becoming more and more difficult to speak freely. I kept hearing that Japanese citizens who were known to be friendly with foreigners, especially Americans, were being questioned sharply about their relationships. I didn't want to cause my friends embarrassment, or, worse, expose them to danger.

I had another serious problem, too. Haruko's family, and particularly her father, had been steadily more disagreeable ever since her adoption. Having secured me as a kind of relation, her father had put me on his borrowing list. And that was only the beginning. His idea seemed to be to exploit Haruko's relationship with me to extract everything possible from me. Haruko absolutely refused to enter into any of his schemes, and as time went on his attempts to win her cooperation, and his reprisals against her, became so serious that I finally was forced to appeal to the police for protection. I got it, but nothing the police could do was sufficient to prevent this unscrupulous man from making Haruko's life, and therefore mine, miserable. Things had got to the point where her family had succeeded in utterly destroying the happy home we had built in Tokyo. It was clear to me that the best thing for us to do was to leave the country.

I didn't want to stay in Japan unless I could be useful. But neither did I want to go back to the United States, after having worked so hard and so long to reach my goal of living in the Orient. Suddenly, out of the blue, a solution presented itself from a most unexpected source.

Father Eylenbosch came to the house one Sunday afternoon with a young man from Siam. The visitor carried letters of introduction from a number of Catholics in Bangkok, and he was living at the Sophia University dormitory. He was a pleasant, persuasive talker, and I enjoyed listening to him tell stories about his country. He arranged for us to meet some other Siamese who were studying in Tokyo schools, and, ultimately, through him I got to know the Siamese Minister,

Pra Mitrakam Laxar, and his family. The more I found out about Siam, the more interested I became in the country, which was just beginning to take its place among the active nations of the world. For generations it had lived a quiet existence under the benevolent rule of its kings, sending promising members of the royal family and able young officials abroad to study and to maintain friendly relations with both Europe and America as well as the other Asian countries. But three years before, in 1932, a bloodless revolution, spearheaded by a small group of young army officers and civilians who had been educated in France and Germany, had succeeded in setting up a constitutional monarchy. The liberal King Prajadhipok had given his consent to the change, and the country, I was given to understand, was making good progress in the direction of a truly parliamentary government.

Several times I inquired of my new-found Siamese friends what their country was doing for the education of the blind. I always got the same answer: "The blind? There are no blind in Siam."

To say the least, I found such a statement profoundly interesting, for a country in which there were no blind people would certainly be unusual. After persistent questioning I won the admission that there were some very aged blind people in Siam, but positively no blind children. Actually, no one was trying to misrepresent the situation to me. It was just that the people to whom I was speaking never had seen any blind children at home, and honestly believed there were none. I finally obtained a truer picture from a young Siamese psychiatrist, Dr. Fonthong Saengsingkaeo, who had come to Japan to study the treatment of the mentally ill. He told me that there were, of course, a good many blind children and young adults in his country, and that so far as he knew nothing much was being done to improve their lot.

The picture Dr. Fonthong painted for me captured my imagination. This could be exactly the opportunity I had been praying for to keep on working in the Orient, even though I could no longer stay in Japan. I realized that it would be a difficult undertaking to start a school from scratch and put into practice the lessons I had learned at Perkins and Overbrook, but it appealed to me as a challenge worth accepting. I promised myself that, if it were at all possible, I would do it.

Early in 1936, one of the Siamese Ministers of State, Nai Pridi, or, as he was known then, Luang Pradit Manutram, visited Tokyo. He was the Minister of the Interior, and, as one of the principal instigators of the revolution, was a power in Siamese political affairs. I met him at the Siamese Legation in Tokyo, and he seemed very much interested in my desire to open a school for the blind in Bangkok. "The people of Siam," he said, "are very much in need of this kind of social project. A school for the blind will be a good beginning." He suggested that I visit the country in the summer, see how I liked it, and try to determine at first hand how my plan might be received by the Government. "I will do what I can to help you when you come," he said generously.

With such powerful encouragement, I made plans to spend a month in Bangkok during the summer of 1936. It would be my first venture outside of Japan since I had arrived thirteen years before, and I was filled with anticipation. I decided to take Haruko with me and leave Mama to stay with friends in Tokyo. Haruko and I had been invited by Dr. Fonthong to live in his cottage at the Bangkok Mental Hospital during our month in Siam. "You will become much more familiar with the country living in a private home than you ever could in a hotel," he said, and I was sure he was right.

Haruko and I set sail for Siam, on a hot July day, aboard the Mitsui Line freighter *Natchi San Maru*. The ship, which had comfortable accommodations for passengers, made the run to Bangkok in just ten days. On the tenth day we moved cautiously toward the mouth of the Chao Phraya River, slipped over the bar at high tide and stopped at the quarantine station for the night before sailing up the river to the capital city.

These days, far more people travel to Bangkok by air than by ship, and when they come down over the city they are treated to an impressive view of the rich rice fields, stretched out like a finely woven carpet, proclaiming the prosperity of the country. But it seems a pity that they have to miss the pleasure of steaming up the mighty Chao Phraya River, which, with its strangely brown water, its sweeping fruit orchards and its busy people and splashing, screaming children, is one of the greatest charms of Bangkok. Haruko and I were up at four-thirty to hang over the rails and soak up the flavor of the spectacular city. The air was permeated with a heavy, exotic fragrance. It was the scent of *turien,* a great spiked mass of fruit for which many Siamese will trade even their precious rice. I never have learned to like the smell, nor the fruit it so pungently proclaims, but at a safe distance it fills the air with something strange and unforgettable, a touch peculiarly tropical. As we smelled its piercing sweetness for the first time, Haruko excitedly described to me the naked, shouting children, wading and swimming in the river, or paddling tiny boats, and their mothers and fathers in rowboats or launches piled high with a bewildering variety of tropical fruits which they were carrying to market. It was a fascinating introduction to Siam, plunging us right into the very heart of the life of the people.

We docked about an hour ahead of schedule, and Dr. Fonthong, who had promised to meet us, wasn't at the pier yet. But he arrived before all the formalities were completed. It was a good thing he did, for the immigration official was seriously shocked when we gave him, as our address, the Bangkok Hospital for Mental Diseases. At first he thought we were joking, and then, when he discovered that we meant it, he was even more taken aback. But Dr. Fonthong rescued us and vouched for both our character and our sanity.

The pier at which we had docked was in the congested

downtown section of Bangkok. Automobiles were few but pedicabs, little, jinriksha-like vehicles pulled by men on bicycles, were numerous, as were bicycles, bullock carts, and especially people. The people were everywhere, crowding the streets, hurrying about their business despite the oppressive heat which, even that early in the morning, drenched us with perspiration. As we drove along, Haruko said, in surprise, "The people are all Chinese!" She was right. We were passing through the Chinese section of the city and the streets were lined with all sorts of shops selling every imaginable article, from exquisite textiles made in France and Switzerland, and expensive imported cosmetics, to coconut graters and fish hooks.

The mental hospital was a group of unpretentious but well-kept buildings set in a spacious garden and reached by crossing a little bridge upon which a guard was posted day and night. The guard was the only outward indication that there was anything unusual about the character of the institution; otherwise it seemed like any other hospital.

Dr. Fonthong, who was one of the assistant directors of the institution then, lived in a small bungalow in the hospital enclosure. When we arrived at the house we were greeted warmly by his wife, Kun Pravat, a shy but friendly young woman who spoke good English and who had gone to a great deal of trouble to make ready a comfortable room for Haruko and me.

Among her other accomplishments, Kun Pravat was a skilled cook. The art of cooking is dear to the heart of every Siamese woman, and from the delicious pineapple she served us the moment we set foot in her house to the last sumptuous dinner she gave us before we left, Kun Pravat laid before us the whole tempting range of Thai cookery, which I think is the Orient's finest. The people of Siam always have been known as Thai, which means free, and in 1939 the name of the country was changed from Siam to Thailand. In 1945 it was changed back to Siam, but in 1949 it became Thailand again, and for a long time now the world has known the people as the Thai rather than the Siamese.

Whatever you call them, the Thai love to cook and they love to eat. The fruit they serve so generously is always carefully peeled and the seeds removed before it is offered to you. In the families of the aristocracy this is never done by servants but always by the mistress of the house or her daughters. Preparing a Thai dinner is an all-day operation. They don't make their famous curries by mixing a little powder into a sauce or gravy; it's done by chopping and grinding innumerable spices, leaves and other ingredients. When special guests are expected, it's a day-long task for the whole household.

On the evening of our first full day in Bangkok, Dr. Fonthong took me to see Luang Pradit, who had become the Minister of Finance. Remembering the encouragement he had given me in Japan, I was impatient to see him and to lay before him my plans for establishing a school for blind children. The Minister, whose gravely ill father was being cared for by Dr. Fonthong, received us warmly, spreading his famous charm generously over us. He gave me the names of several Cabinet members and other high officials of the Government and suggested that I visit them in order to find out what they thought of my project and what my chances were of obtaining Government help.

I was a little disappointed because I had hoped that he would speak to these people himself, or at least personally introduce me to them. But he assured me that he had mentioned the matter to most of them already and that he was sure they would approve. I felt that it was only natural that he should be preoccupied with the condition of his father, who died a few days after our interview, and I wasn't surprised that I didn't see him again until it was almost time for me to return to Japan.

Dr. Fonthong managed to find time to take me to see all the people Luang Pradit had told me to meet. But, wherever we went, we received little or no encouragement. They all listened politely, but they showed no interest at all. "Blind people can never be taught to do anything," some of the more frank ones said. Others told me that the people would never support such a project. One man, the head of the Department of Elementary Education, said that the idea of educating the blind was the same as trying to teach lessons to wooden tables and chairs. Over and over again I got the feeling that they all thought I was talking about the erection and maintenance of a large building and a substantial staff, which would require a huge sum of money. I couldn't seem to drive home to them the point that a school for the blind could be started in a very modest and inexpensive way and still accomplish its purpose. They listened to me but they didn't understand.

It was terribly discouraging, but I could see their point of view. These earnest men were trying to reorganize their country under a constitution that was only four years old. They already had all the trouble they could handle with people who did not approve of their methods, and they saw no point in going out of their way to inflame the opposition further. It was easy to see, too, that there wasn't full agreement between Luang Pradit and his colleagues, and anything he favored might attract a great deal of opposition simply because he favored it. But my mind was made up. I was going to start that school no matter how little help was offered.

Chapter XI

We had booked passage to Kobe on the Mitsui Line but the ship on which we sailed wasn't one of the line's own; it was a ten-thousand-ton freighter they had chartered complete with captain and crew. If it had been their own I'm sure they would have fired all hands and put the ship in drydock for a thorough overhauling. The accommodations for the twelve passengers were among the worst I have ever encountered at sea, and the food was so bad that Haruko invaded the galley almost every day and personally prepared an extra dish for the passengers. As if things weren't bad enough, we ran into a typhoon in the China Sea, and for a few days not even Haruko's cooking had any appeal. All in all, it was not a voyage to remember with pleasure.

Our reception at Kobe wasn't much better. "Where have you been?" the immigration officer demanded abruptly as I took my place before him.

"To Bangkok," I said cheerfully.

"How long have you lived in Japan?"

"Thirteen years."

"What do you do in Japan?"

"I teach in the Fifth Middle School in Tokyo." I didn't see any necessity for telling this rude fellow anything more than that.

"Why does a teacher of the Fifth Middle School of Tokyo want to go to Bangkok?"

I was becoming angry. "I went," I said coldly, "to find out what is being done there for the education of the blind."

"What made you go there particularly?"

"I was invited by the Minister of the Interior, Luang Pradit."

My interrogator turned to a fellow officer and said, in Japanese, "He's a Communist."

That was too much for me. I dipped into my own Japanese and protested vigorously. "He is not," I said indignantly. "He's the Minister of the Interior of the Siamese Government."

"We know him," the officer snapped, slamming down my passport and turning to the next victim.

As much as I disliked facing the prospect, I knew I couldn't stay for long in the country I had adopted. Reluctantly, I made preparations to leave. It seemed best to go back to the United States, where Mama could live with Henry and Beatrice, whom she hadn't seen for nearly twelve years, and I could devote myself to studying the newest techniques of teaching the blind and to earning some money by giving a series of lectures on Japan. I had written a number of letters to friends at home and had been greatly encouraged by their answers. It looked as though the rising anti-Japanese sentiment in the United States not only would not work against a lecture tour such as I had in mind but actually would insure its success because everyone was much more aware of Japan and more curious about it than ever before.

Breaking up our home in Tokyo was painful but not very difficult. We distributed our furniture and such treasures as we could not take with us among our friends. We booked passage for the three of us, Mama, Haruko and me, on one of the Toyo Kisen Kaisha silk cargo ships going through the Panama Canal straight to New York. The voyage would take a month but we were all looking forward to it. The only cloud on our horizon was placed there unexpectedly by Haruko's family, which suddenly decided it was time for her to marry and insisted that she obey their wishes. She refused point-blank. Haruko had a mind of her own and she wasn't easily cowed. She told them she had no intention whatsoever of leaving me, that she was going to the United States with me, and that if they didn't like it it was too bad. They tried to prevent her from obtaining a passport on the ground that, although I had assumed responsibility for her, I hadn't officially adopted her and her name remained in their family register. But, fortunately, Haruko was over twenty-one, and Japanese law was surprisingly respectful of the rights of unmarried women grown to maturity. Unlike their married sisters, they were allowed to own property and to obtain passports under the same conditions as men. Haruko needed nobody's permission but her own.

On the day of our departure, a cold, rainy day in the middle of February, we said good-by to all of our neighbors and to the shopkeepers on our street and drove off to Yokohama. All our dearest friends were at the pier to see us off, which they couldn't actually do because the rain delayed our sailing until the next morning. But they did say good-by to us and they joined us in the prayerful hope that we would come back to Japan and be with them again. Also on hand was a group of my pupils from the Mita Police Station. When we reached the cabin that had been assigned to us, we found a beautiful Japanese doll in a glass case, a farewell present from them.

There were only eight passengers on the ship, so we formed an intimate circle. Mama and Haruko did a lot of sewing, I worked on my lectures, and, for a few hours each day, I enjoyed having someone read to me from the celebrated novel by Margaret Mitchell, *Gone With the Wind*. It was, of course, a massive book, more than a thousand pages, and before long not only Mama and Haruko, but the other passengers, too, were taking turns reading it to me. The book lasted all the way to New York, and I had the interesting experience of listening to the rich Southern accents of Scarlett O'Hara, Rhett Butler and Ashley Wilkes interpreted by a succession of different readers, including one Japanese.

I spent some time every day, too, on my inevitable English lessons with the captain. Every morning, right after breakfast, he would appear with his lesson books and we would settle down in the lounge or on deck for our day's stint. We read, talked and worked on composition, and while he improved his English I added my highly specialized store of knowledge about the character and interests of Japanese sea captains. My relationship with the captain stood us in good stead when the ship entered the Panama Canal, and we were invited to stay on the bridge all the time we were passing through the locks.

It didn't take the ship long to sail up the eastern coast to New York, and before we were fully prepared for it we were there, hugging Henry and Beatrice on the pier and driving with them to their home in West Orange, New Jersey, where we were welcomed by their three daughters, Mary, Joan and Betty. The girls seemed genuinely interested in the stories Haruko and I had to tell them, and our visit was a pleasant interlude. Mary, who was seventeen, was deeply involved in preparations for college; Joan, a vivacious, fifteen-year-old beauty, already was busy dreaming of and planning the acting career that she since has achieved with such notable success; and I found the baby of the family, Betty, who was only twelve and had been born after I had left New York for Tokyo, a delight to know.

I found sorrow at home, too. Uncle Leonard had died a few years before, and now Aunt Ducky was seriously ill. As soon as we could arrange it, Haruko and I hurried to Goshen to see her. She was still living in the same big house in which we had all spent so many happy days together, but she was slipping fast. To the very end, she encouraged me strongly. "Never forget, Genevieve," she said, "in God's plan, each one of us begins where the other leaves off. I may have to go, but you mustn't waste time regretting that. Go on and build whatever you can. Begin something useful that somebody else can finish after you are gone."

Aunt Ducky left us just after Christmas that year, but even now her spirit gives me courage whenever I feel the need of it.

I had far more success than I had anticipated in setting up my lecture tour. The Maryknoll Sisters—one-half of the two distinct but closely related congregations of the famous Maryknoll foreign mission organization—helped me tremendously. Mother Mary Joseph, whom I had known since the days before she entered the order, when she was doing everything she could to assist Father James Walsh and Father Frederick Price, the founders of the Maryknoll Fathers, had invited Haruko and me to regard the Mother House of the Maryknoll Sisters as our headquarters while we were in the United States. She even assigned Sister Victoria Francis, a remarkable woman who, after a successful career as a social worker and parole supervisor in New York City, had become a Maryknoll novice at the age of fifty, to help me arrange my tour. Even before I arrived at the Maryknoll house in Ossining, New York, Sister Victoria Francis had prepared a long list of colleges, clubs and other organizations which might be especially interested in my lecture subjects, and after we had added others that I regarded as good prospects, we sent out announcements.

When I telephoned Jane Hoey, one of my Trinity classmates, I got the impression that she had been waiting at the telephone for my call. Jane had organized the Bureau of Public Assistance of the Social Security Board in 1936, and she had work of national importance on her hands, but when she talked to me she gave me the feeling that my plans were her only concern in life. For years, Jane has been like a sister to me. Whenever I come back to the United States she makes it a real homecoming. Her home is mine, and she always seems to know exactly what I am trying to do and how to make it possible for me to get it done.

We crowded an astonishing amount of activity into those relatively few months in the States. Haruko went to Overbrook by herself to study handicraft work and to find out everything she could about the special problems of the blind, so that she would be better equipped to teach in our school. I was determined not to do or say anything to push her into joining me in my Bangkok project. I made it very clear to her that I had adopted her because I loved her and wanted to give her every possible opportunity to be happy. I was, of course, glad to have her companionship and her loving help, but I hadn't adopted her for the purpose of providing a permanent companion for myself or a crutch upon which I might lean in my declining years. One of the reasons why I encouraged her to go to Overbrook was that studying there would give her the experience she needed to make the right decision about her future. If, after working with the blind for a while, she felt that she would be happier building a career as a dress designer, which she certainly was qualified to do after her tutoring by Miss Odette, she was free to make the choice.

When I joined her at the end of her Overbrook stay, I was finally convinced that Haruko had a genuine vocation for working with the blind. She had a gift for it; without any special training in psychology, she knew by instinct just how to bring out in her pupils their talents and their qualities of self-reliance and self-respect. When she insisted that she wanted more than anything else in the world to go to Thailand with me and help me start the new school, I had no hesitation in accepting her offer.

We added to our qualifications by studying for a while at the famous Lighthouse Institute for the Blind in New York, where Haruko learned art weaving and I observed intently the music, recreation, vision testing and other programs aimed at the rehabilitation and welfare of the blind.

Haruko loved New York City, and, surprisingly, felt very much at home among its teeming crowds and its frighteningly heavy traffic. She even had the courage to learn to drive a second-hand car which I bought so that we could more easily make trips to Ossining, West Orange, Goshen and the other places we visited so frequently. Our car was a 1928 Reo, which, in spite of its nine years of use, was still in excellent condition. It was so big, though, that tiny Haruko could hardly see out over the hood. I remember one day a friendly policeman went so far as to open the door and peer inside, saying, in an Irish brogue, "Indeed, and I wondered if there was anybody driving this car!"

It was Haruko's contention that New York's reputation for noise and bustle was greatly exaggerated. She thought the city was much quieter than Tokyo. I think I know what she meant. The noise in New York is a continuous roar, steady and constant, and therefore less noticeable than Tokyo's staccato clatter, punctuated by the pounding of wooden clogs on the sidewalks, the incessant tooting of automobile horns, and, on many streets, the raucous shouts of itinerant vendors crying their wares.

From time to time, that summer, we traveled to Washington, D.C., to see Jane Hoey. Haruko loved it when we stayed over in Jane's attractive apartment. She was able to display her culinary gifts to the fullest in the marvelously equipped kitchen. Whether Jane was there or not, the apartment was at our disposal, and we came and went as though it were our own.

On one of our Washington trips we heard the ominous news of the clash between the Japanese and Chinese at the Marco Polo Bridge near Peiping. The incident at the bridge occurred on July 7, 1937, and after that the fighting quickly spread over much of China. As was to be expected, the "China Incident," as the Japanese always euphemistically referred to it, aroused hot resentment in the United States. I was afraid for a while that people wouldn't want to hear anything objective about Japan. But on the contrary, as I began to fill my first speaking dates in cities like Chicago, Cincinnati and

Buffalo, I found that my audiences were glad to listen to what I had to tell them. They welcomed the opportunity to obtain the point of view of an American who had lived among the Japanese for a long time.

The main point I tried to make was that, while the reckless Japanese militarists might be out of hand, the situation was by no means hopeless if we could approach it with understanding rather than a ready-made, inflexible prejudice. I knew that my audiences were small and weren't likely to be able to exercise any great influence on American public opinion, but I did my best to show that the Japanese people weren't cruel, dishonest monsters seeking to devour whatever they could get their hands on, that they did have very bad leadership, but that, to some extent at least, they had been forced by external pressures to follow that leadership. I pointed out that our country was being bombarded with propaganda aimed at pushing us into war with Japan, a war which the unscrupulous Japanese leaders were only too willing to thrust upon their people.

The greater part of each talk I made was confined, however, to a description of the manners, customs and outlook on life of the Japanese, with only occasional references to the tense international situation.

Haruko was a decided asset to me, and, for that matter, to her country, on the tour. The friendly way she met and mingled with the people who came to hear me, and the attractive way in which she obliged the women in the audience by showing them exactly how a kimono is put on and taken off, won friends for us everywhere—even in Boston, where I found myself booked to speak on the very night America heard the news of the sinking of the U.S. gunboat *Panay* in the Yangtze River by Japanese airplanes. I was so provoked by the outrage that I found it hard to speak objectively, but my listeners were surprisingly restrained and showed an earnest desire to understand what lay behind Japan's hostility. Haruko's mysterious kimono even attracted the attention of the President's wife when, on one of our Washington trips, Jane Hoey introduced us to Mrs. Roosevelt at the White House. "Of course, I've seen these often," Mrs. Roosevelt said as she examined Haruko's dress. "But I've never had a chance to find out how they're put on. Would you be kind enough to show me?" This Haruko did with the greatest pleasure, and I'm sure it was the proudest and happiest moment of her entire visit to the United States, except, perhaps, the day she graduated from a Girl Scout leadership course in the summer of 1938. The trainees were congratulated by the ubiquitous Mrs. Roosevelt, and as the First Lady moved down the line of young women, shaking hands and saying a few words to each one, she recognized Haruko and placed her instantly. "Why," she said warmly, "you're the girl I met at the White House last year. When are you leaving for Bangkok?" Haruko was so overcome that she barely was able to respond that we were planning to go in September.

It was, indeed, time for us to be about our work. We didn't have anywhere near as much money as I would have liked, but there would be about eight hundred dollars left over from our expenses when we got to Bangkok, and that would have to do. I had written to Luang Pradit, telling him that, even though the Government wasn't interested in my school idea, I still wanted to come to Bangkok and would do so if he thought my work could be useful. He answered in his own handwriting that I certainly should come ahead, that, in spite of the Government's inability to assist me, he personally would do everything in his power to help me found the school. I think I would have gone even without Luang Pradit's encouragement, but it made me feel better to know that a responsible Cabinet minister was behind me.

Our last arrangements were made without difficulty. Since Bangkok was just about halfway around the world from New York, it made little difference whether we went by way of Europe or Japan. We had already been to Japan, Haruko and I decided, and it would be foolish to pass up the opportunity to see something of Europe. So we plotted a route that would take us to London on the *Britannic,* to Paris by air, to Rome on the Rome Express, and then by train to Naples, where we would board the Japanese liner *Terakuni Maru* for the voyage to Singapore. We planned to take passage on a coastal steamer from Singapore to Bangkok.

The hardest thing for me to do was to leave Mama. She was going to stay with Henry, Beatrice and the girls, but it was clear that she wanted to go back to the Orient. It was out of the question, however, for her to come with us. The tropical climate of Bangkok would not be good for her, at her age, and our project was surrounded by so many uncertainties that I didn't dare even consider taking her along. Mama knew all this, of course, and didn't expect that she would be able to join us for quite a while, if then, but that didn't make it any easier for us to part. I was grateful, at least, for the comforting knowledge that she would be with others of her own family who loved her every bit as much as I did and would be better able to take care of her. Henry's growing children, too, would be a tonic for her.

My favorite niece, Joan, confided to me several times before I left that her ambition to become an actress was a serious one, and that she wanted very much to study drama. I told her that I thought she had the personality, and clearly everyone agreed that she had the looks, but I couldn't help wondering what sort of impression her high, flat voice would make on prospective casting directors, not to mention audiences. "If you want to be an actress," I told her, "you'd better do something about that voice." I took her to an old friend of mine, Edith Beck, a voice teacher with a reputation for a sound teaching method, and by the time I was ready to leave for Thailand Joan was hard at work, taking her first step along the road to fame. Anyone who has ever heard Joan Caulfield's clear, resonant voice in motion pictures or on television can testify to the success of Edith Beck's instruction.

Just about the only cloud on our horizon, as the day of our

departure drew near, was the fact that the international scene looked gloomier than ever. Hitler, the demonic Chancellor of Germany, was looking with greedy eyes toward Czechoslovakia, and that beleaguered little country was appealing to the rest of Europe for help. Combined with the warlike attitude of Japan in the Far East, it added up to a disturbing world-wide tension. In the face of such a prospect of cataclysm, it was harder than ever to say good-by to the United States. Life here was so secure, so pleasant; everything was so convenient, and I had so many friends. But I had worked hard to make something useful of my life, and if I were to give up and stay home now, all my work would have lost its purpose.

The *Britannic* sailed at midnight on Saturday, September 3, 1938. Mama, Henry, Beatrice and the girls, along with Jane Hoey and some of our other New York friends, were at the pier to see us off. We had left Maryknoll that afternoon, sped on our way by the same gentle ceremony that attends the departure of Maryknoll's own Sisters when they leave for a foreign mission. Mother Mary Joseph even had pressed into Haruko's hand the little mission crucifix that is always given to a Sister going to a strange land. As our ship moved slowly down the broad Hudson River, through the harbor and out into the open Atlantic, our hearts were filled with a strange mixture of sadness and hope.

On another ship, a Mitsui Line freighter, our equipment for the adventure in Bangkok was stowed away in the hold, packed in a strong wooden box. They were Braille slates, Braille writing paper, elementary school books and two complete sets of embossed maps, all presented to us by the director of the Perkins School. The New York manager of the Mitsui Company had offered to ship this treasure, without which it would have been impossible to start a school for the blind, to Bangkok for us without charging a cent for it. It reached there, safe and sound, only a few days after we did.

My overnight bag, which I carried with me every minute, contained my other great treasure, the Thai alphabet which

I had transcribed into Braille in Tokyo and which had been embossed on metal plates for me at Perkins.

The *Britannic,* one of the largest of the Cunard Line ships, was the first great ocean liner I had ever been on. It was inevitable that some of the passengers should prove to be Orientals. The first day we were on board, as we were stepping into an elevator to descend to our Tourist Class cabin, Haruko said to me, "There's a lady who looks as though she might be from Thailand."

"No," a pleasant voice came back in perfect English. "I'm from Burma. My husband and I have been in the United States for two years and we're going back home."

Later on we met some Indians, and in a few days we discovered a Thai. I was sitting on deck, listening to the other passengers playing deck tennis and bridge, when a young man sat down next to me. "Pardon me," he said courteously, "but I was wondering, ma'am, are you going to Bangkok?"

"Yes," I said, "are you?"

"Oh, yes," he said, "but not right away. I'm a Thai. I graduated from West Point and I've just finished a year with the Army Air Force. But they wouldn't teach me bombing in the United States, so now I'm going to England to study with the Royal Air Force." There was understandable pride in his voice. He was a wide-awake, energetic young man with a real zest for living. His name was Manob Suriya, and he was a lieutenant then; the last I saw of him he was a general, the Chief of Intelligence of the Royal Air Force of Thailand, familiarly known to his American friends in Bangkok as Nobby. I found him a delightful companion.

I noticed, though, that there wasn't any love lost between Lieutenant Manob and the Burmese couple, with whom I also talked often. I hadn't read enough of the history of the region to be aware of the considerable antipathy between the Thai and the Burmese, a result of their frequent armed clashes over the years.

While I talked to the two Burmese, Haruko saw to it that

Lieutenant Manob enjoyed the crossing. She had learned to dance American-style, and so had he, and they were among the most enthusiastic patrons of the ship's dance band all the way to England. I would be less than honest if I didn't confess to having suffered a gnawing sense of uneasiness about the effect this romantic idyll might have on my adopted daughter. I was afraid that she might be swept off her feet. But, although she enjoyed every minute of the voyage on the *Britannic,* she was still the same level-headed Haruko when we reached London.

I gave several lectures in London, principally on Japanese customs and history. The British, unlike the people who had come to my talks in the United States, didn't want to hear about political or military matters at all. While Americans invariably expressed curiosity about what the Japanese thought of them, the British had no such interest because they already knew what the Japanese thought of them. They knew, and they didn't care. The Anglo-Japanese alliance had been broken, the British Government was grimly aware of what Japan was up to, and the average Englishman had other things to think about. Japanese culture—painting, literature and all the rest—always had been more interesting to the British than to Americans, but the people of Japan, who had refused staunchly to accept the theory of the White Man's Burden, were looked upon as impossible nonconformists and were treated accordingly.

Haruko and I met a number of Japanese in London, including the captain of the *Terakuni Maru,* the ship we were scheduled to board at Naples. As usual, I made friends with the captain, and he was kind enough, when he heard about our plans, to invite us to let his company take charge immediately of all the baggage we weren't going to need until we got on the ship. I was most grateful, for baggage always has been a headache to me. Packing it, carrying it, counting it, watching it, checking it, waiting for it, losing it, and, if you are lucky enough to get it to your destination safely, unpacking it. It all seems such a nuisance. I'm convinced that at least part of my expiation in Purgatory will be packing and unpacking suitcases and trunks. That kindhearted captain deserved a better fate for his act of charity than to be killed by a mine explosion at the very beginning of the European part of World War II.

We were in London at the time of the Munich crisis. I listened to the news broadcasts from Germany as well as the English broadcasts, and I wished that I had kept up the German which I had studied so hard at Trinity, so many years before. I understood just enough of it to wish I were able to grasp the rest. Fortunately, our landlady was married to a German and spoke the language fluently. She frequently came into our room when the broadcasts were on and translated for us.

It was hard for me to concentrate on the work ahead as the people of London dug trenches and sent up barrage balloons to guard against air attacks. It had a dampening effect upon the most indestructible enthusiasm to be issued a gas mask, told to guard it carefully, and instructed to carry it wherever you went.

From London we flew to Paris, where we stayed with Odette Maniglier, the same Miss Odette who had been so important to Haruko in Tokyo. We enjoyed every minute of our short visit. The French cooking, so venturesome and so piquant, made the English food seem like mere subsistence in comparison. Instead of rain we had sunshine every day. And best of all, Odette smuggled Haruko into the showing of a new "line" at an exclusive fashion salon, an experience Haruko had dreamed about for years.

Next, after a dreamlike journey through the Alps, we found ourselves in Rome, where we were able to count on obtaining assistance from two priceless sources. Mother Mary Joseph had written to Brother Leo, who was in charge of the Maryknoll House in Rome, asking him to look after us, and I had written to Msgr. Joseph Hurley of the Vatican State

Department, whom I had met in Tokyo when he was secretary to Archbishop Edward Mooney. Brother Leo met us at the station and took us to the convent at which he had arranged accommodations for us, then took our breath away by announcing that we were to be ready early the next morning to go with him to Castel Gandolfo, the summer palace of the Pope, to meet the Holy Father, Pope Pius XI, in an audience which he and Msgr. Hurley had arranged for us.

Neither Haruko nor I had any difficulty getting out of bed in time the next morning. The prospect of meeting the Pope was enough to get us up, even to face the chilly dawn of the unheated convent. I put on a black dress with long sleeves and Haruko chose her best kimono, for we had been told that His Holiness liked visitors from far-off lands to wear the costume of their own country. The bright Roman sun warmed us as Brother Leo, Haruko and I drove up to Castel Gandolfo, where we were conducted past the Swiss Guards and into an anteroom. At the appointed time we went into a small audience chamber and stood waiting for the Pope to appear.

It was one of the few times in my life I have passionately wished I could see.

As the white-clad Vicar of Christ on earth came into the room, Brother Leo whispered a brief description of the scene to me. Then, as an expectant hush gripped the room, the Pope spoke briefly to us in Italian, gave us his blessing, and withdrew, accompanied by cheers from inside and outside the palace. I wondered how anyone could raise a loud shout at such a solemn moment, but I suppose we all have our own ways of expressing emotion.

The next day Msgr. Hurley took us to the Vatican, where we visited most of the places of interest and regretted only that Eugenio Cardinal Pacelli, Msgr. Hurley's immediate superior, wasn't there to meet us. Our regret at having missed him was sharpened when, some time later, Cardinal Pacelli became Pope Pius XII.

In the afternoon, after a sumptuous luncheon at the famous restaurant Alfredo's, the monsignor took us to the Mother House of the Ursuline Sisters, where we were able to talk to two Sisters whom we had met in Bangkok, Mother de Lourdes and Mother Gemma. When he left us, Msgr. Hurley promised us a rare privilege the next day. He was going to pick us up at the convent early in the morning and take us to St. Peter's, where, in the sacred crypt, over the tomb of St. Peter, he would say a Mass for the success of our work in Bangkok.

So it was that on Friday, October 22, 1938, Haruko and I descended into the depths of the crypt of the great cathedral with Msgr. Hurley and knelt there in solemn prayer as he said Mass for the blind children of Thailand and the consecration of the work we hoped to do for them. When we left that holy place, our resolution was greatly strengthened. For that matter, our all-too-brief three-day stay in the Eternal City had proved to be exactly the inspiration we needed on the long trip to Thailand, which we began in earnest on Saturday morning when we took the train to Naples, where we were to board the *Terakuni Maru* the next day.

Except for the few bags we had with us, our luggage was, as the captain had promised it would be, waiting for us in our cabin, and with nothing to worry about Haruko and I spent the evening hours walking around Naples before going to bed and waiting contentedly for the early-morning hour of sailing.

It was a quiet, unremarkable trip. We didn't have a single day of stormy weather, and even the stifling heat of the Red Sea, which I had been warned to expect, didn't materialize. The most interesting aspect of the voyage was the presence on board of an unusual honeymoon couple, a young Thai who had been studying at an English university and his English bride.

It is impossible to live long in the Orient without giving a good deal of thought to the problem posed by international marriages, especially those between an Oriental and a Westerner. Although there is no doubt that some such marriages turn out well, it is equally plain that many of them run into trouble. I have always had the theory that an international marriage is much more likely to prove successful if it is planned and carried out in the country of the man rather than of the woman. An American woman, for example, living in Japan and being aware of the Japanese family system and all that it involves, would hesitate to marry a Japanese unless she had given considerable thought to the necessity of adapting herself to the system and was sure she could do so. And the chances are that the Japanese man, with so many girls of his own kind close at hand, would be quite sure of his feelings toward his Western bride-elect. Thus, from the point of view of both partners, the marriage might have an excellent chance of working out.

Too often, however, an Oriental man living in the United States or one of the other Western countries becomes lonely and finds it easy to succumb to an attraction for a Western girl who appears to share his interests, and who is tantalizingly present, while the girls of his own country are discouragingly far away. The girl, on her part, is apt to find the very different young man from overseas a highly romantic and glamorous figure, possibly even confusing her picture of him still further by assuming that, because he seems to have an abundant allowance, he is rich—perhaps, most dramatic of all, of royal blood. The chances are, of course, that the allowance he spends so carelessly is sent to him by a tirelessly sacrificing family in distinctly moderate circumstances, or paid by his company to enable him to live up to his position. When two such young people marry and go to the groom's land to settle down, he may find his Western bride pallid in comparison with the attractive girls of his own country, and she may discover that life in a faraway country with an exacting mother-in-law demanding obedience to a strange code of customs is anything but glamorous.

Of course, the prospect is vastly different if the bridegroom intends to make his home permanently in the country of his wife. Under those conditions he would be conforming, more or less, to the customs with which she is familiar, and trouble is much less likely to result.

Storm warnings were clearly apparent in the relationship of the young Thai and his English bride. The young man had lived in England for four or five years, spoke the language with ease, and was familiar with English customs. On the other hand the girl never had left her home city, knew nothing about the country to which she was going, and saw no reason why she should learn anything about it. I gathered that, in her blissful ignorance, she was planning to live in Bangkok exactly as she had lived in England. I tried to give her some idea of what Thailand was like, but she simply wasn't interested. "My husband is virtually English, anyway," she said, "and we'll just live in pure English style."

I've often wondered what happened to that poor soul. I'm sure that something had to give.

We were late getting into Singapore, just late enough to miss connections with the coastal steamer we had hoped to take to Bangkok. But we were met at the dock by no fewer than ten Japanese who had been notified by our friends in New York and London of our impending arrival, and they reconciled us to the necessity of staying in their city until the following Thursday, when the train to Bangkok would leave. We spent a few restful days at the home of the Singapore branch manager of the Mitsui Company, and then we boarded the Malaya State Express for the last lap of our journey. It was a two and a half day train ride, and we had to make it in two stages; at Penang we changed to a Siam State Railway train for Bangkok.

We crossed the Malay-Thai border at about noon and, almost without warning, plunged into rain. As the afternoon wore on, the water rose noticeably higher. The land appeared to be flooded as far as Haruko could see, and still it kept on raining. To conserve our meager funds, we had taken curtainless second-class berths, and the water leaked into the car so freely that we had to pile our luggage on two fortunately empty upper berths and lay ourselves down fully dressed on the lowers. It was a miserably uncomfortable night, and, for the first time since I had begun making my preparations for the trip, I was assailed by misgivings. I wondered why I was going to an unlikely place like Thailand, with the world about to explode into war, with only eight hundred dollars in capital to open a school in which nobody appeared to be very interested, and with the rain dripping down on my unhappy face.

In the morning, though, the rain stopped at last; the ceaseless plopping of the heavy drops gave place to the confident, rhythmic clacking of the speeding train as it raced over the drying tracks toward the city of Bangkok. The flood lay behind us, and so did my misgivings.

Chapter **XII**

When the train pulled in at the big new Bangkok station,
Dr. Fonthong was waiting for us. I don't know what we would
have done without him. He had rented a house for us, near
the mental hospital in Thonburi; he had hired a maid and an
English-speaking Thai housekeeper to act as interpreter; he
introduced us to Mr. Namba, the manager of the Yokohama
Specie Bank, with whom we could transact our banking business; and he made an appointment for us to see Luang Pradit
on the first Monday after our arrival. His wife, Kun Pravat,
brought a delicious Thai dinner to our house on our first
night in the country.

We arrived on Saturday. On Sunday, we went to Mass at
Santa Cruz Church near Thonburi, and spent the rest of the
day settling ourselves in the house. On Monday, Haruko and
I took a pedicab into town to the bank to cash a traveler's
check and do some necessary shopping. Mr. Namba introduced us to the members of his staff and told us to call upon
them whenever we needed anything. He advised us not to
open a regular account but to keep our traveler's checks.
The value of the baht, which was then two and a half to a
dollar, might, he said, change for the worse. Very soon it did,
going down to three for a dollar, and we came out well ahead
by following his advice.

I was looking forward impatiently to my meeting with Luang Pradit. I will never live long enough to forget the scene that unfolded in his reception room.

"I hope," he said cordially, after greeting us, "that you will be successful in your noble enterprise. I have arranged for you to live in this country without paying an alien tax."

At the time that meant two hundred baht, a little over forty-five dollars, and I was properly grateful. I told him so. I also thanked him for making it possible for me to enter Thailand without paying customs duties, and I told him I appreciated everything he was doing to help me get started.

Luang Pradit wasted no time puncturing my bubble of enthusiasm. "I must tell you," he said coolly, "it will be impossible for you to solicit donations for your school until you form a foundation. And every member of the foundation, and for that matter the organization itself, will have to be approved by the Government."

I still didn't grasp what he meant. "That's very understandable," I said innocently. "Would Your Excellency do me the honor of serving as chairman of this foundation, or, at least, of sponsoring it?"

"I'm afraid," he said, "that would be impossible. As I'm sure you understand, I'm very busy. I couldn't possibly take on any additional responsibilities. But I'm certain you won't have any trouble finding someone to serve as your chairman."

By now, even I could sense the coolness in his tone. But I wasn't going to give up so easily. "Could Your Excellency introduce me to such a person?" I asked persistently. "As Your Excellency knows, I'm a stranger in Bangkok. I only came because I understood that Your Excellency would give me personal assistance."

Luang Pradit was unmoved. "It would be difficult for me to single out anyone suitable for your purpose," he said. "If I did pick someone, he probably would do it only from a sense of wishing to please me. But I doubt if he would be really interested or very helpful to you. I think it would be much better, and more satisfactory to you, if you would select your own board of directors."

I was stunned. This was the last thing I had expected. How could I form my own board of directors when I didn't know anybody in Bangkok, and almost nobody there knew me?

"I might suggest," Luang Pradit said blandly, "that the Mayor of Bangkok Municipality might be able to help you. I think Dr. Fonthong knows him, don't you, Doctor?" For a minute or two, he spoke rapidly in Thai to Dr. Fonthong, who told me afterward that the Minister had suggested that Khun Samahan, the Mayor of Bangkok, probably would be willing to serve on the foundation. When Dr. Fonthong countered by saying that the Mayor undoubtedly would accept if Luang Pradit introduced me to him personally, the man I had been counting on to sponsor my work just smiled and said that Dr. Fonthong's introduction would be every bit as good as his.

As we walked out of the Minister's residence, Haruko made no attempt to hold back her fury. "Let's go back to Japan!" she said angrily.

But I didn't want to go back to Japan. I was angry, too, angry enough to be determined to stay and prove to Luang Pradit that the school for the blind was worth trying to establish even without his help. "We're not going anywhere," I told Haruko. "I'm not, anyway. I'm going to stay right here and do my work. How about you?"

"I'll stay," she said loyally. "But I'm still mad. Mama, I hope you won't be a doormat."

I had no intention of being a doormat. But I had too much at stake to give up so easily, and I still had Dr. Fonthong to help me. "I don't know how much I can do," the doctor said, "but, whatever it is, I'll do it with all my heart."

The first thing we had to do was make an appointment with Mayor Khun Samahan, who appeared to be interested, although he made no outright commitment. Then, with Dr. Fonthong's help, we made up a list of all the Bangkok people of influence whom I had met on my first visit. From these, we intended to try to assemble our foundation. Finally, we plotted a series of radio talks, newspaper interviews and public appearances, hoping to generate enough publicity to attract some applications from prospective pupils. Even if we got our school, it wouldn't last long without pupils.

When I found out that the boy king Ananda, his younger brother, Prince Phumiphon, and the Princess Mother were in Bangkok on a state visit, I made up my mind that I would try to see her and tell her about my plan. I had met the American Minister, Edwin Neville, several times in Tokyo, and I was sure he and his wife wouldn't mind trying to help me by arranging an interview for me with the Princess Mother. It turned out to be surprisingly easy.

Mrs. Neville was with Haruko and me as the King's mother came into the large, quiet palace room into which we had been shown. Mrs. Neville rose from her chair, curtsied, and squeezed my hand hard, the prearranged signal for me to do the same. Then the Princess Mother shook hands firmly with all of us, and we sat down to talk. We talked about Switzerland, about Bangkok, and about Haruko's kimono, and then we talked about the school for the blind that I wanted to open.

I had been told that the Princess Mother had trained as a nurse at Massachusetts General Hospital before she married Prince Mahidol, who was a student at Harvard then, and it was plain that she had a genuine interest in the kind of work I wanted to do. "I think starting a school for the blind is very important of itself," she said understandingly, "but even more important is the fact that it can lead to much more interest on the part of the people in all sorts of work for the handicapped."

Just before we left, two young boys came into the room and the Princess Mother introduced us to Ananda and Phumiphon. She sounded just like any mother. "I'm having a terrible time keeping them in the house," she said. "They're so interested in everything that's going on in the street that they'd like to be out there all day. We have to keep our eyes on them every minute."

Princes and princesses, I was beginning to find out, are just like any other children.

As we drove back to the American Legation, I felt greatly encouraged. After the bitter disappointment of my meeting with Luang Pradit, my spirits were rising again. Mrs. Neville promised to do all she could herself to help, including serving as a member of the foundation board, but we agreed that the first step was to round up a sufficient number of Thai members. Above all, we needed a suitable chairman.

Publicity, of course, was essential. Dr. Fonthong arranged to have some Thai newspaper reporters interview me, and I was able to give a talk over the Bangkok radio station. Then, late in November, a golden opportunity presented itself when a young army officer, Lieutenant Nonen, came to see me. The lieutenant recently had been elected to the national assembly and apparently had won a considerable degree of popularity during his campaigning in Bangkok. He questioned me closely about the school, and offered the suggestion that I might be able to accomplish a lot of good if I would go to the Constitution Fair, which was to open on the tenth of December, and give a demonstration of what a trained blind person can do.

It seemed to be a good idea. The fair, I had been told, lasted about a week and attracted tremendous crowds. My only problem was to figure out a way to dramatize the capabilities of blind students. Miss Pintu, the housekeeper Dr. Fonthong had hired for me, had been studying the Thai alphabet in Braille, but that meant there were only two of us in the whole country who knew it. It wasn't going to be easy to work up a program.

Lieutenant Nonen promised that he would not only make arrangements for our booth at the fair but would send a car every afternoon at four o'clock to transport Haruko, Miss Pintu and me, and all our equipment. The evening before the fair was scheduled to open, he picked us up at five o'clock to take us to the fairgrounds for an inspection and reconnaissance trip. He had said he would call for us at four but we didn't mind waiting the extra hour.

After we had checked our booth, which was furnished simply with a table and three chairs, and had walked around the grounds for a while, we made our way back to Lieutenant Nonen's car. He asked us if we would like to take a ride around Bangkok with him, but we told him we couldn't because Dr. Fonthong had invited some guests for dinner and we were due back before six-thirty. We got there just in time.

I was greatly encouraged, the day the fair opened, to discover that, despite the exciting variety of things to see and do, our booth held a considerable fascination for the fairgoers. Our biggest problem was to convince the curious crowds that I was really blind. They were so impressed with my demonstration of typing, Braille reading and writing, knitting, and my reading of embossed maps, that they couldn't believe I actually was unable to see. Miss Pintu was kept busy interpreting their questions and passing along our answers.

One man asked me to type a few paragraphs for him. When I did, he said, challengingly, "Now, read it."

"But I can't read it," I told him patiently. "I can't see it."

"Oh," he said in his own language, his voice taking on a respectful tone. "She really can't see!"

Another man tested my ability to read the maps. "Where is Bangkok?" he asked through Miss Pintu, handing the map to me wrong side up. I turned it around carefully as I ran my fingers over it and unhesitatingly pointed out Bangkok, which was indicated by a little raised circle. I also pointed to the Chao Phraya River, indicated by a line of tiny points. The audience clearly was impressed.

One amateur sleuth with a lively imagination suggested ominously to Miss Pintu that I probably was a spy armed with a sinister code to communicate the secrets of the Government to foreign enemies. When this colorful theory was translated to me, I laughed and told the suspicious fellow that I would be happy to teach him the code, and then he would be able to use it to help us copy books for blind children to read. The Thai relish a good joke, and everyone standing outside the booth enjoyed my heckler's discomfiture. There was no further talk about espionage.

I've always been convinced that our little performance at the fair helped mightily in getting our operation under way. One practical result of it was the recruitment of several foundation members, including Phya Prijanusasana, a former Minister of Education.

Gradually, we assembled a working board to head the foundation. The chairman was a gentleman who had no real interest in the work but was perfectly willing to serve in a strictly honorary capacity. But Phya Prijanusasana was genuinely interested, and so was Princess Bichitr Devakul, the head of one of the largest and most progressive girls' schools in Bangkok. Mrs. Neville accepted a place and so did Dr. Fonthong, who generously agreed to serve as secretary. We coaxed one of the local Thai ophthalmologists into becoming treasurer, although there wasn't much treasuring for him to do yet.

We sent the names of all the proposed board members to the Ministry of the Interior, requesting official approval. But, not knowing when the approval would come through, I decided to go ahead with plans to open the school. Haruko and I went twice to see Khun Samahan, the Mayor, and finally wrested from him an agreement that the municipality would pay the rent of a small house for the school's use if I would move from Thonburi into Bangkok proper. I accepted instantly, and we promptly set about the business of house-hunting. Fortunately, it was nowhere near so difficult to find a house to rent in Bangkok in 1938 as it is now. Depending upon the size of the house, it was possible to obtain one for anywhere from twenty to eighty American dollars per month. We settled upon a well-built house that we were able to rent for fifty baht, or approximately twenty dollars. Unlike many Thai houses the kitchen was under the same roof, not separated from the main house, and the first floor included a living room, a dining room and a little concrete enclosure off the living room which we could equip with desks and chairs and convert into a usable classroom. Upstairs were two bedrooms, one of which I could share with Haruko while the other was turned over to Miss Pintu. There also was a small sitting room upstairs. It was all we needed. Only Bunmee, our maid, came out on the short end; there were no servants' quarters, and she had to face the prospect of sleeping in a tiny outside enclosure near the kitchen.

We were so busy that Christmas came and went with startling suddenness. Cashing a few more of our precious traveler's checks, we got together enough furniture to serve our purposes and moved into our new house the day after Christmas. Mr. Gottsche, the owner, had told us that we could move in whenever we were ready but that he wouldn't begin to charge us rent until the first of January. From then on, the rent would be payable at the end of each month. Since the city government was going to pay it anyway, I didn't trouble myself greatly with these details.

I was able to enlist a few Thai women volunteers to begin copying books into Braille, and then I turned my attention to the number one problem of all, enrolling pupils. Not one had appeared. I began to wonder, in a fleeting moment of panic, if my friends in Tokyo had been right when they said there were no blind children in Thailand.

The ice was broken, finally, by a candidate who couldn't qualify as a child but who was definitely blind, and in fact was also partially deaf. She was a princess, the daughter of the late Prince Damrong, one of the great scholars of the country. I had met her sister, who was taking care of her, at a conference of Red Cross workers in Tokyo. I visited the sister and urged her to let us see if we couldn't help the blind girl.

"But she's too old," she said. "She's nearly thirty."

I explained to her that, while my goal was to operate a school for children, my principal need at the moment was for a willing blind pupil of any age, someone I could use as an example to demonstrate that the blind of Thailand could learn just as much as the blind of any other country. The sister agreed that it was worth a trial and I left with the exciting knowledge that we had signed up our first pupil.

We still hadn't heard anything about Government approval of our foundation board, but I didn't see why we should wait. Without a qualm, I assembled the whole staff, Haruko, Miss Pintu, our interpreter, one of our volunteer Braille transcribers, and myself, in the classroom of our makeshift schoolhouse on the morning of January 2, 1939, to await the arrival of our one and only pupil.

Tahn Ying Lec, or the Little Princess, proved to be an eager pupil, and in the year she stayed with us she learned a great deal. She picked up the Thai alphabet in Braille quickly and very soon was able to read and write, an accomplishment which pleased her so inordinately that she could scarcely contain herself. We obtained a table loom and taught her to weave as well as to knit, and, by the time her sister decided that for the sake of her health she would have to forgo the daily trips to the school and make whatever progress she could on her own at home, she had the sort of foundation that she should have been given twenty years before.

The time she spent with us was just as profitable for us as it was for her. By the time the Ministry of the Interior notified us, late in May, that our board had been approved, we had enrolled five more pupils.

Not all of them, of course, were successful. One little boy, we discovered, had been permitted by a good-for-nothing father to come to the school only in the hope that he might learn a few things that would make him a more skillful beggar. The second boy who appeared at our door had a brain tumor and was in no condition to learn anything. Another, a boy of about sixteen, came from a good family, was bright and studied well. The only problem we had with him was that his family were so dubious about the usefulness of the school that they wouldn't even take the trouble to transport him back and forth. Our other two pupils were girls, one seventeen and the other nearly twenty, both from good family backgrounds and both avid to learn everything we could teach them. With our little group of volunteers working hard to increase our supply of elementary textbooks, the Bangkok School for the Blind was very much in business.

The first thing I tried to do was to make our pupils understand that it was entirely possible for them to become useful and independent members of society. "It's up to you," I said, "to make the most of what you've got and to convince people that, even though you're blind, you can work effectively and fill a real place in the world." I knew it would be years before we could count on having enough books in their own language for them to read anything except necessary textbooks, so I began to teach them English as well as Thai, which, of course, I still had a lot to learn about myself. For every hour we spent on Thai, we had an hour of English, and I was pleased to see that not only did they learn the language rapidly, thus opening up for themselves the wide range of Braille literature available in English, but they also reacted with a sharp sense of pride in the fact that they, the hitherto despised blind, were able to study English just as the educated people did. It worked wonders for their morale.

Things were going so well that it was inevitable we should run into trouble. It came from a most unlikely source. An intrepid airman had talked the city fathers of Bangkok into sponsoring a balloon ascension from a park just across the street from our house. Unfortunately for him, and, as it turned out, for us, too, the balloon did not go up. The people were so disappointed that the Mayor, feeling himself personally responsible, felt it necessary to resign. At the time, it seemed to be merely a comical bit of Oriental face-saving business, but when I went to the Municipal Building to pick up the rent money for our house, I found out that it was a serious matter.

"I'm sorry," the new Mayor said politely, "but I am afraid there is nothing I can do for you. It isn't possible for the municipality to pay the rent of your house."

I was flabbergasted. This was the last thing I had expected. "But," I said, indignantly, "Mayor Khun Samahan entered into an agreement with us. He promised to pay it!"

"That was only his personal promise," the new Mayor said firmly. "It has nothing to do with me. I'm very sorry but the municipality cannot be responsible."

There was nothing I could do except pay the rent myself, and I had to keep on paying it out of my painfully small nest egg until our foundation board was able to apply pressure to the Bangkok officials and hold them to the original agreement. By that time, too, we were beginning to attract some donations from interested people, and our precarious financial situation was eased considerably.

We soon realized it was going to be impossible to operate the school without an automobile. Whether we could afford it or not, we had to have a car to pick up our pupils in the morning and take them back home in the afternoon. We asked all our friends to watch out for the kind of car we needed, and finally we were able to acquire a little Morris Minor, of seven and a half horsepower, for seven hundred and fifty baht, about three hundred dollars. We had to pay two hundred baht down and we agreed to pay the balance at the rate of twenty baht per month. The car was seven years old and well used, but it served us faithfully for a long time, and Haruko drove many a mile in it.

We had to provide pupil transportation only for the first two school terms. After that, there were so many children in the school that we would have had to buy a bus. That was clearly beyond our means, so we solved the problem by bravely insisting to the parents that, unless they positively couldn't manage it, they would have to provide transportation for the children themselves. By that time everyone was able to see how much the school was doing for the children, and no one wanted to give it up. We won our point. I think that was our first major victory in the battle to convince the Thai people that their blind children were worth spending a little money on.

Dr. Jacobson, a German ophthalmologist who had left his homeland for Bangkok when Hitler came to power, had offered to give each of our pupils a thorough eye examination. If an operation was required, he performed it; if treatment was called for, he provided it without charge. When we took the little boy with the worthless father to him, Dr. Jacobson found that an operation might restore the child's sight. He removed the cataracts that had robbed him of his vision, and within a few months the boy was able to see. His eyes badly needed training, though, and Dr. Jacobson said he should be sent to a school for sighted children where he could be closely supervised while his eyes were becoming accustomed to reading and other school work.

I took the problem to Father Caretto, a young priest who was stationed in Bangkok to handle business matters for the Salesian Fathers, who operated a large school and mission in the south. Haruko and I met him often and felt that he was interested in our work. We thought perhaps he would agree with us that the Salesian school would be an ideal place for our young ward. Father Caretto agreed with enthusiasm, and the next time Father Casetta, the head of the school, visited Bangkok, we had a long talk with him. It was decided that he would take the boy back to the southland with him when he returned two days later.

First, of course, we had to obtain the permission of the boy's parents. One of our Thai volunteers went to talk to them and came back with the report that they were pleased that their son was going to have an opportunity to attend such a fine school. Everything was settled. But the night before the boy was due to leave his father came to the house and demanded to speak to me.

As soon as I met him, I knew we were in for a bad time. Apparently he had bolstered his courage by filling up on strong Thai brew, and he was very much the worse for wear. He wasted no time making it clear that he had no intention of allowing his boy to go away to school. "He's thirteen years old," he said in rapid Thai, translated for us by Miss Pintu. "He's old enough to go to work, and now that he can see I want him to work for me."

"But what can he do?" I argued. "He doesn't know how to do anything yet."

"He can sell things on the street. Anybody can do that. I need money. Why should he waste time going to school?"

I hated to give up. "If you send him away to school now," I said, trying to appeal to the man's selfishness, "he can earn a lot more money when he comes back home than he ever will otherwise. The school won't cost you a penny, he'll get a good education, and he'll be able to help you more."

"I don't want him to have a good education. I just want him to go to work. And I'm warning you, if you try to send him away, I'll get the police after you."

There was nothing we could do. He was the boy's father, and he had the law on his side. The boy became a street peddler and a street peddler he remained until we lost track of him. "Don't take it too hard," Father Caretto consoled me. "You've got to do your best and leave the rest up to God. If you worry too much, you won't have any strength left for the next task."

He was right, of course. The other children helped me get over my disappointment. They were a never-ending source of surprise and delight to me. I've seen blind children in many schools, schools that are equipped to provide wonderful training, but I have never seen any move about and play with the utter fearlessness and lack of inhibition of the Thai. It's hard to believe that these running, jumping, swinging children, competing vigorously in the most strenuous games, don't have at least some sight. But the largest proportion of our pupils have always been totally blind.

Between the progress they were making in their classwork and the confidence they showed in their recreational activities, our pupils were a revelation to the visitors who came to see how the school was coming along. Princess Bichitr, who had agreed to join the board after she saw our demonstration at the fair, was so surprised that it changed her whole attitude toward the school. Evidently she had been willing to take a place on the board because she thought it was her duty to do what little she could to help the blind, but she hadn't really thought anything important would come of the project. When she saw how much the children already had learned, she was astonished. "Why, this is a major educational project," she said. "It's got to be helped. I'll have to think of some way to make the school better known and get you some more money to work with." When she said good-by, after having given the children the wonderful thrill of feeling that such an important person was genuinely interested in them, she promised me, "You will hear from me soon." One of our girls, Sahataya, who was the niece of one of the wives of King Rama V, told me jubilantly that, if Princess Bichitr became interested enough in what we were doing to press our cause, the school was assured of success. Sahataya, who was seventeen then, was quick tempered, temperamental and hard to manage, but she loved the school with an unquenchable devotion, and she couldn't restrain the excitement she felt over the Princess's visit. I prayed that she would not be disappointed.

The Princess didn't keep us waiting long. She came back in a few days with one of her relatives, a young woman lawyer, Sermsri Kashemsri. They told us they were planning to hold a three-day festival at Princess Bichitr's own school just before it closed for a two-week vacation in August. There would be plays by the students, various exhibits, and, as a climax, an elaborate tea prepared and served by the domestic science classes. The Princess expected a large crowd of visitors and her idea was to solicit them for donations to our school. With this in mind, she wanted to know if I would be willing to bring our pupils to the festival and have them give a demonstration of what they were learning.

It was a priceless opportunity, and I accepted gratefully, even though I wasn't at all sure what we would be able to show the Princess's guests. Our school had been open only six months, and the children were still working on their first readers. In other respects, too, they were still in the elementary stages, and, of course, they had never appeared in public before. As I thought about it, I had a few bad moments; I was afraid that the only thing the children would be able to demonstrate was that the blind couldn't do very much. But then I remembered the tremendous interest the visitors to the Constitution Fair had shown in the exhibition Haruko, Miss Pintu and I had put on for them, and my confidence came back quickly. I was sure that the sight of their own blind Thai children working patiently to master the arts of reading and writing, in two languages, would make a deep impression on them.

I wasn't mistaken. The crowds of people who attended Princess Bichitr's benefit were amazed by the progress our boys and girls had made in such a short time. They not only did not expect too much of them but they extravagantly praised everything they saw them do, reading and writing Thai in Braille, and even more astounding, learning to read and write English. The people showed their interest by responding generously to Princess Bichitr's appeal for funds, and we found ourselves with enough money on hand to take care of our entire first year's budget of approximately a thousand dollars, with enough left over to assure us of a safe start on the second year. We were even able to hire one teacher at a small salary. It was, I thought, an excellent beginning for a brand-new school in a country in which the education of the blind had been looked upon as an unnecessary and even useless undertaking.

I was doing very well with my private pupils, too, so that my personal needs, and Haruko's, were amply provided for. We felt free to look around for some opportunities for a little social life. Haruko, in particular, had been working very hard and needed some contact with young people. Soon she was going out to small parties in the evening, and in turn inviting her friends to our home. Such things were done by the Thai on an informal basis; each guest brought something to contribute to the refreshments, and everybody was able to have a good time at very little expense.

The Girl Scouts provided Haruko with a good measure of interesting activity, too. The Mater Dei School for Girls sponsored a troop, and the American mother who was in charge of it welcomed Haruko with her U.S. training. She made her her lieutenant, and Haruko took her uniform out of the trunk and plunged into the work with enthusiasm. She had always liked Scouting, and luckily the troop meetings were in the afternoon and on Saturday, when our school was not in session, so there was no conflict.

Haruko was a born teacher. During her training at Overbrook and at the Lighthouse in New York, she had caught the fundamental idea of educating the blind, the idea that they must, as far as possible, be taught to live and act like sighted people. Haruko behaved toward our pupils with warm affection and kindness but she would not tolerate any bad habits or mannerisms. She quickly learned the Thai expressions for such commands as: "Hold up your head! Take your finger out of your eye! Pick up your feet!" and she never hesitated to bark them at a forgetful offender. But the pupils knew how she felt toward them and they loved her no matter how persistently she corrected them.

Things were happening in Thailand outside the confines of our little school. Phya Pahon, the Prime Minister, had resigned, and Luang Phibul Songgram was chosen in January, 1939, to replace him, beginning a career that saw him serve as Prime Minister until 1944 and again from 1947 to 1957. Just after he took office, the newspapers carried stories alleging that a plot against his life had been discovered and a number of army officers arrested. One of them was our old friend of Constitution Fair days, Lieutenant Nonen.

The news shocked me. In our experience with him, Lieutenant Nonen hadn't seemed at all like a man conspiring to take someone's life. It was hard to believe, and even harder after his wife came to see me at the school one morning. She asked me agitatedly if I knew where her husband had been between the hours of five and six-thirty on the day before the opening of the Constitution Fair.

It didn't take me long to remember that that was exactly when he had been with us. I recalled right away that he had kept us waiting an hour before he picked us up that afternoon. He had said he would come at four but he didn't get there until five o'clock. I told his wife that, and also told her about the lieutenant's offer to take us for a drive around the city and our refusal because we had to be back at Dr. Fonthong's for dinner at six-thirty, which we just made. "So, you see," I said, "he was with us constantly from five o'clock until six-thirty."

"That's what he says, too," Mrs. Nonen said in a strained voice, "but at the trial they said that was when he was attending a meeting at which the assassination of the Prime Minister was planned."

"He may have been at such a meeting some other time," I said, "but not during those particular hours on that particular day."

"Would you be willing to testify to this at the trial?" Mrs. Nonen asked.

"Of course I would," I said. "Wouldn't it be possible for me to offer to testify, without waiting to be asked?"

"It would be better for you to wait," she said. "I'm sure that, when I tell the authorities about this, they will ask you to come." She seemed greatly reassured when she left.

I wasn't quite so confident. The trial was a military one, and secret, and I couldn't escape the feeling that it was quite likely that we would never get a chance to tell what we knew. The only Cabinet minister I knew personally was Luang Pradit. Though he hadn't done anything to help me with the school, I felt I knew him well enough to consult him about such a serious matter, so I wrote to him and asked if I might speak to him on a matter of great importance, not connected with the School for the Blind.

Haruko delivered the letter herself to Luang Pradit's wife, but I never heard from him. Three days later, Lieutenant Nonen and the men who had been arrested with him were shot. Whether or not he was guilty was a matter for the court to decide, but if the only proof of his guilt was that he had attended that meeting, he was surely innocent. I believe that his unselfish contributions to our school, which was anything but a popular cause at the time, showed beyond question that he did not have the heart of an assassin.

It seemed as though there was always something for us to worry about. One major problem was that our house was no longer big enough to accommodate our growing number of pupils. I didn't want to turn away anyone who appeared likely to profit from an education—except those who were so obviously subnormal that their presence in the school would have interfered seriously with the standards and the progress of the others—so we began once again to look for a house. I wanted one that would be large enough to give us expanded classroom and work area downstairs, and a couple of extra bedrooms upstairs which could be used by deserving pupils who had special problems that made it necessary for them to live at the school. What we really were going to require, I could see already, was a dormitory, but I knew it wasn't likely that we would be able to aspire to anything so grand for quite a while. I would be glad to settle for two spare bedrooms.

While we were looking for a house, we were also wrestling

with a serious household problem. Miss Pintu had left us, and Bunmee, our other helper, was getting ready to return home and be married. We needed someone to manage the house for us, do the cooking, serve the meals, keep an eye on the part-time gardener and hire someone to do the heavy housework. "What we need," Haruko said to me wistfully, "is someone like Fern. If we had her, we wouldn't have to worry about a thing."

Fern, who was the number one girl in the home of our next-door neighbor, a Danish gentleman who also happened to be our landlord, had been our friend and unpaid assistant ever since we had opened the school. She was a remarkable person, a wonderful specimen of wildflower girlhood, lithe, brimful of zest for living, a rare combination of boundless energy and exquisite grace. At all hours of the day and night we would hear her cheery "Kah," in answer to the orders of her employer and his family, and we became accustomed to her speeding past our front door on the way to buy noodles, to get some ice, to call a pedicab or to mail a letter. As Haruko and I began to learn a little Thai, Fern came into the house to talk to us whenever she had a free moment. She called me Ma'am Yai, or the large Ma'am, and Haruko was Ma'am Leck, the little Ma'am. She loved Haruko with a fierce, intense devotion, and whenever we were going out in the evening, Fern was sure to pop in to admire Ma'am Leck all dressed up in her best clothes. And, no matter how late it was when we returned home, Fern's tiny figure would be sure to spring out of the bushes, pointing a flashlight to light us safely to our door. Sometimes when we had guests for dinner, she would slip away from her own house and assume complete charge of serving the dinner in a style which made Haruko and me feel we ought to apologize for what must have appeared to be an uncommonly luxurious mode of living. Fern was a treasure, and Haruko was understating the case when she said that we would have nothing to worry about if we could get someone like her.

When Bunmee was preparing to leave and we were wondering whom she would provide as a successor, she told us that Fern was going to come to work for us. Soon afterward Fern came to see me.

"But you can't, Fern," I said sadly. "You're working for my neighbors. I can't take you away from them."

"I don't want to work for them any more," she said firmly, "and I'm free to leave any time I want."

"That's true," I admitted. "But I'm not free to take you. Don't you see, if you came to me now, it would look as though I had deliberately tried to take you away from him."

"But, Ma'am Yai, you know that's not so. You'd know it was my idea."

I was determined that I should not covet my neighbor's servant. "Anyway, Fern," I said, "I can't possibly pay you as much money as you're making now." I was sure that would settle the matter. But I had underestimated our Fern. She didn't retreat an inch. "I don't care," she said stoutly. "I'd rather work for you for less money. All I care about is working for you and Ma'am Leck."

It took me a long time to convince her that I wasn't going to give in, but she finally went away, promising that she would do what she could to help us find a suitable girl. She kept her promise, too, and it wasn't her fault that Bunmee's departure was followed by a whole series of horrors. At least, I think it wasn't; I must admit sometimes I've wondered.

The first girl who came was a thief, pure and simple. The next one said she was a victim of the evil eye and proved it by succumbing to one strange malady after another, showing an uncanny knack for timing her attacks so that one always came upon her when we were expecting company. We finally relieved her of her duties when she broke out in a rash that Haruko said looked suspiciously like smallpox.

We had found the house we wanted and were just about to move into it when the evil-eye girl's replacement arrived on the scene. This girl said she was a Catholic and had worked at St. Louis Hospital in Bangkok. In my trusting innocence I didn't check with the hospital; I engaged her and said a silent prayer that she would put an end to our problems. Her request for permission to go to confession every Saturday afternoon and to Mass every Sunday morning seemed reasonable enough and carried the promise of a good character. I don't know whether she ever went to Mass on Sunday or not but I'm sure her Saturday-afternoon expeditions, which were regular as clock-work, were not to confession. After she had been with us for about four weeks she left the house on an errand one afternoon and never came back. A day or two later a friend of mine told me that she had been looking at some things in a second-hand shop when a girl had come in and sold the proprietor a dress that looked very much like one of mine. When I went to check my cupboard, I discovered that five of my best dresses were gone. One thing I must say for the girl is that she was an excellent judge of materials. She took only the best dresses I owned.

While we were pondering the problem of how we might recruit a dependable and honest helper, Fern suddenly appeared on the veranda, surrounded by all her baggage and worldly possessions—Fern, the jewel of all Thai domestics. Her voice made it plain that she had not come to conduct a debate. "Ma'am Yai," she announced firmly, "I've come to work for you. You're not our neighbor any more, so it's all right for you to take me if I want to come. I've already left there for good and I have no place to go. Will you let me work for you?"

Fern had won the day. But, of course, it was really Haruko and I who had won. From that moment on, we never had any more household problems. Fern coped successfully with everything and everyone. If, for example, the incumbent laundress proved deficient, Fern took full charge of the situation. The offender automatically disappeared and another took her place. Haruko and I didn't have to concern ourselves with the matter at all. As a result we were much better able to concentrate on school affairs.

The school usually was fairly quiet, but one morning in early February, 1940, it was disrupted by a violent scene that brought all of us hurrying to see what was the matter. A woman was standing just inside our front door, shouting at the top of her lungs in Chinese. "She's got a little girl with her," Haruko said to me. "At least, I think it's a girl. It's hard to tell. Her head is shaved and she's wearing Chinese trousers and a blouse." As we moved closer to the noisy woman, Haruko drew in her breath in a little gasp. "The poor child must be starving to death. Her mouth is sticking out like the snout of a pig. She looks bloated."

The woman who was doing all the screaming turned out to be no relation to the child. She had been guided to us by Dr. Jacobson's son, who explained to me that she was just a neighbor trying to find a place for the little one, whose mother had just died. "The mother," Dr. Jacobson's boy said, "was a patient at my father's clinic. She had tuberculosis and she went blind. She used to bring this little girl with her all the time, and the girl always seemed to be all right. But this morning this woman brought her to the clinic, and she was blind. My father says it's from malnutrition."

Haruko and I tried to make some sense out of the bedlam. Understandably, the neighbor woman didn't want the responsibility of taking care of the blind child. An older sister of the little girl also was in the group, talking volubly, and her argument seemed to be that, since she was married and had to worry about her husband, she couldn't look after the girl, either. I had lived in the Orient long enough to understand this almost incomprehensibly callous attitude. Under the ancient Chinese family system, when a girl marries, she relinquishes all responsibility for her own family and becomes an integral part of her husband's household. She is expected to maintain cordial relations with her own family but she is no more responsible for its members than she would be for a family of strangers. It was a perplexing problem. Somebody had to provide for the child's care, but who?

After a good deal of discussion, I suggested that perhaps we could solve the question by pooling our efforts. If her sister and the neighbor would get together to take care of her the rest of the time, we would pick her up every morning, take her in to school, give her a good lunch and see to it that she got home safely every afternoon. Later on, perhaps, if we ever acquired the dormitory we were dreaming of, we might be able to take care of her entirely. Reluctantly, the two women agreed; it was obvious that they had hoped to get rid of the child completely, but they were unwilling to turn down this much assistance.

The other pupils promptly dubbed the new arrival Nit, meaning the little one, but I wasn't too keen about the connotation of the word, so I changed it to Nittie. Fern, however, thought I was calling her Knitting, and Knitting she remained for a good many years.

The first morning she was in school, one of our volunteer workers made the exciting discovery that Knitting wasn't quite so helpless as we had assumed. She could sew. What's more, she could sew well. She had learned by helping her mother make Chinese trousers to sell in the shops. The only trouble was that the poor girl was in such bad physical condition that she could sit up and work only for a few minutes at a time. Then she would collapse over the table. It was plain that we couldn't let her go on living with people who didn't want her and who either couldn't or wouldn't give her enough to eat. One meal a day, at lunchtime, wasn't going to be enough to arrest the steady deterioration of her health and put her on the road to recovery. Dormitory or no dormitory, we would have to take her in and keep her with us. Haruko put a cot in our room for her and she became one of our "living-in" pupils. Dr. Jacobson, who already had removed one of her useless eyes, took out the other and fitted her with a pair of artificial eyes that everyone said made her look altogether different and far more attractive.

Knitting became Haruko's constant companion. Haruko sewed a collection of pretty dresses for her and always took her along when she went out in the car. Knitting was absolutely stolid when she first came to us, capable of going through an entire day without speaking a word to anyone, but she soon melted under the warmth of Haruko's affection. The other children made a special point of coming and telling me the first time they heard the little girl laugh, but once we broke through the sound barrier we heard all sorts of noise from her. It wasn't all laughing, either. Knitting had been brought up in a congested neighborhood where everyone had to fight with both tongue and fist to preserve his place in the world. Her voice was the voice of the typical Chinese street child, sometimes shouting gleefully in play, often violent in anger, sometimes screaming in an uncontrollable tantrum. I'm sure that every now and then the neighbors, hearing her, must have thought she was being killed, and I'm equally sure there were times when Haruko was tempted to do it. But this untamed little creature had two redeeming qualities that more than made up for her hair-trigger temper. She was quick to learn, and she was scrupulously honest. She would never put so much as a piece of fruit inside the precious little bundle of possessions she always kept with her unless it was given to her by someone in authority.

As time went by, she bore little or no resemblance to the nearly dead child we had taken in. Knitting, whose family name was Lee and who was subsequently baptized Aurora, became a familiar figure on the streets of Bangkok, and often even today, when I meet someone in Japan who was in Bangkok in those days, I am asked what happened to the little Cantonese girl who was always with Haruko. I'm happy to tell them that, after she graduated from our school, Knitting studied in the United States for four years and then went back to Bangkok to teach English, both in our school and to private pupils. I have often thought that, if the Bangkok School for the Blind had done nothing except produce this one successful student, the whole undertaking would have been well worth while.

It seemed no time at all before we had fourteen pupils, far more than we had dreamed we would be able to take care of. Partly because we felt that we needed large quantities of school materials that weren't available in Bangkok, and partly because we had a great longing to see Japan and all our old friends again, Haruko and I decided to go to Japan for our vacation. We made arrangements to sail on a Mitsui ship to Kobe, travel by train to Tokyo for a week's stay, and then pick up the ship again at Kobe for the trip back to Bangkok.

I had no idea what Japan would be like, after the three years of the "China Incident," but I was impatient to find out. I needn't have been. From the time our harmless little cargo ship docked at Kobe and was handled like a captured enemy man o'war, until we left on the return trip, we were treated to one indication after another that the country was in the grip of a war party. There were noisy, smelly, charcoal-burning engines in the taxicabs, ersatz coffee in the restaurants, inedible cakes in the bakeries, and sheets and towels made out of so-called staple fibre that distintegrated after one or two washings. Much harder to bear were the restrictions on free speech and thought. Our old friends were still the same, but the atmosphere was tense and artificial. Haruko was just as glad as I was when we started back to Bangkok.

Chapter XIII

The sixteenth of October, 1940, began just like any other day, but before it ended the entire course of our lives had been changed. Neither Haruko nor I would ever be quite the same again.

I was giving a piano lesson to one of the boys upstairs just before lunch when Khun Ying Roseline, one of the members of our board, came up to me and said, "There's a Thai gentleman downstairs who wants to talk to you." I had no idea who it might be, but I was just about ready to start down when I heard a quick, decisive step on the stairs and a friendly voice saying, "Is this Miss Caulfield? My name is Utagawa. I came to see if you can take time to meet a friend of mine. His name is Mr. Goshima, and he heard about you in Japan. He wants to see if there is anything he can do to help you."

Mr. Utagawa wasn't a Thai at all; he was a Japanese.

"Well," I said, "I'm delighted to see you, and I certainly can meet Mr. Goshima any time he wants to come."

"How about now?" Mr. Utagawa asked in a friendly but businesslike way. "He's staying at the Hotel Thailand and he could be here in a few minutes."

I was somewhat taken aback by such speed, but I agreed there was no time like the present, and Mr. Utagawa hurried off to the hotel. "Why," I asked Haruko after he had left, "did Khun Roseline say he was a Thai?"

"Oh, he looks more like a Thai than a Japanese," she said. "He has curly hair and big eyes."

Apparently she had taken a good look at him.

Meeting Mr. Goshima was a pleasant experience. "I'd like to do something to help you," he said as soon as Mr. Utagawa had introduced him. "What do you need most?"

I didn't have to think long about that. "I need a dormitory," I said unhesitatingly. "We're doing the best we can with what we've got. There are five children staying with us now. But that's nowhere near enough. If we had a dormitory, we could take in a whole lot more."

Mr. Goshima hesitated. "I can't build you a dormitory," he said, "but I'll be glad to give you a hundred baht a month to help take care of the children you're keeping here now. Then I'll see what I can do to help raise money for the dormitory." This from a man I had never seen or heard of before. I found out later that the hundred baht a month he gave me didn't come from any charity fund given him to administer. It was right out of his own salary. But as grateful as I was for the wonderfully generous assistance Mr. Goshima gave me, my memory keeps returning to that day in October, 1940, mainly because it was the day I first met the man I have known ever since simply as Nobu.

Nobutsugu Utagawa had just come from three years in Burma, where he had been the manager of the Japan Burma Association, a propaganda effort of the Japanese. Since the Burmese spoke English fluently, Nobu had learned the language fairly well. But he was an indefatigable student, and as we got to know each other better he arranged to come to the house two or three evenings a week to read with me, and just to talk, in order to improve his already excellent grasp of the language. I found myself looking forward to his visits; we talked about all kinds of things—politics, economics and philosophy—and I found him a stimulating young man.

Nobu was born in Tokyo, the son of a Christian family, just before World War I. Usually the upbringing of children in the section of Tokyo in which he lived is conservative and old-fashioned, but his mother was a woman of foresight and she desired advantages for her son. While he was still only a child, she sent him to an American missionary to learn English. He was an energetic and independent boy, and he worked his way through middle school and the university, a distinctly unusual course for a Japanese boy of that time. After his graduation from the university, he fulfilled his obligation for military service, then set about preparing himself for the diplomatic service. Just at that point, he was offered the opportunity of going to Burma as the manager of the Japan Burma Association, and now he was in Bangkok working for the Showa Tsusho Company.

Haruko liked Nobu as much as I did—in fact, more, and in a different way. It wasn't long before I became very much aware that improving his English didn't interest Nobu half as much as being with Haruko. Nor was she unconscious of his presence in the house. She responded with all her outgoing personality and loving warmth to his interest. I could see that it wasn't going to be long before we would have an announcement to make.

Christmas, 1940, still stands out in my mind as one of the happiest times of my years in the Orient.

The school was progressing wonderfully. A gift out of the blue—well, not quite out of the blue, because Mr. Goshima was behind it—had provided the money to furnish the dormitory I had wanted for so long, and that meant we would be able to take care of more pupils with special problems, the kind who needed our help the most. The money, a tremendous four thousand baht. was given to me by Mr. Asada, the Japanese Consul General, who told me that he had collected it from some of the Japanese business firms in Bangkok and that it was mine if I would agree to one condition. I listened intently to hear the condition. "It's just this," he said, speaking deliberately in a peculiarly languid, almost indifferent manner. "As you know, our Government carries on all sorts of propaganda here in Thailand. It's the policy of the Government. But this assistance to you isn't propaganda. It comes from our hearts. That's why we don't want you to tell anybody, not even the members of your board, where the money came from. Just say it came from an anonymous foreign donor."

I promised readily. It was enough for me to know that Mr. Goshima had started this particular ball rolling. I had learned from Nobu that Mr. Goshima's interest in the school stemmed from a talk he had had before he left Japan with a man I had visited once in a Japanese prison as part of my work for Caroline MacDonald's Shinrinkan in Tokyo. Surely that small act of charity was bread cast upon the waters.

The burgeoning success of the school was only part of our family's happiness. Nobu and Haruko were making plans for Christmas with the special excitement and anticipation of young people in love. We were going to have a big party on Christmas night, and they divided the work between them. Nobu decorated the veranda and even surprised us by magically producing a Christmas tree, a scarce item in hot Bangkok. He'd had it shipped all the way from the north of Thailand. Haruko cooked all sorts of good things to eat, and the four of us, with little Knitting filling out our family group, had a wonderful Christmas that began with Midnight Mass in the Cathedral and ended with a party. It was one of the last great days we knew before the war engulfed us.

We had another memorable party on a night late in January, when Nobu and Haruko and I sat at a table in the garden of the Oriental Hotel, overlooking the busy Chao Phraya, and celebrated the official engagement of my daughter to this fine young man from Japan who had come to make her life complete and into whose capable hands I was glad to entrust her.

It wasn't hard for Haruko to obtain the necessary dispensation to marry a non-Catholic, but we ran into trouble with Bishop Peros, whom we knew well, when it came to planning the actual wedding. Suspecting that he might be difficult about granting permission for the wedding to take place in a church because Nobu wasn't a Catholic, I went to see him privately, saying nothing about it to Haruko. "I was wondering," I said to him tentatively, "if you had any thoughts about where Haruko and Nobu might be married."

"Why," he said decisively, "there's no question about that at all. The wedding will have to take place in the house of the pastor. That's the rule."

I didn't like it at all but I wasn't sure exactly what I could do about it. I took the problem to my good friend Reverend Mother Raphael, the head of the Mater Dei School, and she reacted just as I had hoped. "This will never do," she said indignantly. The Reverend Mother had been greatly interested in Haruko's wedding plans. "Don't worry," she assured me, "we'll do something about it. I think the wedding ought to be right here in the Chapel of Mater Dei."

We soon had another ally. Father Eylenbosch, my old friend from Tokyo who had baptized Haruko there, was coming to Bangkok to conduct a retreat for the Ursuline Mothers, and he had agreed to marry Nobu and Haruko toward the end of his month's stay. When he arrived, and I'd had a chance to tell him of the troublesome matter of the Bishop's refusal to permit a church wedding, he, too, said it would spoil everything. Surely, he said, we ought to be able to do something about it.

I wasn't so sure. "The trouble is," I pointed out, "the Bishop doesn't want to set a precedent."

Father Eylenbosch instantly seized upon what proved to be a winning argument. "It wouldn't be any precedent," he insisted. "Both Haruko and Nobu are Japanese. Making arrangements for them isn't the same as making arrangements for local people. This wedding ought to be treated differently, anyway. It's a priceless opportunity for the Japanese com-

munity in Bangkok to attend a Christian marriage ceremony
in holy surroundings." The Bishop thought Father Eylenbosch had a good point, and he gave in. The wedding was
set for the Chapel of Mater Dei.

Neither Haruko nor Nobu knew anything of all this back-
stage maneuvering, so they approached the great day with
untroubled minds, and the wedding went off beautifully. It
was a scorching April day in the middle of the hot season,
just after Easter, and the chapel was filled to overflowing with
a cosmoplitan gathering of Japanese, Americans, Thai and
friends of other nationalities. Father Eylenbosch read the
marriage ceremony in English, then gave an eloquent explanation in Japanese of the significance of Christian marriage. Thus my Japanese daughter and her Japanese husband
were married by a Belgian priest in the Siamese city of
Bangkok, and afterward there were toasts proposed to the
health and happiness of the young couple by the Ministers
of both Japan and the United States, and for a little while
nobody thought of the black prospect that our two countries
were coming closer and closer to war.

Both Haruko and Nobu insisted that I should continue
to live with them, and after much consideration I finally
agreed. We decided that we would stay in our present house
and look for another one in which to set up the school dormitory, which could be supervised by our paid Thai teacher,
Miss Vedhi. In a way, it represented another step forward,
for a separate house for the school meant that we could accommodate even more pupils. Soon after the wedding, Miss
Vedhi and I took a trip to the North to see if there were any
blind children in the area whom we could invite to occupy
the additional space.

We stayed in Chiengmai at the home of an American missionary, Dr. Court, who was in charge of the McCormick
Hospital, a joint American-Thai undertaking. This hard-
working doctor was the idol of the countryside, for good
reason. Both the hospital and he were at the service of the

people day and night without let-up. We saw very little of him during our visit because the people of the outlying villages, that could be reached only by barely passable roads, claimed most of his time and strength. But we fully appreciated the hospitality of his home. I especially liked the bathtub with its hot and cold water, a rare luxury in Thailand in those days. The Thai method of bathing was to dip cold water out of a large stone jar, or, if outdoors, out of a pond or stream, and throw it over the body, using the other hand to do whatever soaping and scrubbing might be considered necessary. Most bathrooms in the city of Bangkok were equipped with running water, but it was cold. Of course, the Thai like it that way. Sometimes, in the summer, the sun will heat the pipes sufficiently to make the water noticeably warm, and the Thai who is about to take a bath will carefully run off water into a stone jar so that it will have a chance to cool off before he uses it. I've always tried to adapt myself to the way of life of the country I am in, but I will bathe with cold water only when I have no choice at all. If I can manage it, I try to get at least a kettleful of hot water. The bathtub in our own house had a Japanese-style charcoal furnace underneath it, which enabled us, with a little work, to have a hot bath whenever we wanted.

We found half a dozen good prospects in Chiengmai, and after arranging for them to follow us in two weeks Vedhi and I took the train back to Bangkok. I was glad we had made the trip. The addition of the children from the North seemed to make our school more truly national.

To handle the expanded enrollment I had the help of Haruko, Vedhi, two additional Thai teachers, and the part-time services of Khun Ying Roseline, who came twice a week as a volunteer. Even after Haruko discovered that she was going to have a baby, she kept up her work at the school until it was no longer safe for her to make the trip to the new schoolhouse, which, conveniently, was only a block from Nobu's office. I continued to teach English during my free hours in the afternoon, in order to earn my share of our living expenses, and in the evenings we read, entertained guests or went out to visit our friends. It was a pleasant, satisfying life, and we were as happy as we could possibly be considering the terrible tension that was gripping the world.

In June, 1941, the German *Wehrmacht* invaded Russia, breaking the non-aggression pact that had been signed by Hitler and Stalin and presenting the United States an ally that has proved more and more menacing with each passing year. Japan occupied French Indo-China and her relations with the United States became worse. It was a sick feeling to have to sit there and watch our world tumbling around us and to endure the bitter frustration of not being able to do a thing to prevent it.

A few months after we came back from a pleasant summer vacation at the seaside resort of Hua Hin, Haruko's doctor reported that X-rays showed she was going to become the mother of twins. Both Haruko and Nobu were excited, and the only cloud in view was the doctor's suspicion that the babies might be born prematurely. They were due in January but we were told to expect them any time from late December on.

Early in November, I made up my mind that the times were so uncertain and dangerous that I didn't dare leave the school's funds, amounting to some two thousand baht left over from the money Mr. Asada had given me, in the bank. I went to the Yokohama Specie Bank and spoke to one of the cashiers whom I knew. "Don't you think it might be a good idea for me to withdraw my deposit?" I asked him. He didn't hesitate. "Yes, Sensai," he said sadly, "I think it would." So I transferred our precious hoard from the impressive surroundings of the bank to the more doubtful security of my trunk, where it remained as long as it lasted, which was almost two years. What we would have done if Providence hadn't, for the second time in my life, prompted me to take my money while the taking was good, I don't know. As soon as the war began, all the American deposits in that Japanese bank were, of course, frozen stiff.

Thailand's position as the tension increased was, to say the least, difficult. She had friends on both sides. Ever since the Thai delegates to the League of Nations had supported Japan's position in Manchukuo, relations between the two countries had been growing more and more friendly. It was natural enough; they were neighbors, and they did a brisk trade with each other. In 1940, after France fell to Hitler, the Japanese had returned the earlier favor by supporting Thailand's military drive to reclaim some of the land on its northeastern border that it had lost to French Indo-China in the 1800's. On the other hand, there also was a strong traditional bond between Thailand and Great Britain. Highly placed Thai, including members of the royal family, eager to study abroad, almost invariably went to England. Economic ties, too, were strong between the two countries. So, with the Japanese poised restlessly on the Indo-China border, and the British on the Malayan border, the unhappy Thai were between the Devil and the deep blue sea. Adding to the anxiety was the fact that Premier Phibul Songgram had asked Prime Minister Winston Churchill if Thailand could expect any British help in the event of a Japanese invasion and had been given a flat no. There wasn't much the Premier could do except announce that any hostile force invading the borders of Thailand would be met by instant resistance. After that there was nothing anybody could do but wait. With the calm of utter resignation, like people in a dream, we went about our daily affairs, knowing that a terrible storm was about to break over our heads but powerless to do anything about it.

I spent hours every day listening to the radio with its drum-fire of reports of diplomatic discussions, threats, recriminations, boycotts and ultimatums. It was as though all of it was happening in another world. Bangkok seethed with rumors. The American Embassy notified us that, if we desired, we could obtain transportation to Manila or to the United States, but I had no intention of leaving my school. We were issued new passports because, the Embassy officials said, so many fraudulent ones existed throughout the world. Events rushed toward the inevitable climax.

Early in December we had word that a nun who was the daughter of a Japanese family we knew well had died in Shanghai. I arranged for a Mass to be said for her on the sixth of December, a Saturday. Haruko and I were very disappointed when Nobu told us that he had been ordered to make a business trip to the South and would have to leave on Friday. We asked him if he couldn't at least manage to wait until after the Mass on Saturday morning.

"I don't know," he said. "It really isn't such an important matter. Maybe it will be all right if I have someone else go in my place." When he later told us that he had been able to arrange it, we were pleased. We had no idea what a fateful decision it was.

On Sunday, some of Nobu's Japanese friends from Burma came to the house for a visit. They had come in by ship and they reported that there were a large number of Japanese ships of every description anchored at the mouth of the river. That evening, Nobu went out to dinner with some Japanese officials, and when he came home he said that things looked very serious. No one knew exactly what was going to happen but the feeling was strong that something was.

At eight o'clock the next morning I turned on the radio to hear the news and was shocked by the horrifying report of the attack on Pearl Harbor. I sat there numb as one shattering report followed another. The long-dreaded war was on, and from now on my friends the Japanese were, because of the reckless actions of their ambitious military men, the enemies of my country.

I told the awful news to Nobu and then I walked to a little bridge near our house, got into a pedicab, and hurried to the school. I was responsible for twenty blind children, and war or no war, I had to see that they were cared for. I told Miss Vedhi to do her best to lay in an ample supply of food and to carry on as usual until we were able to get some idea of what was going to happen next.

When I returned home at noon, Nobu was back from the office. He told us that Bangkok already was crowded with Japanese soldiers, that there had been some brief fighting in the South, but that Premier Songgram had flown back from the provinces early in the morning and had signed an agreement with the Japanese.

The man from the Showa Tsusho Company who had gone south in Nobu's place had been killed in the fighting.

On Tuesday morning I had a telephone call from the American Legation. There were about a hundred Americans in Thailand, and the Embassy invited all of them to take refuge there. Also, I was informed, the Minister was trying to requisition a train on which Americans might ride as far north as the railway was able to take them in the direction of the Burma border, after which they could get out and walk to British territory. This unappetizing project never was carried out because no train was made available, but quite a few missionaries in the North managed to cross the border on foot and make their way to India.

I thought long and seriously about my situation. I was living in a country not yet at war with mine but allied with our enemy. I had worked long and hard to establish a school that meant everything in the world to twenty blind children, I had an adopted daughter, as dear to me as if she had been my own, who was expecting to give birth to twins, her first-born. I didn't want to leave the school, and I couldn't possibly leave Haruko. I had to stay where I was.

My dilemma was made even more painful by the fact that Nobu and Haruko were Japanese. I knew that under the circumstances I couldn't hope to go on living with them indefinitely, but I decided that I would stay with them until the babies were born and then move into the schoolhouse with Miss Vedhi. I felt sure that everyone would appreciate my reasons for not accepting the asylum of the Embassy and would understand that my personal ties with my Japanese family did not imply sympathy with the war aims of their country.

Haruko and I had one wry laugh on that grim morning. Nobu had been trying for months to gain admission to the Bangkok Sports Club, the center of social life among foreigners and foreign-educated Thai. The board of admissions, which was predominantly English, wasn't enthusiastic about admitting a Japanese, and Nobu's sponsor, Dr. Viehover, the American advisor to the Ministry of Agriculture, had been having a hard time getting him in. A few days before Pearl Harbor, he had told Nobu that he thought he would be able to push it through very soon. Then, on the morning of the fateful eighth, the telephone rang and Dr. Viehover's voice came regretfully over the wire. "I'm terribly sorry," he said, "but we weren't able to have a board meeting this morning to decide upon Mr. Utagawa's admission to the Sports Club."

A few hours later I heard that the club's extensive grounds were the first premises occupied by the Japanese when they entered Bangkok. So far as I know, no one voted upon their admission.

Because the American Legation was guarded by Japanese soldiers who spoke no English, Nobu went over every day to interpret for his American friends. It didn't trouble him that the Japanese officers might look upon him with suspicion. He drove Americans around Bangkok, interpreted for them, and made deliveries of food to their homes without ever suffering any unpleasant consequences.

I was genuinely anxious about what would happen to the school if I were interned. I might have been less brave about the future if it hadn't been for the steadfast encouragement of Dr. Fonthong. He told me that, in case of an emergency, I could count on him to return the children to their homes or find suitable places for them. But he urged me not to break up the school unless I was forced to. It would, he said, be almost impossible ever to revive it. I assured him I would hold on like the Old Man of the Sea.

With my course plotted as firmly as possible, I submitted philosophically, on the sixteenth of December, to house internment. A Thai policeman was stationed at our gate and I was forbidden to leave the house. At that, I was lucky; a week later, on the twenty-third, all American, British and Dutch nationals were sent to an internment camp. The only exceptions were Government advisors, who were permitted to remain at home. Since I had been admitted to the country with semi-official status, I was considered a member of this privileged group. It was one time Luang Pradit's help stood me in good stead. In any case, whether it was because I had come to Thailand at the invitation of a member of the Government or because the officials of the internment camp weren't eager to take a blind woman into their charge, I was allowed to stay at home and was able to continue my supervision of school business by telephone.

Chapter XIV

Christmas, 1941, was a far cry from the happy, carefree cele-
bration of the year before. Being interned, I couldn't even
go to church with Nobu and Haruko. But the sadness we felt
on what should be the greatest feast day of the year was
nothing compared with what came next. My mind still re-
sists going back to those days.

The doctor's prediction that Haruko's twins might be born
prematurely proved to be accurate. We took her to St. Louis
Hospital three days after Christmas. I made up my mind that
no internment regulations were going to keep me from going
with her, and I put on my hat and coat and marched out
past the guard. He never said a word. Nobu said he seemed
to be looking hard in the other direction.

Like all mothers, Haruko was glad that her time had come
and she entered the hospital with eager anticipation. The
Sisters gave me a room right next to hers, and I stayed
outside on the veranda, with my typewriter and a few books,
through the long vigil. It was a very long time. Haruko's
labor lasted from noon on Sunday to late Monday afternoon.
Finally, the doctors, two German and one French, decided
upon a Caesarean operation, and Haruko's two babies, a boy
and a girl, were born at six o'clock Monday evening.

Haruko was still under anesthesia when Nobu and I had

our first look at the twins. He could hardly believe their good luck in having both a boy and girl. "I never knew I could be so happy," he said to me as he left the hospital to go home for the night. "If only there wasn't this terrible war."

By the next morning, Haruko was conscious, but very weak. She smiled when the Sisters showed her the babies. They were so tiny that they had been laid in the same crib, one at the head and the other at the foot. But she was suffering much pain. I stayed on in the next room, unwilling to leave until I knew that she was better. She seemed greatly improved that evening, but the next day she became worse. The three doctors gathered at her bedside and prescribed what medication they could for her; there were, of course, none of the wonder drugs that are available today to fight such infections.

In the morning, her condition was so serious that I called Nobu at home and told him he had better come right in. Then, doing what I knew had to be done, I called Father Caretto and asked him if he would come and give Haruko the last Sacraments.

Nobu was with me at her bed, holding tightly to Haruko's hand, when she spoke to us with the last of her ebbing strength. "I want to live," she whispered. "Nobu, the babies. I have everything to live for. I'm trying to live. But if God wants me now, I'm ready."

Minutes later, she was dead. The grief that flooded me, and that left Nobu shocked and bewildered, cannot be described. We were like sleepwalkers, going through the necessary motions with a mechanical unreality. I forced myself to hold my despair at arm's length. I still couldn't believe that Haruko was dead but I knew that she would be counting on me to look after her grieving husband and her motherless babies.

We buried Haruko from Assumption Cathedral, less than nine months after her wedding day, and Nobu and I went home to a desolately empty house.

I tried to think what to do next. The nurse we had hired to take care of the babies had come up to me at the cemetery, just after the service was ended, and said, "Ma'am, I think it's best to take the babies home."

I didn't understand. "Why?" I asked her. "We're not ready for them yet. They're much better off there."

"They're afraid to stay in the hospital," she said nervously, and then I understood. The three-day-old infants weren't afraid to stay in the hospital, but apparently the nurse was. She was afraid of ghosts. I settled the problem by dismissing her and arranging with the Sisters at the hospital to leave the twins there until they were three weeks old. By that time I would be ready to take care of them at home.

The babies made their first trip outside the hospital on January 6, 1942, when we took them to Mater Dei to be baptized. Bishop Peros himself performed the ceremony, baptizing the boy Nobuyuki Joseph Samuel and the girl Haruko Marie Thérèse. The first part of the boy's name was, of course, the same as his father's, and the second part, Yuki, is one reading of the character used in writing my name in Japanese. "Caul" is, in the complex Japanese language, pronounced "Koru" and is written with a character which means "fortunate child." Another reading of the same character is "Yuki" and still another is "Sachi." Haruko and Nobu had intended to name the twins Nobuyuki and Sachiko, but now we wanted to have another Haruko, so Nobuyuki and Haruko became the Japanese names of the children and Joseph Samuel and Marie Thérèse their Christian names.

The day after the baptism, while we were having lunch in the house, my considerate police guard appeared and asked to speak to me. "Now, ma'am," he said politely, "you must not go out any more."

He had been turning his head every day as I went back and forth, unmindful of his presence. But now he felt that it was time for him to enforce the rules, and I, wanting to reciprocate his understanding, submitted without protest.

One result of our sorrow was that Nobu decided to take instruction in the Catholic faith. He had been so impressed by Haruko's trusting spirit of acceptance and resignation that he wanted to know more about, and even embrace, the religion that had the power to bring such peace and tranquillity to the soul. He went to Mother Gemma at Mater Dei and began studying the faith.

My first big problem, in preparing for the babies, was to obtain a supply of milk. Fresh milk from cows was unsafe. What we had to do was to buy as much powdered milk as we could lay our hands on, but it wasn't going to be easy because all imports had stopped. The product that was recommended most highly to us was a British baby food called Cow-and-Gate, and I commissioned all of our friends to scour the markets for it. They co-operated so enthusiastically that we accumulated fifteen cases, a whole year's supply, and the twins thrived on it. Our friends never stopped looking for it. Every now and then, during the long years of war, I would find one of them standing on the veranda holding out a package or two of Cow-and-Gate that they had discovered hidden away on some tradesman's shelf.

There was plenty to eat in Thailand all through the war, although imported foodstuffs were unobtainable. The occupying Japanese were on their best behavior. They wanted to set a good example in the only truly free country in their Greater East Asia Co-Prosperity Sphere, which I heard the Delhi radio refer to, with bitter humor, as the Greater East Asia No-Prosperity Sphere. They paid for what they bought in the markets and they displayed considerable caution in disturbing the economic balance of the country, although they didn't hesitate to print large quantities of military baht. Despite the fact that Japanese soldiers were everywhere, we had no trouble buying fresh vegetables, fruit, eggs and meat. Prices, of course, were something else again. The Government published a long list of ceiling prices which accomplished nothing except to make the black market blacker and to make illegal what might just as well have been done in the open.

Once, after Fern had checked the Government list, I telephoned a Bangkok grocer and asked him what price he was asking for coffee. "The Government price is two baht a tin," he told me candidly. "I'm selling it for four."

"Send me six cans, please," I said meekly. I was certain it would never again be sold at that figure, and every citizen of Bangkok can testify that it never has been. Prices for everything—house rentals, servants, clothing and food—skyrocketed all during the war. But, at that, the rising costs of wartime were nothing compared with the dizzying inflation that has taken place since.

I substituted pressed coconut milk for cream in coffee and used it successfully to make banana ice cream. We had rice flour which could be used to make bread and cake which tasted fairly good if you ate it on the day it was baked, although it tended to dry up into a tasteless crust if you kept it overnight. Later on we learned how to combine rice bran with the flour, and that greatly improved the taste of our bread. White sugar was hard to get but palm sugar, although expensive, was available. Butter, of course, was unobtainable.

Soap and paper were precious commodities, and so was cloth. Most people had trouble replacing worn-out clothes, and sheets, mosquito nets and similar articles were at a premium. Nobody had to ask us the familiar question being asked all over the world: "Don't you know there's a war on?" We knew it well.

At the beginning of the war, we were required to file a report with the police if we possessed a short-wave radio. I had one, an excellent RCA model, and I dutifully reported it. I fully expected that it would be confiscated, but as the days wore on and nothing happened, I assumed that there had been a bureaucratic oversight somewhere, and I thanked my lucky star that I still had this priceless contact with the outside world. About a year later I heard once again that a careful check was being made of all short-wave radios, and, fearful of getting into trouble, I called up the Ministry of Commerce, whose concern it was, and asked if they had the license number of my radio on file. "I reported it a year ago," I said, somewhat defensively.

"Just a moment, ma'am," a polite Thai voice said. In a few minutes, the man was back on the telephone. "We have the license number of your radio on file," he said briskly, and then, more softly, he added a sentence that I have always treasured. "May I suggest, ma'am, that the less you say about that radio, the better."

That was all I ever heard about the matter. I kept my radio all through the war. Of course, anyone who had a short-wave set was supposed to listen only to Radio Tokyo and dutifully shun all broadcasts from Allied countries, but this order was obeyed the way free-thinking people usually obey such absurd regulations. Our hearing was strained as we listened intently to faintly murmuring voices from Delhi, Manila and even London. Sometimes someone forgot to keep the volume down, as when we plainly heard the strains of "God Save the King" coming from the Japanese house opposite us.

In the middle of January, we heard that Thailand officially had declared war against the United States and Great Britain. It made little difference in the actual situation because the treaty of alliance with Japan had had the same effect.

Nobu brought the babies home on the nineteenth of January. I had hired a highly recommended Chinese nurse, and Fern, who had been married herself a few months before Haruko, had set up a comfortable nursery for them on the second floor. There were two bassinets in it, a supply of bottles, a sterilizer, and everything else that we had been told we would need. Fern's husband, Sompong, worked in Nobu's office, and he was going to help Nobu bring the twins home. Everything was going smoothly, and Fern and I were checking last-minute arrangements when, at just about three o'clock, the air-raid siren sounded shrilly.

Ever since the first raid on Bangkok the day of the baptism, when a number of bombs fell on the city, including one on Assumption Cathedral, and machine-gunning planes swept the downtown streets, every signal had been obeyed fearfully by the Thai. If they couldn't find any better shelter, they would duck underneath a table and hope for the best. Some people, especially the Chinese, responded to the wails of the siren by hurrying out of the city proper, on the theory that nobody would bother to drop bombs on the more thinly settled areas. This time, among the group of refugees was our Chinese nurse. She sent word of her defection to me by messenger but the messenger didn't show up until long after Nobu had come home with the twins. At first, when he heard about the nurse, he wanted to take the babies back to the hospital, but I talked him out of it. "We're going to have to learn how to take care of them ourselves," I told him, "and we may just as well start right now."

We got through the night all right, and the next day I was able to hire another Chinese nurse. Although she knew next to nothing about taking care of infants, she helped Fern and me get through the days until our problem was solved by the miraculous appearance of an efficient Thai nurse who had been trained in a strict British home and who really knew how to look after babies.

Early in February, Nobu had to leave us. The army had arranged to borrow him from the Showa Company for a special assignment in Burma. The Japanese-trained Burma Independence Army, originally created with the idea that it could help expel the British from the country and thus play a part in Japan's master plan, was showing altogether too much independence. The Japanese were displeased; something would have to be done. Nobu's services were requisitioned because he knew so many of the Burmese leaders as a result of his work there with the Japan Burma Association, and as much as he disliked leaving the twins he had to go.

I said good-by to him with a heavy heart. I couldn't even count on getting letters from him for there was no way of sending mail between Burma and Thailand except by the ancient method of hand-to-hand delivery. Nobu promised that he would write to me whenever someone he could trust was traveling between Burma and Bangkok, and it was remarkable how many letters we were able to exchange.

Nobu, who was young and a little naïve, went to Burma believing firmly that Japan intended to give the Burmese their independence. He expressed real indignation when I ventured to suggest that the army probably had no such purpose. Gradually, however, during the two years he spent in Rangoon, he came to realize that the Japanese Government's only motive in promising independence to Burma was to create another Manchukuo. Meanwhile they proposed to drain everything they could from the country.

Nobu's awakening came as a bitter disillusionment to him, but he was too honest not to recognize it and react to it with anger. Some of his letters to me described his feelings in unmistakably blunt terms, and it was a good thing the men who served as his couriers were true friends. If some of those letters had fallen into the hands of army censors, Nobu's letter-writing career would have been cut short.

Nobu continued to take religious instruction in Rangoon, and sometimes his letters to me contained enclosures from the Bishop of Rangoon to Bishop Peros, and my return letters carried the answers.

The Japanese had been seizing Church property indiscriminately in Burma and had been making life miserable for the religious. Nobu stepped into the situation by arguing with the military authorities that this scarcely was calculated to help Japan's relations with the Vatican, which the Government in Tokyo was trying hard to foster. He told them that all Church property belongs, in the last analysis, to the Vatican, and he solemnly urged the army to be careful. He must have been persuasive; before long, he was given the job of dealing with the matter himself. He proceeded to bring back communities of Sisters from the country, to allot sufficient rations of food to Catholic hospitals and other institutions, and in every way he could to re-establish order.

Years later, when I visited Rangoon armed with a letter of introduction from Nobu, I was welcomed lavishly. The warmth of my reception was, I knew, not so much for me as for Nobu, a lone Japanese civilian who, in a dangerous and inflammatory moment, had stood up against the authority of a mighty military machine and extended the hand of friendship to people working in the name of God.

My house internment ended with the unexpected visit of a policeman who informed me that the restrictions were being relaxed to permit me to make daily visits from the house to the school, and back, with a guard accompanying me. The guard at the gate had disappeared long ago. "Your guard," the policeman said, "will be here tomorrow morning, and he will come every day to make the trip with you."

I was pleased. It would be a blessing to be able to move about even a little. Furthermore, my guard, Kun Sorn, proved to be a pleasant and obliging young man who wore no uniform, went with me to and from school in a pedicab tricycle, and acted as though his assignment was more to protect me than to guard me. The first morning he came, he told me that I should feel free to go other places than to school. "All you have to do," he said in friendly fashion, "is to tell me, and I will go with you. That is the only rule." I was grateful, and when Mother Raphael asked me to go to Mater Dei once a week to teach colloquial Japanese to the Sisters and Mothers there, so that they might be able to communicate at least a little bit with the Japanese soldiers, I was glad that Kun Sorn's kindness made it possible for me to perform this small service for an old friend.

Kun Sorn, for his part, seemed to enjoy his "work." He always waited at the school for me until I was ready to leave, usually about noon, and during the children's free periods he sang songs and played games with them much as though he were an older brother. I learned that he had a brand-new

baby at home, and, guessing that he might be able to put some
of the twins' outgrown clothes to good use, I gave him odd
garments from time to time, and he warmly appreciated
them.

One day I discovered that I had bent the frame of my eye-
glasses and would have to visit the office of a Bangkok op-
tician. I told Kun Sorn about my problem and asked him
if he would be kind enough to take me there after school.
He didn't know where the shop was, and he asked Miss Vedhi
to give him directions. She went over the matter carefully
but he became only more confused. Finally he shrugged and
told her, "Look, you know where it is. You go with Ma'am,
and I'll stay here and take care of the children."

We took him up on it. Feeling like a naughty child running
away from school, I got into a tricycle with Miss Vedhi and
fared forth unguarded into the perils of occupied Bangkok.

"What on earth do you suppose he'll try to teach the children?" I wondered out loud.

Miss Vedhi laughed. "Nothing," she said. "I gave him an
easy book to read but he'll probably spend most of the time
singing with them."

We got the frames for my glasses without any trouble and
then stopped for lunch at one of the famous Bangkok drive-in
shops, the Rachawong. We had a substantial meal of rice
gruel with pork and vegetables, treated ourselves to coconut
ice cream for dessert, and then pedaled back to the school
and relieved my extraordinarily co-operative guard.

As the days went by the war seemed far away from us
despite the presence of so many Japanese soldiers and the
ceaseless reports on the radio of Japanese victories and Allied
defeats. Only the ominous, chilling screech of the air-raid
siren brought it home. When the planes came over, usually at
night, we would hurry across the street to take refuge in a
crude shelter one of our neighbors had built in his garden.
The nurse, Mae Son, carried one of the twins; Prom, the
cook, carried the other; and I brought up the rear with a

cloth bag containing our medicines and money hanging around my neck and in my hands a huge basket filled with the babies' bottles, formula, diapers and other necessities. Fern and Sompong never could be induced to leave the house; they argued that thieves were more dangerous than bombs, and they stayed behind to protect our property.

We had a shelter at school, too, at first a surface structure and later on two enormous cement jars, sunk into the ground, each of which was capable of holding ten people. Visitors to the school used to enjoy seeing us conduct an air-raid drill. It was amazing the way those blind children would rush out of the school, scamper straight for the shelter and climb easily down the crude steps cut inside the cement containers. Any time you dig a few feet below the surface in Bangkok, you strike water, which was why we couldn't have a genuine underground shelter.

With Nobu in Burma, and only the Thai servants to keep me company, I had nobody to read to me, except when I visited Mater Dei and Mother Gemma was able to read to me for an hour or so. Finally, though, Mother Gemma found a Eurasian girl who knew English whom I was able to hire for a four-hour stint every week, a period which became a great treat for me. "The only trouble," I told Nobu, "is that the reader just gets through things as fast as she can, which is what she's supposed to do. She doesn't enjoy things as you do. But we can't have everything, and, in a way, this is better for the purpose of covering the most possible ground in the time allowed. There is no temptation to stop and talk over the things that are being read, which, of course, is what makes reading with you and Mother Gemma so delightful."

Rumors kept spreading about arrangements for the repatriation of all the foreign internees in Thailand. So I wasn't surprised when one day the Swiss Consul called to inquire if I wished to go home to the United States. I hadn't, of course, waited until then to consider the problem. I had thought about it for months. Home, in a country that probably never would become a battleground or even know the impact of a bomb, was an enticing prospect. But I hated the idea of turning my back on the school after carrying it this far, and I couldn't bring myself even to think of leaving Haruko's babies with their father away with the Japanese army in Burma and their mother buried in a Bangkok cemetery. I had to stay right where I was and see the war out.

Telling the Swiss Consul that I had decided to stay was easy; saying good-by to the repatriates when they left, in June, was much harder. After they had gone I found myself one of only five Americans in Bangkok. My fellow citizens were three Mothers of Mater Dei and Sarah Davies, the American widow of a British professor who had died in Bangkok just before the war began. Mrs. Davies hoped to go to England, where her son was, but after waiting in vain for a year she settled for transportation back to the United States by way of Africa. I found myself one of a tiny group of foreign nationals living in a distant country that had declared war on mine, even though mine had not returned the favor, and that was allied with a country that was locked in a death struggle with mine. It took all of the resolution I could muster to stamp out my uneasiness and focus my attention on the survival of the Bangkok School for the Blind and the care of my twins. A lot of people were counting on living out the war in Thailand; I would be one of them.

It sounds comical now but one of the principal wartime annoyances the Thai people had to put up with was a ruling by their own Government that everyone appearing on the street had to wear both hat and shoes. This might not be such a startling ordinance in New York City or London, but in Bangkok it hit the people hard. The normal dress of the country was informal and wildly varied. Many of the men wore loose Chinese trousers, and the custom was to wear a different color for each day of the week, which made the streets a riot of color. The women wore *passin,* a saronglike skirt, also of the appropriate color for the day. With white shirts for the men and white blouses for the women, the result was a pleasant combination of comfort and neatness. For dress-up wear both sexes favored the more formal *panung*, a long piece of cloth folded in such a way as to form trousers, topped off with a buttoned-up coat. Only business and professional men wore Western-style suits. Most of the ordinary people went barefooted; those who put anything on their feet settled for comfortable slippers, or, at best, sandals. Shoes were reserved for the most formal occasions, and nobody ever wore a hat. Contrary to custom throughout the world, Bangkok's Catholic women didn't even wear hats in church. It was simply too hot. So it was a shock when the Prime Minister handed down an edict that everyone, without exception, who ventured out on the street was to wear both hat and shoes. Women were, as far as possible, to wear blouses and Western-style skirts or one-piece dresses. There were to be no Chinese trousers worn on the streets at all.

The new law was strictly enforced. No one was allowed to enter a public building, buy food at a market, or even obtain treatment at a hospital unless he was wearing these badges of culture. A pedicab driver couldn't pick up a hatless or shoeless passenger.

It was more than a nuisance, it was an expensive nuisance. Many families, hard pressed to buy enough to eat, now had to invest precious baht in hats and shoes they not only didn't need but didn't want. Most country people solved the problem by buying a family hat and a family pair of shoes. When the mother went to buy something in the market, she wore the newfangled regalia; when the father had to go into town to sell his produce, it was his turn. One or the other, and in many cases both of them, developed painful limps from wearing shoes that didn't even come close to fitting.

The schoolchildren were dressed in Nazi-style uniforms, organized into two youth associations, the Juvachon for boys and the Juvanari for girls, and put through military drill. The uniforms were even worse than the drill. Long-sleeved and high-necked, they were suitable for Germany but utterly unfit for the tropics. After drilling in the broiling sun, the poor children, dripping wet, were marched back into their classrooms where the breeze soon cooled them off and, as often as not, left them with colds.

Late in May the routine of my days was broken up when one of Nobu's couriers handed me a letter from him saying that he was making a trip to Saigon and then on to Tokyo, and that on his way back to Burma he would be able to stop off in Bangkok for two weeks. I had missed him, and I looked forward excitedly to seeing him again.

By tacit agreement, we didn't discuss the war much on that visit. Nobu knew I had no sympathy for Japan's war aims, and I knew that no matter how much he might disagree with them he was a loyal Japanese. But he was so indignant about what he had encountered in Burma that he couldn't keep from telling me about it.

"They keep telling the Burmese that they're going to be independent," he said angrily, "but at the same time they say that this national resource or that one has to remain under Japanese control. Naturally, the Burmese don't like it, and how can you blame them? They won't be very independent if they can't even control their own national resources."

I smiled faintly to myself but said nothing.

Nobu had made his protests to the military authorities on the scene but their answer was that as a local command they were merely carrying out orders from Tokyo. So Nobu arranged to fly to Saigon and talk to the area commander, then go on to Tokyo and lay his case before the high command. "They listened to me politely," he said, "and they said they would look into it, but they didn't make any promises."

Among the things Nobu brought me from Japan was a beautiful *haori*, or scarf, a present from his sister-in-law. I had to confess to him that I wasn't enthusiastic about wearing it. "Everybody says the design is beautiful," I told him, "but from the way they described it, whenever I put it on, I feel like an old lady." The one I habitually wore was a gay thing splashed with big, bright flowers. It probably was intended for a girl of about eighteen, but I was convinced that it looked well on me. "Anyway," I told Nobu, "I know all the reasons for assigning the old and wise to dress in somber colors, but I've always wondered why such an artistic people as the Japanese would subscribe to such an upside-down concept. Young people don't need brilliant colors and flaming garments. It's the pale cheek and the saddened eye that should be framed in something colorful and gay."

While he was with us, Nobu completed his religious instruction and was baptized into the Church. Bishop Peros, who had married him and Haruko and had baptized their children, poured the waters of Baptism on Nobu's forehead while the twins watched the scene calmly from Mother Gemma's arms and mine. All we needed to make the scene in the Mater Dei Chapel complete was Haruko, but we felt sure that she knew what was happening and was gladdened by it.

I know I was. I tried to explain how I felt in a letter I wrote to Nobu some weeks later: "When you went away before," I told him, "you really went. It was very lonely, and the house seemed half empty. This time I have the feeling that you are still here, that you know what we are doing and that your spirit is in our home. The invisible connection among those who follow the True Church on earth, and the still more wonderful connection between us and those who have left this world—the Communion of Saints—is one of the most comforting things our faith brings to us. It isn't a product of our own minds or feelings; it's actually there, just as the grace of the sacraments is actually there. After your baptism, you said you felt different. That was, of course, partly a sense of security and accomplishment. But to a far greater degree it was that you *are* different. The sacraments don't help you simply because you make up your mind to receive them. They in themselves possess the power to strengthen and guide you. Thus, confession is not only the telling of our faults, the sorrow for them and the resolution not to commit them again, it's a sacrament, carrying with it the grace which strengthens and fortifies us. The more we use this help, the stronger we become and the clearer becomes our insight into the will of God. It will be hard for you in Rangoon, because of the poverty of human contact and the absence of any personality that can stimulate you. But you have what is far more important than any human contact— the Mass, the sacraments, and the ever-present help God is giving you."

I wrote at least part of a letter to Nobu almost every day. I tried to touch upon all the subjects that interested both of us, always, of course, beginning with the children.

"I wish you could see Nobuyuki in his long white night clothes," I wrote once. "Everyone says he looks like a little angel. He has a wonderful dramatic sense, for he seems to know that as soon as he puts on this long white garment, all activity should cease, and he lies quiet and gentle in my arms, waiting for the moment to go to bed. Haruko is too practical to resemble an angel, and too matter-of-fact to be dramatic, but she is an adorable little girl. I am so anxious to show them to you. What a wonderful time we shall have when you can be here all the time. By here, I mean at home, not necessarily in this place. We shall try to have a real Catholic home with our daily lives filled with the spirit of what we learn from the holiest of all Families. If we can give that kind of spirit to the children, they will be fortified to meet anything in the future. Spiritual, intellectual and physical balance is what is required. It is that lack of balance that has thrown the world into its present state. Overemphasis on the intellectual and physical, with no thought of the spiritual, has brought us to the present pass. Too many people are erecting what they call spiritual values which in reality are nothing but the exaltation of an ideal based upon pride. They call it spiritual simply because it is not material, but it is leading them to destruction. People are seeking for something, but they are making the mistake of attributing to nations or human leaders what belongs to God. We are instruments in the hands of the Creator, not almighty beings to whom nothing is impossible. Pride is the curse of the world."

A few days after Nobu left on his return trip to Burma, the police department presented me an impressive document which notified me that henceforth I would be permitted to go wherever I wished without the necessity of being accompanied by a guard. It was signed by Luang Adoon, the Chief of Police.

I was happy about my new freedom but I couldn't help regretting that I was losing Kun Sorn. However, when I showed him the document, he merely nodded and said, "But, inasmuch as I haven't received any orders yet, I will still go to school with you every day."

"Good," I said immediately. "I'll be very glad to have you. Of course, if I have to go somewhere without you after school, I'll go."

Kun Sorn agreed. "Certainly," he said. "You've got written permission from the Chief of Police. But I will go to school with you as usual."

So my guard and I went on as before. I waited faithfully for him every morning and he returned me to my house at noon. In the afternoon, if I wanted to go shopping or visit Mater Dei or go somewhere else, I went with Sompong, who could drive our faithful Morris Minor, or with Miss Vedhi. Kun Sorn went about his own concerns.

Toward the middle of September, we began to hear disquieting rumors of floods in the North. High water is a regular thing in Thailand at the end of the rainy season, but these floods were something else again, the kind that come every thirty or forty years. I knew it was serious when Fern, Sompong and Prom began to move all of our furniture up to the second floor. I wondered why they didn't lay in a supply of food to tide us over the flood period, but when I urged them to they assured me there was nothing to worry about.

The rising waters came closer to us every day until, one morning in the middle of October, we awoke to find the garden flooded. The first thing I thought of was the car. It meant so much to us that I shuddered to think of it being damaged. "What can we do about the car?" I asked Sompong. "If the water gets any higher, it will be ruined."

"Don't worry, ma'am," he said reassuringly. "I'll take care of it."

That evening, when he came back from work, Sompong led a troop of strong young men up to the house. Where he had recruited them I have no idea, but they all seemed to know me and greeted me warmly. They went to the car, which was parked on a small bit of higher ground, and pushed it up next to the veranda. Then they all bent down, caught hold of the little automobile, and lifted it bodily right up onto the veranda, where it perched, high and dry, until the waters receded and the same strong-muscled young men came back with Sompong to lower it to the ground again.

At the height of the flood the entire city of Bangkok was a huge lake, studded here and there with little islands of high ground. If you wanted to go anywhere, you had to go by boat. Because the country people always brought in their produce by water, food was, as Fern and Sompong had said it would be, plentiful in the market; meat, fresh fruit and vegetables appeared just as regularly as if they had been trucked in on dry roads. But you had to do your shopping in a boat. I went to school, as often as I could, in a boat, and if I wanted to take the twins for a ride I had to wait for a friend who owned a boat to come along and invite us out. This amphibious existence lasted for a month. For people like us, living in two-story houses, it wasn't so bad. The ones who suffered the most were the ones who lived in one-story houses, which were completely flooded. Unless they could find a boat to sleep on, they had a bad time of it.

One amusing thing about the flood was that there was no easing of the Prime Minister's hat edict. Enforcement of the shoe ordinance was more difficult, but, even though you might, of necessity, be wearing shorts or a bathing suit, you still couldn't buy food at the market or stamps at the Post Office unless you had on a hat.

The high waters were good for young lovers, who had a whole month of moonlight boating parties, and for fishermen, who were able to let down their nets from the windows of their houses and haul in good catches of shrimp and fish; they were bad for professional thieves, although some of the more adventurous ones adopted the expedient of moving about on stilts, and for the Allied bombers, who found it impossible to detect profitable targets when the land was covered with water. There wasn't a single raid during the peak flood period. But as the waters started to go back in November, we began to cock our ears apprehensively toward the skies, certain that the time was coming soon when we would have to dive into the wet shelters again.

They came, U.S. Army planes, on the night before Thanksgiving, and after circling the city in deliberate fashion two or three times, they did a nice piece of precision bombing on the Bangkok gasoline factory. The Thai expressed satisfaction and relief at this "gentlemanly" type of bombing, which they vastly preferred to the haphazard dropping of bombs that had characterized the earlier raids. It seems grotesque now to think of categorizing bombing raids that way, but we were grateful for small favors.

The highlight of my Thanksgiving Day was a farewell dinner with Sarah Davies, who was due to leave in a few days for the United States. She had sent me a note a week before, inviting me to come for dinner on the holiday, but we found that it wasn't so simple. We internees weren't supposed to have any social intercourse at all. Hopefully, though, Sarah applied to the police for special permission, and finally it was granted, on condition that Kun Sorn accompany me.

It was an odd Thanksgiving dinner we had, two American women in wartime Bangkok, guarded from the next room by Kun Sorn and Mrs. Davies' personal policeman, neither of whom spoke a word of English. We felt like dangerous spies.

Before I knew it, it was time for Nobu to come home for Christmas, which he had promised to do. We had a party for the children at the school on Christmas Eve, and then I settled down to wait for Nobu. There was no way of knowing when he would come; he would have to take his chances on squeezing aboard a Bangkok-bound airplane. Christmas morning dawned clear and cool, but no Nobu. I decided to delay dinner until the evening, in the hope that he might make it, and after a light lunch I took the twins to Mater Dei for a visit with the Mothers. We were all sitting there, in the shade outside the house, when Nobu rushed in. He had almost given up hope of coming when he heard about a special flight to Bangkok. He packed a few things and hurried to board the plane. When he landed he decided that we probably would be at Mater Dei, and he had come straight there, suitcase and all. His appearance, and his announcement that he could stay for a week and help celebrate the twins' birthday, made it a much happier Christmas.

Little Haruko and Nobuyuki were a year old on the twenty-ninth of December, and we decided to have a highly exclusive Twin Party. Margaret Vichien, who had helped us at the school from the beginning, had twin girls six years old; another of our Thai friends had two-year-old twins; and we rounded out the party group with a set of three-year-old triplets, all boys, whose mother had been awarded a prize by the Government for having them. It was a highly successful and noisy party, with Haruko gracefully presiding in her high chair at one end of the table, and Nobuyuki at the other end, laughing joyously and clapping his hands vigorously to show his pleasure.

Their father's visit was quickly over. Sompong drove us

to the airport on New Year's Day, 1943, and Nobu gave the babies a last hug and hurried aboard the airplane that was waiting to take him back to Burma. We didn't see him again for a year, and by then the course of the war had changed considerably.

One day, soon after Nobu left, the French priest from the Cathedral, who was supposed to look after foreigners, suddenly appeared at my door. It was the first time I had seen him since the war began.

"Do you speak Japanese?" he asked abruptly.

"Yes," I said, wondering what was on his mind.

"Here is a Japanese soldier with a letter of introduction to me from a priest in Singapore. He wants to become a Catholic. Can you teach him?"

"I think I can," I said, "but isn't it a difficult situation? What will his superiors think of his coming to the home of an American to study anything?"

"I don't know. I'll leave him with you. Maybe you can do something for him."

The young man, Takesaka San, was a sergeant. He told me that he had wanted to become a Catholic for a long time but had been unable to find anyone to instruct him during the seven years he had served in China. He said that he had met some Nisei Catholics who had been born in Singapore, but they couldn't speak Japanese. Finally, he met a Chinese Catholic, with whom he read part of the Catechism in Chinese, but it hadn't gone very well. They could both understand the written characters but they couldn't talk to each other because the Japanese and Chinese pronunciations are entirely different.

When he was transferred to Bangkok, he almost gave up hope of becoming a Catholic. But, just in case, he had asked for a letter of introduction to the French Fathers in Thailand, and here he was. "Could you teach me?" he asked eagerly.

"There's nothing I'd like better," I told him. "But how can I? If you come here for instruction, and your officers find out, what will happen to you? I'll be very glad to teach you, but first you've got to go to your commanding officer and tell him there is an American internee who would be glad to teach you Catholic doctrine if he will give you permission to visit her twice a week for instruction. Will you do that?"

"Yes," he said without hesitation. "I'll ask him today, and tomorrow I'll come back with the answer."

I was pretty sure that would be the last I'd ever see of him, but I was wrong. The next day, he came to the house just as he had promised he would and said, simply, "The captain told me he's willing for me to study with you to become a Christian, provided I become a good one."

Instructing Takesaka San was a complicated business. I had to copy parts of the *Kokyo Yori,* the Japanese Catechism, into Braille and then ask him questions to see if he knew the answers. The rest I just let him read, both questions and answers, and explained it to him as we went along. I was sorry that he had to be satisfied with so little, but I was sure that the Holy Ghost would help me to manage. He must have wanted me to do it or He would never have sent this soul to me all around through China, Indo-China, Burma and Singapore.

When I thought my soldier was ready to be baptized, I arranged for the ceremony at Mater Dei. It is customary for a priest to examine any candidate for Baptism who has been instructed by a layman, or even a Sister, but in this case, because of the insurmountable language barrier, Bishop Peros took my word that Takesaka San was properly prepared.

Soon after he was baptized, Takesaka San was transferred away from Bangkok, and I never heard of him again. But, whether he was killed in action or survived the war and returned safely to his homeland, I'm sure that he found on that day something he had sought for many years. For my part, I think of it as one of the most satisfying experiences of those grim and anxious days.

Chapter XV

The skies that welcomed 1943 were faintly streaked with hope for the Allies, but there still was a long way to go, especially in Asia. Except for occasional air raids and the incessant rumors upon which everyone fed avidly, life in Bangkok was comparatively quiet.

The school was coming along well. The pupils were showing the results of their training, especially in their dramatic efforts. Our temperamental but talented Sahataya had a genuine gift for writing plays and training the other children to perform in them, and some of the entertainments they put on were surprisingly good. They performed mostly in Thai, but after a while they added a few playlets in English. I was very proud of them, and I encouraged them to keep it up. One of these days, I thought, we would be able to put this flair for dramatics to good use, perhaps even to raise some money.

Money was beginning to become a problem to me. The durable dormitory fund Mr. Asada had given me, that I had withdrawn from the bank in the very nick of time, finally was running low. The wartime inflation had been hard on it. What I would do when it was all gone I didn't know. We kept hoping that the Government would recognize the usefulness of the school and give us a subsidy, and from time to time various officials called upon me to ask about our needs, but nothing ever happened. I heard vague rumors that the Japanese Culture Association, which maintained an office in Bangkok, was thinking of taking over the school, but that didn't appeal to me at all. It would mean that I would have to give up my connection with the work, for I could hardly be in the position of accepting a semi-official appointment from my country's enemies. Hoping to forestall such a step, I begged our board members to do everything they could to win a subsidy from the Thai Government, but it was months before we got any results.

I had no problem at home, so far as money was concerned. I had saved a little from what I had earned before the war as a teacher of English, an occupation which had vanished with the coming of the Japanese occupation troops, and Nobu had arranged for the Showa Tsusho office in Bangkok to pay an allotment to me every month for the maintenance of his home and children. So I was getting along very well. But the school was a different matter entirely. I calculated that I had just about enough money to last through 1943; after that, we would have to see. I was sure that God would find a way.

Then, one day, Madame Phibul Songgram's secretary called and asked me if I thought our pupils were capable of putting on an entertainment for the Women's Culture Association, of which the Prime Minister's wife was president. Without hesitating, I said they most certainly could. On my birthday, they had surprised me with two plays, one an original work in Thai, and the other, "Cinderella," in English. I was sure they could work up a thoroughly respectable program out of these two plays with the addition of a piano solo and perhaps a few other musical numbers. When I asked Sahataya if she thought they could do it, she agreed enthusiastically, and in a matter of hours rehearsals were under way.

The children had courage. They had never given a public performance of any kind, but they were unafraid, even though they knew the Prime Minister's wife would be in the audience. They understood it was a golden opportunity for them to do something for their school and they were determined to make the most of it.

The Women's Culture Association numbered among its members the wives of all the prominent officials of the Government, and on the day of the performance, as I sat, resplendent in hat and gloves, in my seat, I was nervous. I was sure that the people in the audience were wondering why the Prime Minister's wife hadn't just asked them to contribute to the school fund and spared them the ordeal of sitting through an entertainment put on by such pitiably handicapped children. But, from the moment the performance began, I breathed a deep sigh of relief. The children were as cool and as self-possessed as seasoned actors and actresses.

The surprise and pleasure of the audience were measured by the spontaneous applause that broke out again and again. When the performance was over, Madame Songgram thanked the children and announced a substantial donation to the school. This was followed, a little later, by another from the Prime Minister himself, coupled with an invitation for all the pupils and teachers of the school to have lunch with the Prime Minister and his wife the next day. We had much to be happy about that night, and I took full advantage of the opportunity presented by the luncheon the next day to inform the Prime Minister not only of the school's aims, but its needs, too.

It wasn't many days later that Miss Vedhi telephoned me one morning in a state of great excitement. "Has anyone," she demanded, "told you what's in the newspaper?"

"No," I said. "Why, is something the matter?"

"May I come to your house right away?" she asked, breathlessly.

"Of course," I said, wondering what was up. "It's nothing bad, is it?"

"No, no," Miss Vedhi said, hanging up abruptly.

In an incredibly short time, she was at the house, carrying

a newspaper. "It says here," she read at the top of her voice, "that the Department of Public Welfare, of the Ministry of Health, is going to appropriate twenty thousand baht a year for the support of the Bangkok School for the Blind."

"Oh, no," I gasped. "It must be a mistake. That's impossible!"

"I agree with you," Miss Vedhi said. "It must be a mistake in the type. But that's what it says!"

"Well, the only thing for us to do is to find out," I said firmly. "Let's get a tricycle and go to the Department of Public Welfare and ask them."

As we rode along, I thought about the possibilities. Up to now, our budget, not counting the dormitory, which I had operated out of the special fund, had amounted to approximately thirty-five hundred baht a year, about nine hundred American dollars. If this newspaper story was correct, it was suddenly going to be raised to twenty thousand baht, or five thousand American dollars. It was not to be believed.

I had met Khun Chamnong, the Director General of the department, in Tokyo, so I had no hesitation about asking to see him, and when I was ushered into his office I came right to the point. "Can this story in the newspaper be true?" I asked impatiently.

"It's true," he said, laughing at my attitude of disbelief. "We've been so pleased with what you've been doing for the blind children that we want to help."

Even when he had said it, I had difficulty grasping the scope of our good fortune. This was more than we had ever dreamed of; our wildest fantasies were becoming reality. I trembled with joy as I thought of what this would mean to the school, and to the children.

"Does the department intend to take over the running of the school?" I asked, trying to collect my thoughts and still searching instinctively for the inevitable catch that I was sure had to be lurking somewhere.

"No," Khun Chamnong said. "It will remain a private

institution. We have no thought of operating it, merely subsidizing it. The money will be paid over to your board, and the board will provide whatever is needed to run the school. Nobody in this department knows anything about how to run a school for the blind, and we don't intend to interfere in the work in any way. We only want to help."

These are the generous conditions under which the Bangkok School for the Blind has received its Government subsidy ever since that electrically exciting day in the middle of the war. Twenty thousand baht a year! It was like winning the grand prize in the national lottery.

Fate smiled on us in another way that year when Khun Ying Roseline, the treasurer of our board, told me that her cousin, Princess Visakar Svasti, was coming home from Malaya after having been trapped there ever since the war broke out. I was greatly interested because I had heard much about the Princess from Khun Ying, and I was hopeful that she might be willing to help the school by serving as a volunteer teacher. At any rate, I intended to ask her, and I told Khun Ying to be sure to let me know when she arrived home.

Princess Visakar was a great-granddaughter of King Rama IV, the celebrated hero of *Anna and the King of Siam* and *The King and I*. Her grandmother, who, at ninety, was still living, had married one of Rama IV's sons. Visakar's eldest sister, Queen Rampai, was the wife of King Prajadhipok, who had abdicated a few years after the bloodless revolution of 1932. As the father of the Queen, Princess Visakar's father, Prince Svasti, had wielded considerable power at court, but when the revolutionaries set up their constitutional monarchy, and assumed the power of Government, Prince Svasti took his family to Penang in Malaya, where he remained until he died. He entered his two daughters in the highly regarded girls' school of the Convent of St. Maur, and while she was there Princess Visakar became known as Mary, the name she adopted as her own when, after a long struggle with her family, the Sisters of the convent, and her conscience, she became a Catholic.

A number of Thai girls were attending the convent school, and it was their habit to return home every year for the Chistmas holidays. As a result, almost all of them were safe at home when the war began. But Mary and one other girl from Bangkok had stayed behind in order to take their Cambridge entrance examinations, and they were caught. They had a bad time of it. Penang was heavily bombed, and the girls were evacuated to other convents in safer parts of the colony, returning to Penang only when all resistance was ended and the Japanese had settled into their role of occupation troops. There was nothing benevolent about this occupation. Unlike Thailand, which the Japanese dealt with as an ally, Malaya was conquered territory and was treated as such. The army cared only about feeding itself and couldn't be bothered worrying about whether or not the Malayans starved. Mary said that from the beginning of the war to the day she finally was allowed to leave, in the spring of 1943, she ate exactly two eggs. Meat was unobtainable. Their diet consisted principally of tapioca, potato leaves and rare pieces of fruit. It took weeks of rest, good food and vitamin injections to restore Mary to health after the Thai Government, prodded by her grandmother, finally managed to convince the Japanese general in charge of the Malayan occupation to allow her to return to Bangkok.

Princess Mary's feeling toward the Japanese was bitter. I went to see her soon after she had returned, and I was immediately taken by her. She was twenty-one years old then, a slender girl with a reserved manner but cordial, intensely interested in people and events, anything but self-centered. She was a girl of character and determination, as she proved in the matter of her adopted religion. Throughout her years in the convent school, Mary had felt a longing to become a Catholic, and for five years before the war she had taken serious instructions. But her family objected, because the royal family of Thailand had always been strictly Buddhist, and, aware of the family's attitude, the Sisters had been reluctant to allow her to enter the Church. "At least," the Reverend Mother told her, "let's be sure you're a thoroughly convinced one. It won't hurt to wait. There's too much at stake for you to act on impulse."

When she was trapped in the war, Mary decided that five years was long enough to wait. If anything was going to happen to her, she wanted to have the consolation of the faith she believed in. Confronted with the combination of Mary's resolution and the dangerous times, the Reverend Mother gave in, and Mary was received into the Church.

When she told me about her baptism, I realized that it had taken place on the very same day that the twins had been baptized, and at the first opportunity I had her meet them. She was captivated by them, but her enthusiasm was tempered by one big reservation. "If only," she said, sadly, "they weren't Japanese."

I laughed. "Don't worry," I said, "you'll soon forget about that. Those people in Penang were just the product of war. They weren't the real Japanese."

"It will take a long time to convince me of that," Mary said. But, even as she was talking, she picked up baby Haruko in her arms and kissed her cheek affectionately.

As soon as she was well enough, Mary accepted my invitation to teach in the school. She came as a volunteer teacher of English, but her influence on the pupils was far greater than that modest role might indicate. From the first day she appeared, the pupils were overjoyed to have a princess as a teacher. The Thai have a great love and respect for their royal family, and these blind children, who only recently had been ignored even by their own families, were profoundly impressed that a princess, the granddaughter of a king, should consider them worth her time and attention.

Mary soon was as absorbed in the progress and personalities of the children as I was. She laughed along with me at little

Piac, one of our youngest boys, the day he was caught by some of his schoolmates stealing money out of the contribution box. A delegation of the pupils reported the matter to me, and I sent for Piac. The terribly young criminal stood before me expectantly. "Well, Piac," I said, "did you take money out of the contribution box?" He shuffled his feet a little. "Yes," he said, "I took some."

"What did you do with it?"

"I put it back."

"You did? Then why did you take it?"

"I would have kept it if it was real money," he confessed unashamedly. "But it was only paper, so I put it back."

Nobu came home on the nineteenth of December to spend Christmas with us, and I was shocked to learn that he had had a narrow escape in an airplane crash flying from Rangoon to Tokyo. He had been traveling as an advisor to Dr. Ba Maw, the head of the so-called Independent Burmese Government, en route to a Greater East Asia Conference to which Hideki Tojo, the Japanese Premier, had summoned representatives of all the members of the Co-Prosperity Sphere. Luckily, both Nobu and Dr. Ba Maw survived the crash; they were picked up and flown the rest of the way to Tokyo in Tojo's personal plane.

Nobu's long stay in Burma was telling on him. He showed marked signs that life there was anything but easy. He was thin and nervous, and he complained that both his eyes and his ears were giving him trouble. When he told me the sort of food he was accustomed to eating in Rangoon, I didn't wonder that his health had been affected, and I was happy when he said he had decided to return to his Showa Tsusho office in Bangkok for a few months, put himself in the care of a doctor, and try to restore his strength before going back to Burma.

Nobu's position was an unenviable one. He wanted to do his work well and he wanted to live up to his own ideals, and it wasn't always easy to do both.

Partly because of my despair that the Japanese army would ever allow him to accomplish any real good there, and partly because of my very human fear that he was exposing himself to needless danger, I sometimes tried to talk Nobu into giving up his work in Burma. Once I wrote to him: "I just heard that yesterday nearly thirty tons of bombs were dropped on Rangoon. It is terrible. Nobu, for pity's sake, do not wait until it is too late. You surely cannot do much organizing with raids like that. Thirty tons. Sixty thousand pounds. It is incredible. Remember, you are needed for the future. Do not throw away opportunities by taking chances now. You do not need to be told that I am the last one to advocate running away from anything, but this is not running away. It is preserving for your country a life which will do it no good if it is thrown away uselessly, but which will do much good if it is used at the time it is needed. I know God is taking care of you. If I did not know that, I wonder what I would do."

Part of the time, I'm afraid, I lectured Nobu in my letters, fast and furious, on life, politics, child raising, philosophy and religion. I still have a copy of a letter I wrote to him in February, 1943, in which I told him of listening to a B.B.C. broadcast of a Sunday-evening service from Westminster Abbey. "This service," I told him, "was especially dedicated to Russia. The sermon, preached by a responsible minister of the Church of England, was devoted to praise not of the bravery of the Russian armies but of Russian ideals. He spoke of the struggle of the Russian people to attain true community life, and of their devotion to the welfare of mankind. 'Of course,' he said, 'there are atheists among them, but we shall pray that they will see the light.' Etc., etc. It simply made my blood run cold. Some Protestants are always trying to compromise when it suits their purpose, especially the Anglicans. Compromise with divorce, compromise with birth control. But to compromise with atheism is beyond the limit. These people are willing to overlook the horrible persecutions of Christians that have taken place in Russia and that are taking place in the Baltic states, in Poland, and everywhere that Russia has set her foot, simply because the Russians are fighting Hitler. Hitler is a menace, there is no doubt, but the fact that Stalin happens to be fighting against him does not turn that same Stalin into an angel, to be heralded from British pulpits as the savior of mankind. They are doing too much wishful thinking about Russia and they are going to get into real trouble, which, I fear, will be deserved. Imagine a Catholic Bishop broadcasting a sermon in which he declared that Communism as practiced in Russia is an evidence of the struggle of mankind for better things. He would be excommunicated."

It was plain that the tide of war was turning, gradually but irresistibly, in favor of the Allies. America's massive productive capacities, so grievously underestimated by Germany and Japan, were beginning to tell. Even though they were fighting many thousands of miles from home, the Americans were better equipped, better supplied and better fed than the Japanese. We became accustomed to Japanese soldiers and civilians returning to Bangkok in a half-starved condition. Provided with little in the way of supplies from home, they had to live off the land, and the pickings were slim, despite their ruthless depredations. What little they did grab had to be distributed among a great many hungry men. It was no wonder Nobu was so badly undernourished.

The changing fortunes of war were reflected, too, in the increasing number of air raids on Bangkok. Things got so bad that I set about trying to arrange for a temporary rural location for the school, in case it should prove necessary to get the children out of the city. The Salesian Fathers had a school at Bangtarn, and they generously offered to make available to us two rooms in their building there, for which I was very grateful. I told them I would take advantage of their offer only if I had to, but the time came sooner than I had expected.

When the air-raid siren sounded on the night of December twenty-third, I was glad that Nobu was still with us. We decided to stay in the house with the babies and the servants. The shelter in the yard across the street was still there, but the neighbor's dog took refuge there in every raid and we were afraid his presence would be dangerous for the babies if he were frightened by a hit or a near miss. So we stayed home, and, as the exploding bombs striking all over the city made it appallingly clear that this was the biggest raid of them all, we prayed that Miss Vedhi and the children were all right in their cement-jar shelters.

It was the kind of air raid that shouts the horror and stupidity of war. The planes dropped flares first, to light up the blacked-out city and allow them to see what they were doing as they went about their deadly work. Then, in wave after wave, they let go their bombs. They may have had some specific targets in mind, but it didn't seem to us as though they were trying to do anything except create as much havoc as possible. Most of the earlier raids had been aimed at targets of genuine military importance, such as the gasoline factory, the railway, bridges, and the shipping in the harbor, but this one appeared bent merely on indiscriminate destruction. Mixing incendiary bombs with the ordinary explosives, they started fires raging all over the city. There were a great many casualties.

We didn't know whose planes were involved in the raid, and we don't know to this day. Whoever it was probably was ashamed of it. Whenever, after the war, we asked British or American military men about it, they vigorously disclaimed any part of it, although they didn't hesitate to acknowledge responsibility for other raids on the city. It was the guess of the Thai that it was the Chinese from Kunming, using this means of letting the Thai Government know how bitterly they resented the discriminatory treatment being meted out to the Chinese in Thailand.

At the time it didn't matter much who was responsible

for the raid; what mattered was living through it. And what mattered desperately to us was that the blind children at the school should live through it. The bombing went on for hours. Every time there was a lull and we thought it would be safe for Nobu to take off for the school, another wave would come over and the earth would begin to rock again from the thunderous blasts of the bombs. While we waited in an agony of apprehension, I promised myself that this would never happen again. I would send the children to Bangtarn immediately; they would be crowded there, but they would be safe. I was just beginning to plan the details of the move when Nobu called to me that they were all walking into our garden, the whole school, with Miss Vedhi, almost exhausted but triumphant, at their head.

"There were fires all around," she said, "and I was afraid some sparks might land on the school. So I decided we'd be better off here, and I was sure we could make it."

"You have no idea how glad I am to see you," I told her. "But how did you know our house wasn't on fire?"

"We didn't," one of the children cried out. "But we were sure that, even if it was, you and Mr. Utagawa would know what to do."

"How did you manage?" I asked Vedhi.

"I told them all to come out of the jars," she said, "and then I lined them up two by two and told them we were going to walk to your house and that they would be all right if they would just stay very close behind me. I would guide them. We walked along Sathorn Road, where there weren't any fires, and whenever an airplane flew over us I made them all lie down in the road, right where they were, until it passed. I wasn't sure that would do any good if the plane shot at us, but it seemed better than just walking. We were about halfway here when we met Sompong, who was on his way to the school, and he helped me take them the rest of the way. They were wonderful."

Nobody seemed to mind that we had no beds for all the

children, and as soon as the "all clear" sounded they arranged themselves on the floor in various parts of the house and soon were peacefully asleep.

In the morning I got in touch with the Salesian Fathers and told them I was going to send the children to Bangtarn the next day, which would be Christmas Day. Next I telephoned Kun Prapat, the head of a Bangkok boys' school, a kindly man who generously lent us his school bus whenever we needed it, and asked him to have the bus pick up the children in the morning and take them to the railway station, where they could get on a train for the two-hour ride to Bangtarn, about fifty miles away.

I would have to stay where I was. Vedhi and her Thai assistant would have to run the school while I remained in Bangkok, helped in the formation of our new board for 1944, and saw to it that sufficient funds were channeled to Vedhi in Bangtarn to pay the school's expenses. Besides, I was, after all, an internee, and I wasn't sure how the authorities might react to my disappearance from Bangkok.

Princess Mary spent most of the day of the twenty-fourth with us, helping to prepare for the momentous move. It was obvious that she wanted to go with the school, but her family, like many in Bangkok, was getting ready to move to the country, feeling it would be safer there, and naturally they expected her to go with them. I invited Mary to eat Christmas dinner with us, Christmas Day being of no special significance to her Buddhist family, and she accepted, although I'm sure she was doubtful about sitting down to dinner with Nobu. It was all very well for her to love the little twins, but, after what she had been through in Malaya, to associate socially with a grown Japanese man was something else again. However, the lure of Bubu and Koko, the nicknames little Nobuyuki had fastened on himself and his sister, was more than she could resist.

She appeared unexpectedly early in the morning. The school children already had left; the bus had picked them up before daylight. Mary was visibly disturbed. "My family insists that I go to the country with them," she said unhappily, "but I don't want to. I want to go to Bangtarn with the children. I wish I knew what to do."

My heart went out to her. She was a troubled girl, wanting badly to do what she thought was right, but not wanting to hurt anybody, either. "I wish I could help you," I said softly, "but I'm afraid this is something you'll have to decide for yourself."

"I know," Mary said, "I know." She stood up and made ready to leave. "I'd better not come for dinner," she said. "They're leaving this afternoon, and it doesn't give me much time. I've got to think. I'll let you know what I decide to do."

We had a pleasant holiday dinner, but all the while I was wondering what Mary would do. It was a hard choice she had to make. She loved her work with the school, and I knew she would regard it as desertion to leave the children at a time like this, when they needed all the help they could get. But she loved her grandmother and the rest of her family very much, and it was hard for her to contemplate doing something that she knew would antagonize them.

We had been finished with dinner about an hour when a pedicab came to the front door carrying Mary and all her baggage. "I've decided to go to Bangtarn," she said. "The family doesn't like it at all, but I'm sure they'll get used to the idea."

She wouldn't be able to leave until the morning, when a car was going to Bangtarn with some things for the school, so the three of us, Mary, Nobu and I, had a quiet evening together. I was glad of the opportunity it gave these two young people of whom I was so fond to get to know each other. I was sure that Nobu's perfect manners and his cosmopolitan outlook on the world would convince Mary that there was a vast difference between him and the soldiers who had invaded the convent in Penang and arrogantly ordered the Sisters to burn all their English books. I was interested in hearing Mary tell how the Sisters responded to the order, instead of burning the books, they merely hid them, and calmly continued to teach English to the girls at night, when no one was likely to burst in on an inspection tour.

"It's a ridiculous attitude," Nobu said. "You can't make everybody learn Japanese whether they want to or not, and you can't prevent them from studying other languages. But what are you going to do with people who think they're going to conquer the world?"

At first, Mary's reserve in the presence of one of the despised Japanese was conspicuous. But Nobu exerted all of his considerable charm, and before the evening was over his friendliness had broken down her reserve. She laughed at his little jokes and found herself agreeing with many of the things he said. Her antipathy for the Japanese as a nation was still intact but it was pretty clear that she was beginning to change her opinion about one individual Japanese.

It was a happy evening for me, although I was saddened by the knowledge that I wouldn't see Mary again for some time. I had grown very fond of her, and I was going to miss her. When she left for Bangtarn in the morning, I was proud of her. She was, after all, a royal princess, and she was giving up a life rich in creature comforts for an uncertain existence that would compel her to live and work around the clock in two rooms with twenty-two other people, with no light except oil lamps, no water except what was dipped out of a nearby canal, and no way to obtain food except to ride in a packed train to the nearest market, miles away.

But Mary knew what she wanted to do. The decision she made that Christmas Day in 1944 changed her whole life.

Chapter XVI

Life in Bangkok wasn't the same for me without the school but I managed to keep busy. We had a second birthday party for the twins, this time with only the family taking part; a new board was formed to operate the school for the coming year; and I began searching for larger temporary quarters for the school. The two rooms in Bangtarn wouldn't do for long.

I found the house I was looking for in Hua Hin, Thailand's most popular seaside resort. It was a large brick house, offering plenty of room and located next to the King's summer place just outside the town proper, and it was ideally suited to our needs. The owner agreed to let us have it for a hundred baht a month, which I thought was astonishingly cheap, especially with so many people in the market for a country home that would offer security from the increasingly frequent air raids. As soon as Vedhi and I inspected it, I decided to take it. Then I started back home, dropping off Vedhi at the Bangtarn station and picking up Mary there. Mary made the long trip just so she could spend Easter with me and the twins.

Nobu's health was much better and he was getting ready to return to Burma. This time he was going in a new role, as advisor to the so-called Burmese Independent Government, an extension of the part he had played at the Greater East Asia Conference. He wasn't sure how much good he could accomplish, because he knew now beyond the shadow of a doubt that the army had no intention of allowing the Burmese real independence, but he felt that he owed it to Dr. Ba Maw to do what he could.

The outlook wasn't good for anyone who worked against the interests of the militarists. Mr. Goshima had been arrested by the Kem Petai right in Bangkok, charged with activities directed against the Tojo regime, and when he was finally released he was so sick with malaria that we were afraid it might be fatal. From time to time I heard of other decent Japanese men who had been seized by these despots and whose fate wasn't enviable, and I prayed earnestly that nothing like that would happen to Nobu.

My prayers were answered more swiftly than I dreamed possible. Mary went back to Bangtarn after the Easter weekend, and Nobu left for Burma soon afterward. I was alone with the twins, except for the servants, and I was lonely and uneasy. My state of mind wasn't improved by the gnawing worry that Nobu might get into trouble with the Kem Petai, and, longing for someone to talk to, I sent a note to Mary and asked her to come up and spend a few days with me. It was selfish of me to take her away from the school, but I felt I needed her. I promised Vedhi I wouldn't keep her long.

Mary was with me for two days and was planning to go back to Bangtarn the next morning. Suddenly I heard her run out onto the porch and greet someone, and as they started in, I could hear their voices.

"What are you doing here, Mr. Utagawa?" Mary was asking.

It was Nobu! "I've come home to stay," he said, and it had been a long time since I'd heard a more welcome voice. I got up quickly to greet him and to ask what was going on.

"Right after I got to Rangoon," he said, "I went to see

a civilian friend of mine, and he said to me, 'You know, Utagawa, the army doesn't like you.' I told him that didn't surprise me particularly. 'They say you're pro-Burmese,' he said. 'Is that right? Are you really pro-Burmese?' That struck me as a silly question to ask. 'Of course I'm pro-Burmese,' I told him. 'How could I serve as the Government's advisor if I weren't?' But my friend didn't think that was going to do me any good. 'If that's the way things are,' he advised me, 'you'd better go back to Bangkok fast. The army is out to get you.' So I decided he was undoubtedly right. If the army didn't want me there, doing the kind of work I was supposed to do, I'd be better off coming back. So here I am. I'll just stay here and work for the company."

"But," I said apprehensively, "what about the army here?"

"I won't have any trouble," Nobu assured me. "General Nakamura is a sensible man. I've finished my assignment in Burma and I've come back to the company. That's all there will be to it."

Mary, like me, wasn't quite so confident, but we were happy to have Nobu back safe and sound and we were glad that he would be staying in Bangkok, a relatively safe zone. "Please let me know how it all turns out," Mary said when she left for school in the morning. And in a short time we were able to report to her that all was well, that Nobu had taken up his work in the office just as though he had never been away, and nobody was bothering him at all.

Unquestionably the army was busy worrying about more important matters. The Japanese were suffering one reverse after another, and they couldn't have felt very happy about the D-Day landings on the Normandy beaches on the sixth of June. The Axis powers were learning how it felt to take punishment.

We had box seats at a preview of one symbol of America's growing might. I had taken Bubu and Koko along on a visit to some friends, and we were enjoying the mildness of a sunshiny June afternoon when suddenly the quiet was shattered by the wail of the air-raid siren and, almost simultaneously, the roar of giant airplane engines. There was no place to take shelter, so we all stayed right where we were and put our trust in God. "Here they come!" our host said. "They're the biggest planes I've even seen, like great big white birds. They're American planes!"

Instinctively, I seized a few handfuls of cushions to cover the twins, although what good that would have done if a bomb had landed near us I don't know. It was something to do, anyway. We all sat tight and waited for the planes to pass over, hoping that they weren't heading for the gasoline re-finery, which was nearby. Fortunately, they kept going, great, eaglelike machines of destruction, and dropped their loads of bombs near the railway station.

A few days later I heard a radio broadcast from Delhi that said the United States had produced and entered into service a monstrously powerful new bomber, the B-29 Superfortress, and that the trial raid of the new planes had been made over Bangkok, as a test of their long-distance flying capabilities. All the planes, the broadcast said, had returned safely to their base, and soon an armada of B-29s would be sent into action against the Japanese home islands.

Prime Minister Phibul Songgram resigned that summer of 1944, and Nai Khuang Ahpaiwong, the opposition leader, became his successor. One of the new Prime Minister's first official acts was to rescind Phibul Songgram's celebrated hat edict. "Hats off!" the newspapers shrieked joyously, and the new Premier's popularity skyrocketed.

Shoes, however, had come to stay, and it was just as well, for they have rescued the population from hookworm and other ills that come from going barefooted.

With the school well settled in the comfortable house at Hua Hin, I wanted very much to be there, too. I didn't have to worry any longer about there not being enough room for me; the question was whether or not the authorities would object to an internee wandering so freely around the country. I decided to call up Kun Sorn, and ask for his opinion.

"Kun Sorn," I said, "we've moved the school to Hua Hin, and I want to go there. What should I do?"

"Just go," he said, without a moment's hestitation. "If you file a report on it, or make an application for permission, it will take forever. Just go. Nobody will mind."

With that comforting assurance, I made plans to go. Miss Vedhi came to Bangkok for a few days to settle some business, and, when it was time for her to return, Nobu arranged for his company car to take all of us to the railway station. We had to go to the station on the other side of the river because Allied bombs had destroyed the Bangkok side of the bridge and the trains were unable to cross.

The express which used to make the trip to Hua Hin in five hours had been taken out of service. We traveled on a local that stopped at every station between Bangkok and Hua Hin. It took us twelve hours, but we forgot how tired we were when we found Mary waiting for us at the station, ready with enough tricycles to transport us and all of our luggage to our destination.

The big brick house outside of town couldn't have been better suited to our needs if it had been built for us. I couldn't help wishing it were possible for us to buy it and use it as a summer home for the school.

The only thing I really missed at Hua Hin was my radio, which I had been unable to bring because there was no electricity in our house. But the landlord, who lived nearby, had electricity in his house, and we went there regularly to catch up on the news.

The water we used caused nearly everybody in the school to develop a rash which had to be treated with sulphur and coconut oil. Mary applied the remedy with the skill of a trained nurse. Luckily, we had no serious illnesses, but there were enough minor ailments to keep her busy every day. What the children would have done without her I have no idea. The only other person we could call upon in case of illness was a practitioner who was what the Thai called a third-class doctor, which is a term of definition, not opprobrium. I was convinced, however, that this particular technician's sole aim in life was extorting the last possible cent from his customers for the atabrine and sulfa tablets that he managed to obtain. I became his friend because I possessed a large bottle of atabrine, which he greatly coveted.

I remember going into his shop one day with Mary and hearing him berate an elderly woman in a language that was unfamiliar to me. I couldn't understand a word he was saying, but it was clear that he was chastising the woman. Then Mary interrupted him. "I speak Malay," she said coldly. "You ought to be ashamed of yourself, trying to send that poor woman away just because she hasn't got any money. I'll pay for her medicine. Give her what she wants, and don't be a cannibal."

Nobu joined us for Christmas, and we went to Mass at the Chapel of Mater Dei, which had moved to Hua Hin, too. After Mass, as I stood at the chapel door with Reverend Mother Raphael, waiting for Nobu, Mary and the twins to catch up to us, Reverend Mother whispered to me, "Doesn't Mary look beautiful in that dress? It's made from a Japanese kimono, isn't it?"

"Yes," I said. "It's one of Haruko's. Wouldn't she be pleased if she could see it?"

Reverend Mother pressed my hand and I leaned close to her and said, "I wonder if we're thinking the same thing."

"I wouldn't be surprised," she said gently.

As the new year of 1945 dawned, we had no way of knowing that it was ushering in the last year of the war. There seemed to be more bombing than ever. The railway was under almost constant attack. Reports circulated daily that the British were preparing to land in Malaya, or even in southern Thailand, and soon trainload after trainload of Japanese soldiers began to make their way southward. Before long, a Japanese garrison settled in Hua Hin, and a search got under way for housing accommodations for them. One morning I received a message from Reverend Mother Raphael, asking me to come over to the Mater Dei School right away.

"The Japanese are here," she told me when I arrived. "They want me to let them have one of our houses for a soldiers' barracks. But I can't do it. The house they want is a students' dormitory, and I haven't got any place else to put the girls. Can you explain it to them?"

I had my doubts, but I agreed to try. We walked over to one of the Mater Dei houses, and Mother Raphael led me to the Japanese officer who was in charge of the billeting party. I bowed and said, in Japanese, "Good morning. The Reverend Mother would like to know what she can do for you."

"Good morning," the captain said. "We're looking for a house for our Medical Corps, and we would like to have this one."

"But this house is being used as a dormitory for a girls' school," I told him.

"I know it is," the captain said. "We would be glad to arrange matters so that the soldiers would leave every evening when the girls come back to sleep."

I took my courage in my hands. "These girls," I said firmly, "have been commended to the care of the Sisters by their parents, because Bangkok isn't safe for them. If you sent your daughter away to school, because Tokyo wasn't safe for her, would you like it if the head of the school permitted foreign soldiers to move into her dormitory?"

"No," he said, "I wouldn't." At least he was honest.

"That," I said, "is how the parents of these girls would feel."

The captain pointed to a little house not far away. "All right, if we may have that small cottage over there, I think we can manage."

I told Mother Raphael what he had said, and she readily agreed. I thanked the officer ceremoniously, and he thanked me, and we parted friends.

The war was rushing toward a climax and we walked to our landlord's house every night to hear the news. After the surrender of Germany in May, the Allies, and especially the United States, moved even more strongly against the Japanese. The fall of Okinawa in June, after three months of bitter fighting, signaled the beginning of the end. The frighteningly powerful new B-29s joined the airplanes of the fleet in hammering the home islands through June and July, and everybody knew an invasion was imminent. Then, on August 6, the first atomic bomb was dropped on Hiroshima, and on August 9 another fell on Nagasaki. On August 14, surrender terms were accepted by the Japanese.

Mother Raphael called me the morning after the surrender and asked me if I would speak to the officers who were occupying her little cottage and tell them that, if there was any way she could be of service to them, she would be glad to repay them for the courteous treatment they had extended her. We walked to the cottage together and found two officers sitting on the veranda.

I felt some embarrassment about bringing up the subject but I plunged right in. "Now that it's all over," I said, "Reverend Mother hopes that, if there is anything she can do for you, you won't hesitate to ask her."

"Now that what's all over?" the captain asked in surprise. "What do you mean?"

"Why," I said, hesitating a little, "the war." It suddenly dawned on me that they actually didn't know. I felt uncomfortable being the one to bring them the news, but I had to finish what I had started. "Yesterday," I said, "the Emperor announced an unconditional surrender."

"What about Okinawa?"

"Okinawa has fallen."

"What about Singapore?"

"Singapore is included in the surrender."

The captain got up and went inside the house. The other officer said, softly, "We had heard that a terrible new bomb had been dropped on Hiroshima, but we never dreamed that the war had ended. Do you hear the news every day?"

"Yes. We go to the house of a man who has electricity and we listen to the radio."

"You're sure that it was His Majesty the Emperor himself who surrendered?"

"Yes," I said, "that is certain." I turned to go.

"Sensai," he called after me, "I'm sure we will receive official word very soon and we will probably be ordered back to Bangkok. But until then, if you should meet any of our soldiers, would you mind not telling them? They might misunderstand. Something might happen."

"Certainly," I said. "I won't tell them. I wouldn't have mentioned it to you if I hadn't thought you already knew. I hope you will pardon the presumption."

"It is nothing," the polite young officer said.

But it was a great deal more than nothing. The long and terrible war was over at last.

Chapter XVII

Nobu came to Hua Hin by boat the first weekend after the surrender.

"You must be glad it's all over," I said simply.

"I am glad it's over," he answered solemnly, "and I'm thankful we lost. There would have been no living with us anywhere in the world if we had won."

We spent the weekend planning what we would do. First of all, we had to assume that the country would be occupied, probably by the British, and that the thousands of Japanese soldiers in Thailand would be disarmed. There wasn't any question that the British would come and would stay for a long time, and that Nobu, along with the other Japanese, would be put in an internment camp and, eventually, sent back to Japan.

"I'll stay with you and the twins," Mary announced.

"But what about your family?" I protested. "Surely they've forgiven you by now. They'll be glad to have you back."

"I'll be glad to see them," Mary said firmly, "just as soon as I can. But I'm still going to live with you and help you take care of the twins."

So, in those few short days, we drew up a rough plan for our future. Mary and I would stay in Hua Hin for a while, until the transportation problem was eased somewhat. Then

241

we would take the twins and go back to Bangkok, where we would all live together until Nobu was interned. After that, Mary and I would be able to get along on what we could earn as English teachers. Now that the Americans and British were back in power, the English language would be popular again. At least we would be sure of a place to live, for the house was leased in my name, not Nobu's, and wasn't likely to be taken away from us.

After a fantastically arduous journey, which saw us ride on four trains, including a freight train, and three boats, we got back to Bangkok about the middle of September. Thanks to Fern and Sompong, the house was in excellent condition. The only thing that was in bad shape was the little Morris Minor, which had been stripped of all its tires by enterprising thieves. I was lucky to be able to sell it for exactly what I had paid for it, seven hundred baht. But the value of the baht had taken such a beating from inflation that seven hundred 1945 baht were like seventy 1939 baht.

Our big problem was to find a house for the school. We had given up the old one when we moved to Hua Hin because we didn't think the school ought to be paying rent on two houses at once. Now, with the British and Indian troops commandeering every dwelling they could, it was hard to find one. Mary and I decided to go to British Headquarters and put our problem before the authorities there.

As we made our way through the streets of the city, we were struck by the sudden change. Foreign soldiers, including newly released prisoners of war, were everywhere, most of them speaking English. The streets, Mary reported to me with interest, were filled with jeeps, the marvelous American-built vehicles of which we had heard so much. Soon they were to become as familiar in Bangkok as tricycles.

When we passed the house of Nai Pridi, the Regent, Mary stopped. "That's my father's old house," she said. "Nai Pridi lives there now. Do you think, if we stopped in and asked him, he might help us?" I was doubtful that the man I had known in the prewar days as Luang Pradit would do anything to help me, but I was willing to try. "He could do it if he wanted to," I said. "Let's go."

We asked to speak to Nai Pridi but were told that he was busy and couldn't be disturbed. His wife, Madame Poonsuk, met us, however, and seemed genuinely pleased to see us. "I'm sure my husband can help you," she said when we had told her what we wanted. "You wait here while I send him a note."

In a little while, an answer came back from Nai Pridi. His wife read it and told us, in a surprised tone, "He says he's sorry but he can't do anything about a house." She sighed. "I'm sorry," she said. "I'm sorry my husband can't help you."

The men at British Headquarters were much more helpful. They gave us the name of the sergeant who was in charge of housing in the district in which we hoped to locate the school, and told us that all we had to do, after we found the house we wanted, was return to Headquarters and have the matter confirmed by the officer in charge.

It took us a few days but we finally found what we required. We settled the details with the courteous British and quickly set about the task of arranging the transportation of all our personnel and equipment from Hua Hin.

My biggest worry was how the British and the Americans in Bangkok would receive Nobu. I knew what his feelings had been about the policies of Japan's war party, but the Allies didn't, and I couldn't help fretting that to some of them one Japanese might look just like another. My first indication that the problem wasn't going to be a troublesome one came when some Thai friends of ours came to the house one night with a British army chaplain. I had some misgivings about it when they told me they were bringing him, but I realized that we had to break the ice sometime and I felt it was a good thing to start with a priest.

It wasn't long before Father Telford mentioned that he had just come back from Burma.

"Is that so?" I said, seizing the opportunity. "Mr. Utagawa was in Burma, too. In fact, he was able to do quite a few services for the Sisters and the priests while he was there. He was a liaison man between the army and the Government."

"Is it possible," Father Telford said interestedly, "that this is the Angel Gabriel I've been hearing so much about in Rangoon?"

"I wouldn't be surprised," I said, and we launched into a long, animated discussion of the experiences Nobu and Father Telford had had in Burma and of the troubles of the Catholic missionaries there. From that night on, Father Telford was our good friend, and he came often to visit us, bringing other army friends with him. I soon got over my fear that Nobu's reception might be an unfriendly one. People, I discovered, hadn't forgotten how to judge a man by his own qualities.

Of course, we still had to face the unhappy prospect of Nobu's internment. With the twins growing up so rapidly, I hated to think of him having to leave us. But the evil day finally arrived. One morning in the middle of October, a bus stopped at our door and Nobu kissed us good-by, climbed in and was driven away.

I was glad Haruko wasn't there. Not only because it would have been a sad day for her, but because if she had been the twins would have had to go, too. As it was, Nobu went alone. Mary and I kept the twins with us, and nothing was ever said about them.

There were distinct advantages to being an American in Bangkok now that the war was over and our side had won.

As soon as I found out that the internees were allowed to have visitors, I set about obtaining permission to see Nobu. He was glad to see me and hungry for news of home, of the twins and Mary. The camp life, he said, wasn't too bad. He lived with a congenial group in a small house which they had improved as much as they could. Some of the men in the camp were engineers and mechanics and they were able to purify the drinking water and otherwise improve sanitary conditions.

As the months went by, they began to look around for a major project that would enlist all of their energies and skills, and they decided to build a bridge across the canal, a bridge that might be used by the Thai people for years and that would serve as a tangible reminder of the desire of these Japanese for good relations with the people among whom they had lived for so long. It took several months to build, but, with the engineers among them doing the planning and every able-bodied man in camp working on the job, they completed a beautiful red bridge which is still very much in use.

The first letter I'd had from home in all the long years of war was given to me by the Red Cross. Somewhat inaccurately addressed to Miss Genevieve Caulfield, Prisoner of War of the Japanese, Bangkok, Thailand, it had been written more than a year before. Mary read me the news that Mama was dead. She had died, Henry wrote, in 1942.

I was relieved, as I sat there thinking about her, that she hadn't come to Bangkok. I felt better knowing that she had spent her last years comfortably with Henry, Beatrice and the children. But it was hard to grasp the fact that she was gone from us, and indeed had been gone all these years without my knowing it.

It was a good thing there was so much to keep me busy. The American Legation, which was almost opposite our house, was reopening, and I went there at the first opportunity to register and to pay my respects to our new representatives, Mr. and Mrs. Charles Yost, Mr. Yost's secretary, Helen Larsen, and Edward Barker, the Consul. Helen Larsen came to our house the first afternoon and made friends with Mary and the twins, and soon afterward both Helen and Ed Barker accepted an invitation to have dinner with us. Because I was the only American in Bangkok outside of the three Mothers at Mater Dei, Ed referred to me as "the American colony."

It was like going back home when I was invited to have Thanksgiving dinner at the Air Transport Command mess, and I ate the first old-fashioned American holiday dinner I'd had in a long time. The A.T.C. also did wonders for our morale by making it possible for us to send letters home. Incoming mail was still erratic but before long it was all straightened out and we had good mail service to the United States and most of Europe, although it was almost two years before we had service to Japan.

During the months that Nobu was in camp, Mary and I had some serious talks about her future. She told me it had always been her ambition to study medicine in England, but, although she knew she could do it with her grandmother's help, now she wasn't sure she wanted to. It was evident that something was on her mind, something she wasn't ready to talk about yet, and I thought I knew what it was. At least, I hoped I did. But I was sure she would tell me when the proper time came, and meanwhile it didn't interfere with her busy life, teaching at the school, helping to bring up the twins, and giving some time to her own family.

I knew perfectly well what Nobu had on his mind. On my visits to him, he confessed that Mary was very much in his thoughts. But he felt that his position as an internee, waiting to be sent back to Japan to begin life at the bottom, made it impossible for him to do anything about it.

All I could do was pray for them.

As Christmas drew near, we were faced once again with the specter of house-hunting, this time in our own behalf instead of the school's. Our landlord wanted his house back, and there wasn't anything we could do but oblige him. We finally found a new house not far away, and we made plans to move into it the day after Christmas, which was traditionally moving day in our family. The big problem was to find someone to move us. Nobody had any trucks except the military.

We were discussing the matter at dinner one evening. One of our guests was Captain Dalzell, a young Irish officer attached to the British Veterinary Corps. He interrupted us. "Would you mind," he asked, "if you had to move early in the morning?"

"We don't care if it's in the middle of the night," I said, "if we can only get hold of a truck."

"Well you just be ready at six o'clock the morning after Christmas," Captain Dalzell said easily, "and there will be a truck at your door. What's more, it will be manned by a squad of Indians who are as strong as any men you've ever seen. They'll do the job for you."

I could scarcely express my gratitude, but Captain Dalzell insisted that it was nothing. "I'm sorry to have to send them so early," he said, "but they have to be on duty at nine. If they don't finish in time, though, they can come back in the evening."

With that worry off our minds, we were able to really enjoy Christmas. On Christmas Eve, Mary and I had dinner with the Yosts at the American Legation, and afterward we went to the Cathedral for Midnight Mass. At four thirty in the morning, Prom and I left the house with a big basket packed with all the trimmings of a bountiful holiday dinner. We climbed aboard a launch in the early-morning mist and went upriver to the internment camp, where Nobu and I ate Christmas dinner together. It wasn't exactly the way we would have liked it to be, but it was a lot better than it had been during the war. At least now we could look ahead with confidence and plan the life that we had been dreaming about for so long.

The postwar world, or at least that part of it in which we moved, was slowly taking shape. The boy king Ananda, his brother Phumiphon, and their mother had returned from Switzerland. More and more Indian soldiers were pouring into Thailand, and frequently their behavior made the Thai look back nostalgically to the relatively good old days of the well-disciplined Japanese. Prices rose higher and higher. Luang Phibul Songgram, the former Prime Minister, was arrested as a war criminal.

While the deposed Prime Minister was under arrest, his wife, Lady La-iad, lived quietly in a house across from our school. She had few visitors, but once in a while Sahataya and some of the other older children in the school, remembering her kindness to them when they had performed before the Women's Culture Association, went to see her. One day she told Sahataya, gratefully, "if my husband ever returns to power, I'm going to ask him to see to it that your school has a building of its own, so you won't ever again have to move from one rented house to another." It was a momentous promise that was faithfully kept.

By the spring of 1946, it was possible to begin to forget that there had been a war. There still were large numbers of Japanese soldiers in and near the city, but they were unarmed and the way they worked was the admiration of everyone. "There simply is no need to supervise them," one British officer told me. "Their discipline is marvelous. For a defeated army, it's incredible."

The easing situation was reflected happily, in the month of April, in a way that was very personal to us. Without warning, Nobu appeared at the house, shouting hello to everyone and announcing joyously that the British authorities had given him a pass for a two-week visit at home. Technically, he was supposed to be under guard, but his guard was somewhere in Bangkok, enjoying himself, and had arranged to meet Nobu at the dock on the appointed day of return. Meanwhile, Nobu was free to be with us.

We had invited Commander Alfred Gardes, the U.S. Naval Attaché, to have dinner with us that night, and I wondered if his encountering Nobu at the table would prove embarrassing. I decided that the best thing to do was to go over to the Embassy and tell him the good news that Nobu was home. The twins walked across the street with me to his office.

"That's fine," Skeet Gardes said when I told him. "Shall I have the pleasure of meeting him at dinner tonight?"

"Indeed you will," I said, greatly relieved.

"Good. I want to meet the father of these youngsters." He picked up both Bubu and Koko, with whom he had struck up a great friendship, and, much to their delight, carried them out to the gate on his shoulders. A few hours later, he and Nobu laid the basis of an enduring friendship.

Nobu was convinced that this would be his last visit with us before his repatriation. Actually, he was able to come again, but he didn't have any idea then that he would be able to, and it was obvious that he had made up his mind he had to find out how Mary felt toward him. Like him, I was hoping beyond all else that they would be able to make a life together. But I knew there was much to be considered. The problem of nationality was first, compounded by the reluctance of the Thai royal family to have its members marry foreigners. It wasn't going to be easy.

But I could tell from Mary's unconcealed pleasure in having Nobu at home, and from his earnest conversations with me about her, that love was going to find a way. So I wasn't surprised, one morning during Nobu's first week at home, to return from an errand and find Nobu and Mary, hand in hand, waiting for me.

"Mother," Nobu said, "Mary has made me very happy. She has promised to marry me as soon as I can make a home for her in Japan."

I couldn't keep the tears from coming to my eyes. "That's wonderful," I said. I put my arm around the girl who had come to mean so much to me and kissed her. Then, more practically, I asked her, "Are you sure you can make the sacrifices you're going to have to make?"

"Whatever I'll be giving up," Mary said quietly, "is nothing compared to what I'll be gaining."

A few days later we all went over to Mater Dei, the scene of so many of our family's joys and sorrows since Haruko and I had first arrived in Bangkok, to tell Reverend Mother Raphael and Mother Gemma the wonderful news. Reverend Mother and I exchanged a little "I told you so" handclasp.

Both Nobu and Mary felt that their engagement should be kept secret. They knew that Nobu had to go back to Japan alone on the repatriation ship. I would keep the twins, and Mary would continue to live with us. When Nobu was ready, I would bring the children and Mary to Tokyo, and they would be married there. We thought it would probably take about two years.

Since they were to be separated so soon, and wouldn't even be able to exchange letters for a long time, Nobu and Mary were anxious to have some tangible evidence of their engagement. They wrote out a formal betrothal promise, and, after both of them had signed it, they asked Father Caretto and me to witness it. When Nobu went back to the internment camp, he carried one copy of the pledge with him and Mary kept the other.

We were lucky enough to see him a few more times before he sailed for Japan. He was allowed another short visit home in May, to put his affairs in order, and a few weeks later, on June 9, just before he was due to leave, we all went to see him. It was the first time Mary and the twins had been to the internment camp, and it was Mary's first boat ride on the Chao Phraya since she had sailed in the royal barge when her sister was the Queen.

When we got back to Bangkok that night, we found the city appalled by the sudden and shocking death of King Ananda. His Majesty had been mysteriously shot to death in the palace. Volumes of testimony and conjecture have been written on the matter, and after years of investigation it was decided officially that the King was assassinated. His alleged killers were executed. But at the time it happened, the deep mystery surrounding the affair intensified the grief and bewilderment of the Thai people, who have a deep and abiding affection for their royal family. Prince Phumiphon was immediately proclaimed King, and a regency was set up under Prince Rangsit of Chainat.

Our pupils were especially shocked by the news because, not long before, they had put on a play for the King and his brother, and they had been tremendously excited by the opportunity to meet His Majesty. They could hardly believe that he was dead.

Just before Nobu's ship was to sail, Sompong and I visited him for the last time at the embarkation camp in Bangkok. Located on the site of the slaughter house, it was optimistically called "New Life Camp." No visitors were allowed there, but I sent the ever-resourceful Sompong over to investigate the possibilities. He reported that the camp was situated along the river and that it was guarded at night and in the early morning by Japanese soldiers, with the British taking over during the day. Early the next morning, Sompong and I set out for it. We passed the Japanese guard with a casual greeting in his own language, and Sompong led me straight to the roofed-over platform where Nobu was beginning his "new life."

Nobu was happily surprised to see me, and we sat down together in good spirits and proceeded to enjoy the breakfast I had brought along. One of the things I remember about that breakfast is that the eggs, which I had asked Prom to hard-boil, weren't cooked at all, and when I broke one by banging it against a wooden platform it got all over everything. At that, it lent a little humor to the situation, which was anything but funny. It was with deep misgivings that I said my last good-by to Nobu and hurried away before the British guards came to take over the day shift.

We heard later about the nightmare trip to Japan of more than three thousand men, women and children packed like sardines into a small cargo ship. Amazingly, though, all of them reached home safely.

Mary and I did our best to carry on. We had much to occupy us. There were the twins, the school, private pupils in abundance, and an ever-increasing number of friends. Life wasn't dull, although it wasn't always pleasant.

Among the unpleasant postwar developments was thievery on a scale so grand that it was virtually an industry. One enterprising intruder climbed up the palm tree outside our house one night and broke into Mary's room. Boldly reaching right underneath the pillow on her bed, he stole the pistol that she always kept there. He probably had hoped to find a pocketbook or some jewelry, but when he discovered the pistol he obviously decided to settle for that and vanished out the window. I was relieved that he hadn't forced me to open the trunk in which I kept all of my money, but the incident made me realize how unsafe such banking arrangements were. It was time to go back to a regular bank.

In the morning I went downtown to the Thai Commercial Bank and asked to open an account. It was a routine transaction and everything went smoothly until I was asked for my signature. I took out the little ridged board that I always put underneath any paper I want to sign, in order to be certain that my pen stays within the proper area, and I duly signed my name.

"Can you sign your own checks?" the man asked suspiciously.

"Yes," I said, "I can sign my own checks."

"How do you make them out?"

"I type them, or I have someone make them out for me."

"How do you know that the person making them out puts down the correct amount?"

"I don't," I said, calmly. "I always ask someone I can trust."

"How do you know you can trust them?"

I had been trusting people in more important ways all of

my life. "I'm sure," I said with a touch of asperity, "that I can trust anyone whom I am in the habit of asking to write a check for me."

The official was adamant. "They might change the figures," he said. "As long as the danger exists, we cannot accept your account."

I was, by now, thoroughly perplexed. "Even if they did change the figures," I argued, "it would be I who would be cheated, not the bank. You wouldn't be running any risk. If the account was overdrawn, you simply wouldn't honor the check. I don't understand what you're worrying about."

"Just the same," the clerk said, "we cannot accept your account." What's more, his decision was upheld by the manager. Their attitude was incomprehensible to me but it left me with no choice except to go over to the Chartered Bank of India and open an account there, where no questions were asked. The experience brought home to me the lesson that there was still a tremendous need to educate the public in the rights and capabilities of the blind. To establish a school for the blind, and even to impress people with what trained blind pupils could do, was one thing, but it was quite another to convince them that the blind can be responsible for themselves in the sighted world. Prejudice against the blind was still widespread; not only could they not vote, they couldn't even open a bank account.

Knowing that I would be returning to Japan sometime within the next two years, I began to pay serious attention to the problem of finding someone to take charge of the school. Vedhi was an excellent teacher and assistant, but I knew and she knew that she wouldn't be able to run the school herself. Mary would have been the logical choice, but she would be leaving with me. Someone would have to be found, and I was glad that at least I had lots of time to look.

I was able to strengthen the administration of the school in a different way at, of all places, a Fourth of July reception given at the American Legation by the new U.S. Minister, Edwin F. Stanton, and his vivacious wife, Josephine. I had an opportunity during the party to tell Josephine Stanton about our school, and as I was talking to her it occurred to me that she would make an ideal board member, so I promptly asked her if she would be willing. She insists that I told her she had to become a member, but I have the impression that I put it a little more politely. At any rate, she readily agreed, and from that day on she worked for the school enthusiastically.

Whenever I think of Josephine, I think of the day she brought a group of American visitors to inspect the school, and, wanting to show off the splendid progress the children were making, she asked Tong Chai, one of our older boys, to read something from one of our Braille editions of *The Reader's Digest.* Josephine's guests couldn't keep back a startled gasp of surprise when our prize pupil opened the pages of the magazine and, in a confident voice, began to read "The Political and Economic Principles of Henry Wallace."

The school was in sound condition. Our board chairman was Kun Prapaht, the Mayor of Bangkok, and the Department of Public Welfare was still giving us the subsidy of twenty thousand baht a year. By this time, however, it wasn't enough. Between a steadily increasing enrollment and the impact of inflation, our budget required us to seek donations from the public.

People were amazingly generous. One day, one of our volunteer teachers handed me a hundred dollars and said, "This is from Bill Davis. I mentioned to him that the school needed money, and he gave me every dollar he had in his pocket." I was overwhelmed by such an act of generosity on the part of a total stranger, and I asked the teacher to bring Mr. Davis to the house some day so I might thank him in person. He came, a young ex-serviceman who was operating a small aviation freight service, and he became a good friend. Mary and I had much to thank him for before we said good-by to Thailand.

The Red Cross delivered a letter from Nobu, which relieved our minds greatly. He wrote little about the hardships of life in Japan, although it wasn't difficult to read between the lines, but it was enough to know that he had arrived safely and was hard at work. He had been able to meet some of the people I had asked him to look up—the Sugis, for example—and it was good to hear about my old friends and to know that they had found, as I had, that it is possible to be loyal both to your country and your friends even during a war that places you on opposite sides.

We were taken completely by surprise when the Red Cross brought us another mesage from Nobu in the middle of May, 1947, less than a year after he had left us. The telegram informed us that everything was ready for us to go to Japan; Keiyo University was holding a teaching position for me, and permission had been granted for all four of us to enter.

Coming with such suddenness, it was more than we could grasp. We were still trying to organize our thoughts when the American Vice-Consul telephoned and asked me to come over to see him. When I arrived at his office, he asked, abruptly, "Did you ever apply for permission to go to Japan?"

"No," I said, surprised, "I didn't."

"I thought not. Such an application would have to go through this office, and then be relayed to Tokyo, and then it would have to be sent to Washington. If it were approved in Washington, the whole procedure would have to be followed in reverse until the answer came back here. But listen to this cable:

" 'Endorse passports and make out travel orders for the following four persons: Genevieve Caulfield, Mary Supasvat, Nobuyuki Utagawa, Haruko Utagawa. Signed MACARTHUR.'

"If you wish," the Vice-Consul said, "I will issue passports immediately. But I have to point out to you that anyone receiving permission to enter Japan must do so within sixty days after permission is granted. I'm sorry to tell you that this telegram was received a month ago."

Only sixty days allowed us to get there, and thirty of them already gone! I was stunned. "What happened?" I asked, bewildered.

"I've only just taken over the work," he said apologetically, "and my predecessor didn't list this telegram among the matters to be given priority. I just found it this morning."

"Can't you telegraph Tokyo and ask them to extend the time? It's simply impossible for us to be ready to leave within a month. Two months would be bad enough. I have to settle about my school. I have to arrange transportation. There are all sorts of things that have to be done before we can go."

"I'm sorry," the Vice-Consul said with bureaucratic firmness. "I can't possibly ask them to extend the time. It just isn't done."

Maybe not, but I intended to try. I carried my troubles to Mr. Stanton, and he took an entirely different view of the matter. He was annoyed and angry that such an error could have been made in his office and not even reported to him, and he didn't see any reason why something couldn't be done about it. "I'll send a telegram personally, at once," he said. "Don't you worry. It will be all right."

Diplomatic channels quickly returned an answer to Mr. Stanton's request and the time for our admission to Japan was "indefinitely extended." We couldn't have asked for anything more. All we had to do now was get ready.

Finding someone to take charge of the school was the biggest problem. The board members and I talked over several possibilities, but none of them worked out. I wanted a Thai, if possible, and, failing that, someone who was planning to stay in the country permanently. But no Thai we approached would consider it; most of them were busy with their own work and the others simply didn't want the responsibility. Then we thought of the Salesian Sisters, and there we found our solution. They had been in Thailand for quite a while, had built a fine school in Banpong, just south of Bangkok, and intended to stay. The only objection they raised when I spoke to them about it was that none of them had had any experience teaching blind pupils. I was sure, though, that if even one Sister was willing to take on the work I could train her; all of the Sisters were experienced teachers, and teaching the blind is not the highly technical art that so many people seem to think it is. It's more a matter of aptitude than technique, as Sister Rose, who was picked to operate the school, proved by managing it with great success after absorbing the basic training I was able to give her before I left.

With the school taken care of, our departure plans went ahead speedily. I found myself torn between looking forward to seeing Japan and Nobu again, and hating to leave the school. In a very real sense the school was my child, born among difficulties and reared in the midst of war. I loved it dearly. But I had to go, and I realized that it was better for the school that I should go. It was growing up; it would be better for it to be in the hands of teachers and administrators who had no other responsibilities and could supervise its operation and its growth every minute of the day. The work I had intended to do when I first went to Thailand had been done. The school was well started, the pupils had learned what their capabilities were, the public was aware and interested, and it was time for me to move on to other work.

Nobu told us to be sure to bring ample supplies of clothing and food, and we had a great deal of shopping and packing to do. Then there was the question of our passports. Mine was a simple matter; General MacArthur's telegram had instructed the American Consul in Bangkok to issue one to me, and that was done. But Mary and the twins were another matter. Before he left Bangkok, Nobu had registered the twins as Thai subjects, so, in my ignorance, I had assumed it would be easy to obtain passports for them. But when I went to the Thai Foreign Office, the first question I was asked was the perfectly natural one, "Who is their guardian, please?"

"I am," I said, blithely.

"Have you written proof?"

No, I hadn't. I didn't, as a matter of fact, have a single written word on the subject, not even a letter from Nobu telling me to bring the twins to Japan. I produced the telegram from General MacArthur, but that, they said, wasn't enough to prove guardianship of the children. I didn't know what to do. It would take forever to write to Nobu and get an answer through the Red Cross. I was afraid that nothing would solve this problem except forgery. Then I had a sudden idea. Why couldn't I adopt Bubu and Koko and take them to Japan as my own children?

Adoption in Thailand, though not wound around with the miles of red tape that keep so many children in the United States safely in orphanages, does require the consent of the parents, if there are any. I thought, however, that I might be able to appeal to the reason of the Thai District Officer who had the matter in charge. Luckily, he recognized me. He even remembered the day Nobu and I had come to his office to register the twins as Thai subjects. "Don't worry, ma'am," he said. "I'll arrange the necessary papers for you. Then you can show the adoption papers to the Foreign Office and everything will go through all right. The only thing I ask of you is that you let me see the passports when you get them, so I'll have had visible proof that you're taking the children to Japan."

He filled out a paper, signed it, and handed it to me. I hesitated, as I was about to leave, then asked him if there wasn't a fee attached to the transaction. He stood up, took my hand in his, shook it firmly, and wished me and the twins a pleasant journey to Japan.

That took care of the twins, but there was still Mary. When she made out her application for a passport, she was told that, as a member of the royal family, she would have to obtain the permission of Prince Chainat, the Chief of the Council of Regents. We knew that she would have to have the permission of the King, or, in this case, the Council of Regents, before she could marry a commoner, no matter what nationality he might be. But we had hoped she would be able to obtain her passport first and then ask for permission to marry. We still thought it was wise to keep to that order of business, so we arranged to meet Prince Chainat at tea at the Stantons' and speak to him about our proposed trip.

Prince Chainat, a man of great culture and understanding,

and an old friend of Mary's father, was happy to learn that we were planning to go to Japan, and possibly to the United States as well. Mary had written down several countries on her application, but in our conversation with the Prince we laid stress on the trip to Japan, and he readily gave his consent.

The only persons we told about Mary's engagement were her eldest brother, who was her legal guardian and who knew Nobu and approved of the match heartily, and Khun Ying Roseline, her cousin, who also was happy about it. Grandmother would be told later.

We all breathed a sigh of relief when Mary's passport came through. Now she was free to leave the country, and once she got to Japan she could marry anybody she wished. But all of us wanted to abide by the regulations of the royal household, so we made another appointment with Prince Chainat, and late one afternoon we went to his home to tell him the real purpose of Mary's journey.

We weren't looking forward to an easy interview. Though Thai princes often had married commoners, and some of them, including Chainat himself, had taken foreign wives, it wasn't until very recently that princesses had been allowed to marry commoners, and only one of them had ever married a foreigner. Mary's problem was complicated further by the prejudice which existed among some members of the royal family against the Japanese. But Mary never lacked courage and she didn't hesitate to ask for the permission that meant so much to her.

"I have no objection to the marriage myself," the Prince said soberly. "All I care about is that this man make you a good husband." With the gentleness of a father, he asked Mary to wait a day or two while he considered the matter. "I will let you know then," he said. "You can come back for your answer."

We prayed earnestly, from the moment we left the Prince's house, that his answer would be favorable. For, although

Mary was determined to marry Nobu come what might, she wanted very much to do it properly, according to the customs and traditions of her family.

We were sitting in our living room two days later when a car drew up in front of the house and Prince Chainat got out. "I didn't want to trouble you to come to my house again," he said, "and I was passing by, so I thought I would stop in and talk to you." We held our breath as we protested that he shouldn't have gone to so much trouble. "I've been inquiring about Mr. Utagawa," he went on, "and I hear nothing but good of him. There will be no difficulty about obtaining His Majesty's permission for you to marry him."

"Thank you," Mary said gravely. "You have been very kind."

"I think, however," the Prince said, "you had better go to Japan without publishing your marriage plans. Then, after you arrive, if you find that everything is all right, you can telegraph me in care of Ambassador Stanton and officially request permission to marry. I will answer by telegram, also through Ambassador Stanton. It will be the quickest and safest way to settle the matter."

The Prince didn't have to explain to us what we already knew only too well, that there might be considerable opposition to the marriage among anti-Japanese politicians. Announcement of the news before Mary left Thailand might conceivably stir up such a storm that her passport would be revoked.

It was time to consider the problem of transportation. Our friend Commander Gardes succeeded in booking passage for us on the American ship *Marine Swallow,* leaving Hong Kong early in September for Yokohama. The big question was how to get to Hong Kong. There was virtually no international air service available and the only ships were little coastal vessels that had only one first-class cabin and packed as many as eight hundred passengers on the open deck. We didn't see that we had any choice, so we booked space on one of the ships. We weren't looking forward to the trip with any enthusiasm, but if it was the only way we could get to Japan we were willing.

Then, one morning, while we were in the midst of packing, Bill Davis, the young American who had made the princely donation of a hundred dollars to the school, came to the house. "I hear you're going to Japan," he said cheerfully.

"Yes," I said, "we'll be leaving very soon."

"I understand you're picking up an American ship at Hong Kong," he said. "How are you going to get there?"

"On one of those coastal ships. There isn't any other way."

"How about flying?" Bill suggested casually.

"How could we possibly fly to Hong Kong with thirty-eight pieces of luggage, even if we could get a plane?"

"You could go on one of my planes, that's how," Bill said, smiling. "Actually, you could keep all the personal luggage you'd want to have with you on the airplane, and you wouldn't have to worry about the weight, either. And you could send the rest of the stuff on the ship you were planning to take, and it would be in Hong Kong in plenty of time. What do you say?"

I wanted to say that it sounded perfectly wonderful, but I was still looking for the catch that had to be there somewhere. "Suppose the luggage gets there ahead of us," I said. "Wouldn't it be stolen on the pier?"

"It won't be stolen," Bill said confidently. "I'll notify my agent to pick it up as soon as it arrives and store it in his office. It's a deal, now. You get everything that you want to go on the ship ready and we'll come with a truck and pick it up. Then you can take the rest of your things on the airplane."

I didn't know how to thank him. "I've read about fairy godmothers," I told him, "but you're a fairy godfather."

When our packing cases were ready, Bill's man brought a Thai customs official to the house to examine them. Then they were nailed up, sealed, and loaded on a truck.

"What about the freight charges?" I asked. "To whom shall I pay them?"

"The captain of the ship is happy to carry them to Hong Kong for you," he said, smiling. "There's no charge." Obviously Bill Davis was taking care of the freight charges just as he was taking care of everything else.

We fixed our date of departure so we would arrive at Hong Kong three days before the *Marine Swallow* was due to sail. Those three days we planned to spend with the Maryknoll Sisters there.

Bill's plane, a DC-3 military transport with twin engines and bucket seats, could hardly be classed as de luxe, but I have never, before or since, flown with a lighter heart. The airplane was sturdy, the engines smooth-running, the stewardess fed us generously, and we were four people and several hundred pounds of baggage, all flying from Bangkok to Hong Kong without paying a cent.

Sister Emelda, the Provincial Superior of South China, and Sister Mark, Superior of the Community in Kowloon, saw to it that we had a pleasant few days in Hong Kong. They arranged for us to sleep at a nearby Catholic hospital but we spent our days and ate our meals at the Maryknoll School. Being with the Maryknoll Sisters was like being home again.

We had heard so much about Japanese atrocities committed in Hong Kong that it was a relief to hear from the Sisters a story that helped balance what we had been told. The army had taken over the Maryknoll School but had permitted the Sisters to live in part of the building. On the door leading into the Sisters' section the commanding officer posted a notice which read: "This part of the building is occupied by reverend and respected ladies. They are not to be disturbed in any way."

We had first-class accommodations on the *Marine Swallow* but we had no way of knowing what that would mean. The ship was, after all, an unreconverted troop ship. We were told that we would be billeted in a cabin for twelve, which didn't seem so bad, and on Saturday morning, September 14, 1947, we went on board. The steward who met us at the top of the gangway gave us the number of our cabin and told us that each passenger was permitted to take one suitcase to his cabin. We carried four for our group, one to put underneath each bed, and we were looking forward to getting settled. But when we opened the cabin door we had a surprise. Every bed was occupied. "There's a Chinese woman in every one of them," Mary whispered to me. "I wonder what we're supposed to do."

We quickly found out that we had been directed to the wrong room. Ours was the next one, and when we reached it we found four empty beds waiting for us. I still couldn't understand why all those women in the other cabin had been in bed. "Is there something wrong with them?" I asked the cabin boy.

"They're seasick," he said.

"How can they be seasick? The ship hasn't even started yet."

"They can," he said flippantly. "As soon as some of these Chinese women get on a ship, they're all ready to be seasick and have a good rest."

On these ships, with twelve in a cabin, men and women, even husbands and wives, had to have separate quarters. Our cabin mates were French, American, Danish and British women who had come from the United States by way of Manila; they were all experienced travelers and they knew how to make the best of life on board ship. It wasn't always easy to make the best of it, either, for not all of the passengers subscribed to the same standards of hygiene. I had just finished reading one of Lin Yutang's books, in which he ridiculed the American passion for sanitation. He pointed out that culture, such as had long prevailed in China, can develop nicely without it. I often wished during that voyage that he could have been among us to witness unsanitary culture raised to its highest, or lowest, point.

However, we had broad decks and excellent food, and, thank God, calm weather. There were several priests on board, bound for Shanghai, so until we reached that point on our journey we had Mass every day somewhere in the lower regions of the ship.

As we approached Shanghai, we were warned to keep our cabin doors locked and to maintain a guard in the cabin at all times. The thieves there, we were told, were rapacious, and they had an ingenious habit of pushing long hooked poles through the portholes and lifting pieces of luggage right out from underneath the beds. Our group took the necessary precautions, and we kept our possessions intact.

It didn't seem long, as the ship sailed steadily through the calm Pacific, before word went around, "We're due in Kobe tomorrow." Japan, at last. I told Mary excitedly what Kobe had been like when I was last there, teeming with shipping, one of the great ports of a flourishing nation. Now, as we steamed into the harbor, Mary told me what she saw, and it was a simple summing up of what a difference a war makes. It was empty; there was hardly anything there at all.

When we anchored, a launch carrying American naval personnel appeared. They boarded the ship, examined the papers of the passengers landing at Kobe, and got off. Only English was spoken, and it seemed a strange way to be welcomed to a great Japanese city.

The next morning, Saturday, September 21, 1947, we sailed into Yokohama harbor and made fast to the dock. In a few minutes Mary was catching my arm and saying, "There he is! There's Nobu!" Bubu and Koko jumped up and down and waved and shouted joyously as Mary pointed out their father to them. In a few minutes we were on the pier with him, kissing him and being kissed back, and our long journey was over.

Nobu had borrowed his company's car for the occasion and we were able to ride in style to Seijo, the Toyko suburb where Nobu was living with Mr. Uehata, one of the men he had been with in the Thailand internment camp. Mr. Uehata's spacious Japanese-style house hadn't been damaged by the bombing and he had offered to let us have two rooms in the house and the use of a small wooden garage which could, with alterations that were already under way, be converted into additional living space. As Nobu was telling us this, we were driving through the ruined streets of Yokohama, and for the entire length of our ride I listened in awe as Nobu and Mary described the destruction of the land. For miles there was nothing but chimneys and ruins, broken up only here and there by a new piece of construction of a more or less temporary nature. This was the miracle the militarists had worked for their country.

During the ride, too, we caught up on Nobu's news. The first thing he had done when he returned to Japan was to seek out his family. Two of his brothers had died in the war. His mother and a younger brother were living in the country outside Tokyo. After he found them, and did what he could to help them, he set about the task of gathering together a few trusted friends and starting up a new business. They were bringing seafood down from Hokkaido for sale in the Tokyo markets and were using the profits to lay the foundation for an import and export business. Considering the difficulty of the times, they had been reasonably successful, and as soon as he felt sure that everything was going to be all right Nobu decided to send for Mary, the twins and me.

It hadn't been easy. He had gone from one Occupation official to another, and had received no encouragement at all. They didn't understand why he hadn't brought the children with him. And as for a fiancée, weren't there nearly four million Japanese repatriates? Suppose each of them had the same sort of request? Of course, Miss Caulfield, who had been in Japan before, who could speak Japanese, and who was guaranteed a teaching position at Keiyo University, might be arranged for, although even that was difficult because very few women were being admitted to the country.

Nobu had just about resigned himself to a long, long wait, when he resolved to make one final try. He sat down and wrote a letter to the great General MacArthur himself, telling him the whole story, a letter filled with confidence that the general would understand.

Nobu's confidence was well placed. In a very short time he was summoned to the office of the Director of the Personnel Section of SCAP, the Supreme Command of the Allied Powers. "I understand," an officer there said to him, "that you would like these people to be admitted to Japan." He showed Nobu a typewritten list of our names.

"Yes, sir," Nobu said. "I would like very much to have them come."

"I see no objection to the children. After all, they're yours, and it's only natural that you should want them with you. Miss Caulfield can be arranged for, too. The only problem is the young lady, your fiancée. Suppose, after she gets here, you should decide not to marry her. You know how those things are, sometimes."

"Yes," Nobu nodded. He thought fast and decided to take a chance. Fervently hoping that what he was saying would turn out as well as his insistence that the Church property in Burma belonged to the Vatican, he said, "I have a solemn promise of betrothal, witnessed by a Catholic priest and by Miss Caulfield, and signed by my fiancée and me." He showed the pledge to the officer. "In the eyes of the Catholic Church," he went on, "a promise like this is binding. Not, of course, to the extent of marriage, but sufficiently binding to make it very difficult for it to be broken."

"Is that so?" the officer said. He promptly picked up his telephone and asked for the priest who was the liaison officer between the Catholic population of Japan and SCAP. "Is it true, Father," he asked when the priest came on the line, "that a solemn promise of betrothal, witnessed by a priest, is binding in the eyes of the Catholic Church?" Nobu couldn't, of course, hear what was said on the other end of the connection, but all he needed to hear was the officer saying, "Thank you, Father," and then turning to him and smilingly saying, "You're right. That's all I wanted to know. Your fiancée will be permitted to come with the others."

Chapter XIX

Until our little garage house, with its own kitchen, bedroom and tiny sitting room, could be completed, we shared Mrs. Uehata's kitchen with her. That is, Mary did, for my use- lessness as a cook was well established. The big problem was obtaining something for Mary to cook. The most im- portant word in the Japanese language at this time was *haikiu,* meaning ration. Vegetables, eggs and some fruit could be bought in the market by those who could afford them. Meat, too, could be had at a price, but the price was sky-high. Virtually everything else was strictly rationed, including rice, soya sauce, without which Japanese food cannot be prepared, *miso,* the bean paste which is used for the essential breakfast soup, and salt. Even the great Japanese standby, fish, was in short supply because the countless mines in the coastal waters made fishing extremely hazardous.

Military and other official personnel of the Occupation weren't allowed to buy in the Japanese markets. Their food- stuffs and other supplies were brought over from the United States. The relatively small number of Americans like my- self and all other foreigners who had no official status were given special ration cards entitling us to buy, with Japanese *yen,* specially allocated U.S. Army supplies at a center set up in Tokyo. It was a blessing. We were able to obtain such staples as flour, bread, potatoes, butter, cooking oil and canned corned beef. As Thai nationals, Mary, Bubu and Koko also were entitled to foreigners' rations, including two pounds apiece of precious sugar every month. The result was that Mary was able, by judiciously combining all of our rations with what Nobu picked up in the Japanese markets, to provide us with nourishing and even appetizing meals. Nobu, who had been decidedly undernourished, soon regained his strength. Our staple dish was a mixture of corned beef and vegetables, prepared in different ways, sometimes in the form of hash, sometimes in a stew, but always well seasoned and tasting good. It was a special treat when, at the end of the month, a little surplus corned beef carefully hoarded by Mary could be served as a separate item.

We managed an egg for breakfast almost every day, and we each had a quarter of an apple or a mandarin orange. There were enough potatoes to help fill us up, and, since we regularly got flour and sugar rations, Mary was able to make cookies and, on special occasions, a cake or pudding, much to the delight of Bubu and Koko. We had brought a quantity of dried bananas and canned soup from Bangkok, which helped give the children the food elements they needed, and what with one thing and another we managed beautifully. In fact, when we thought of how little most Japanese families had, we felt guilty.

One of the joys of life was seeing old friends again. Among others who came to welcome me back to Japan and to be introduced to the other members of my growing family were the Sugis, the Horikoshis and the Fukuis, all affected to a greater or lesser degree by the war but still alive, still hopeful, and, above all, still the same good friends. There were others, of course, whom I had hoped to see but who were missing. Many were dead. Some were in Sugamo Prison, awaiting trial as war criminals.

As soon as the garage house showed signs of nearing completion, we began to make plans for the wedding. First we went to see Mr. Bruner, the American Consul, who had been most helpful to Nobu when he was working on the problem of bringing all of us to Japan. Mr. Bruner, the man Nobu had picked to give away the bride, promptly wired Prince Chainat requesting formal permission for the marriage. We hardly dared breathe until, a few days later, the brief but eloquent answer came back: "Permission granted."

Then we sought out Archbishop Morella, who had been Apostolic Delegate to Japan since before the war, and he consented to perform the marriage ceremony. Since this was a marriage between two Catholics, there was no problem about having it in the Chapel of the Jesuit University with the celebration of Holy Mass. We decided upon October sixteenth for the wedding day.

Food rationing made a big reception impossible but, as the best solution, we decided to invite as many of our friends as possible to attend the ceremony.

Not entirely to our surprise, the Japanese newspapers interested themselves avidly in the wedding. Not only was it one of Tokyo's first between a Japanese and a foreigner since the end of the war, but in this case the foreigner was an attractive princess, and everybody loves to read about royal romances.

Even though we couldn't have a proper reception, we felt that the least we could do would be to provide a little hospitality for the wedding party itself. That would total about twenty people, and it was hard to decide what to give them. Coffee and sandwiches would be fine, and we had brought some instant coffee with us from Bangkok. But we didn't have anywhere near enough cups to serve it in, so coffee was out. We finally settled upon corned beef sandwiches and lemonade, which we could prepare from our stock of dehydrated lemon juice, also brought from Bangkok. The success of our little party was assured when Mrs. Bruner volunteered to make a wedding cake. She could obtain the ingredients at the American commissary, and it would be her wedding present to the bride and groom.

Mary's wedding day was a Wednesday, and it dawned bright and clear and crisp. Nobu had stayed the night before with some old friends, but his company car was on hand to take Mary and me, the twins, all dressed in white, Nobu's mother, who had come for the occasion, and Mrs. Uehata to the church. It was a fairly long trip, so Mary brought along a suitcase in which she had packed her traveling dress and other things she would need for the brief three-day wedding trip she and Nobu were going to take. We had been driving for about ten minutes when Mary remembered that she had forgotten her coat. She was going into a mountainous area, and we were sure she would need it, so we turned back and got it. Then, this time after about twenty minutes of driving, Mrs. Uehata realized that she had forgotten the bread for the sandwiches. This was a major calamity. Bread was strictly rationed, and it was impossible to buy it on the way. But gasoline was rationed, too. We had no choice; we would have to keep on and give the guests lemonade and wedding cake. Then I remembered that the University maintained a dormitory and undoubtedly kept sizable supplies of bread on hand for the Fathers. I would ask the Father in charge to lend me some. I did, and he was most helpful. The crisis was past.

Mary looked beautiful in the white georgette wedding dress she had made in Bangkok. Bubu and Koko held up the train with great care and pride as she moved, on Mr. Bruner's arm, to where Nobu stood waiting for her. It was a touching moment as they knelt in the sanctuary, awaiting the words which would unite their lives, and their friends from many different countries welcomed this evidence that the war was over at last.

For a long time after the wedding day, a picture of the bride and bridegroom, with Mary cutting the wedding cake, occupied a place of honor in the shop window of one of Tokyo's foremost photographers.

My mind was crowded with many thoughts as I sat next to Nobu's mother, but principally I thought of that other wedding day in the Chapel of Mater Dei in Bangkok, before the war came to change everything. I was sure that Haruko must be as glad as I was that Nobu had found a loving, trusting partner to share his joys and sorrows, and that Bubu and Koko had a mother to love them. Truly, God had been good. As I listened to the holy words that made Nobu and Mary man and wife, I was happy and grateful that He had chosen me to serve as His agent in joining such a fine young family, walking in His ways and putting their trust in Him.

The wedding made an impression on the twins, even though they had known Mary so intimately, for so long, that it required no adjustment on their part for them to think of her as their mother. I remember each of them making at least one reference to the changed circumstances.

"When aunties marry, do people call them Mother?" Koko asked one day. Assured that, in this case, people did, Koko seemed very satisfied. Bubu made no comment at all. Then, one Sunday afternoon as we were returning from a visit with some friends who lived near the Tachikawa Air Base, Bubu struck up a conversation with a young airman.

"Are you a Catholic?" he asked the serviceman.

"Yes, I am," the airman said.

"I didn't see you at Mass this morning," our young investigator observed.

"I went to Mass at the Air Base chapel," the airman defended himself.

"Oh," Bubu said, apparently satisfied. Then he asked, "Are you married?"

The airman laughed. "No," he said, "not yet."

"My mother is married," Bubu said proudly.

"I'm glad to hear it," his friend said as the train stopped and he hurried to get off.

The succeeding years were crowded with memorable events. I flew home to the United States for a lecture tour and to see my relatives and friends, returned to Tokyo after ten months to meet five-months-old Anne Utagawa, born during my absence, made a flying trip to Bangkok to see how the school was faring under the loving hands of the Salesian Sisters in charge of the efficient Sister Rose, and then settled down with my family in Japan.

Mary loved Japan, although one day when she was driving a surplus jeep that Nobu had purchased for the family's use she was picked up for parking illegally, and, because she wasn't a Japanese, she was put through a long, burdensome routine of questions, scarcely any of them having anything to do with the matter at hand. Finally, after two hours of exhausting interrogation, she was asked, "What was your grandfather's occupation?"

"He was a king," Mary said wearily. "And now, I'm tired. May I go home and come back another time?"

They allowed her to go, and there was no other time.

In August, 1949, the Mayor of Hiroshima invited me to be present at the ceremony marking the fourth anniversary of the explosion of the atomic bomb. I thought Tokyo had been bad enough, but there was a desertlike aridity in the desolation of Hiroshima that struck terror to my heart, a feeling that was accentuated when I was introduced to one person after another who had been burned or blinded or maimed by the bomb. Separate memorial ceremonies were held by various religious groups. I went to Mass at the Jesuit mission, and afterward I attended the official commemoration ceremony dedicated to the memory of those who had been killed four years before, and to the expression of the universal desire for peace. It might easily have been an occasion for bitterness and recrimination, but there was nothing of the kind, only the prayerful hope that never again would anything like this happen anywhere in the world.

Since then a Catholic church has been erected in Hiroshima, and Sisters of Perpetual Adoration pray there unceasingly, day and night, before the altar of God, for peace.

We were all shocked when war was unleashed upon the East once more, in Korea, but it was warming to me to see how Japan stood by us. No Japanese troops fought in Korea, but Japanese workmen, Japanese ground crews and Japanese dock workers were in a position to make a mighty contribution to our cause, and they made it gladly.

In the spring of 1952, I went back to Bangkok for a visit. The little school I had left was scarcely recognizable. Premier Phibul Songgram, in power again since late 1947, had kept the promise his wife had made to Sahataya and the other pupils who had visited her in her time of loneliness. New buildings provided ample classroom space, roomy dormitories, and space for the school to breathe and to expand. The enrollment had grown to eighty pupils. When I last obtained a count, it was up to one hundred and forty, and a beautiful new concrete building, erected entirely by the Board with donations from the public, helps accommodate them. I am satisfied that the blind of Thailand never again will be regarded as helpless incompetents but as people fully capable of standing on their own feet and making useful contributions to their homes and to society.

Five of the pupils who were trained in our school have studied abroad. Tong Chai, who, up to the age of fourteen, had never received a bit of formal education, was the first. On one of my trips to America, I managed to obtain a scholarship for him at Overbrook, where he studied for four years. He is now working for the Delaware Commission for the Blind and is studying for his master's degree at the University of Wilmington.

Knitting, or Aurora Lee, spent four years at Overbrook and is one of our school's most successful teachers.

Piac spent two years at the Perkins School and is doing well as a piano tuner and music teacher.

Talented Sahataya, who writes all of our plays for radio and television, spent a year in Australia and is now our kindergarten teacher.

Watana spent a few months in Burma, studying handicrafts, and is now at the head of a newly opened workshop in the school. He is looking forward to enlarging the work for the adult blind.

Four of our pupils, after taking a two-year course with a teacher we brought from Japan, are professional masseurs. Others are earning their living with handicrafts. Eight boys are studying in higher schools, and a number of others are taking training in typing. We have a good jazz band and a chorus, which may open up career opportunities in music.

And now another door has been opened to me. In 1956, President Ngo Dinh Diem of Vietnam asked me to set up and implement a program for the training of the blind in his country, and the first step was taken in March, 1958, when a little elementary school was opened in Saigon with eight eager pupils and a Vietnamese director trained in the United States. We hope to increase the enrollment to fifteen very soon.

My heart is full as I contemplate the Kingdom within us all that makes it possible for us, despite the worst apparent handicaps, to do the work of God on earth. When I was talking about this book to a friend in America, he suggested, "Bring the story to a dramatic climax." But I don't know how I can. The story and I can only go on and on, for that is what life is, the process of going on and on until the work for which we were created comes to an end.